A TREASURY OF CROCHET PATTERNS

A TREASURY OF CROCHET PATTERNS

By Liz Blackwell

CHARLES SCRIBNER'S SONS • New York

B—5.72(H)

PRINTED IN THE UNITED STATES OF AMERICA
Library of Congress Catalog Card Number 71-143947
SBN 684-12331-2

ACKNOWLEDGMENTS:
*The clever original creators of all pattern
stitches and Spinnerin Yarn Co., Inc., whose
yarns were used in all swatches.*

To the entire handknitting yarn industry—
for the pleasure their products give to
everyone who loves to crochet.

CONTENTS

ABBREVIATIONS

Written instructions for crochet usually strike the beginner as being written in a foreign language. Abbreviations are a necessary evil. Without them, one step would require many lines of copy and be even harder to absorb. Once you learn each abbreviation, you will find it very easy to read and follow crochet instructions.

ch	chain
sc	single crochet
dc	double crochet
hdc	half double crochet
tr	triple crochet
dtr	double triple
tr tr	triple triple
sl	slip
st	stitch
yo	yarn over or wrap yarn over hook
beg	beginning
pat	pattern
rnd	round
rep	repeat
tog	together
inc	increase
dec	decrease
sp	space

* means repeat instructions following the * as many more times as specified, in addition to the first time.

( ) means repeat the instructions enclosed in the parentheses as many times as indicated by the number immediately following.

A TREASURY
OF CROCHET
PATTERNS

Introduction

This book is not an erudite history or study of the art of crochet. Rather it is a simple endeavor to gather together many of the pattern stitches that have survived the years, before they are lost forever from the crumbling pages of books and magazines long out of print. Crochet has had more ups and downs than any other known form of handwork and has even been considered a lost art during many periods of time. But the craft has proved invulnerable and has always survived, even after long periods of almost complete stagnation. Crafts worked with human hands certainly pre-dated the written word and were passed from generation to generation, by a method our modern schoolchild knows as "Show and Tell." The emergence of written instructions can be counted only by hundreds of years, but the craft itself is considered in centuries. The oldest written instructions are the European ones, for crochet was definitely popular long before there was an America. Possibly France deserves the greatest credit for the first written instructions, since the word crochet is the French word meaning hook. But this is only conjecture—not fact.

Imagination is a wondrous thing and must be counted as one of the greatest blessings given to man. Without imagination, few discoveries would have been made. With imagination, all things are possible. So let's take a most imaginative trip back into history and see if we can recreate a believable and logical story of just how crochet came to be.

All crochet starts with a chain, so who made the first chain? Of what? It must have happened accidentally and might very well be considered the first form of doodling. History tells us that the early caveman invented the first crude needle, once he decided to wear clothes. He had animal skins and hides at hand and no doubt decided that if he was going to wear them, they would be less troublesome if joined together in some way. There would be no need for a needle without something to use with it.

1

Possibly the first needle had no eye and was used only to punch holes, which solved nothing. But with all that hide available, his imagination led him to cutting narrow strips to lace through the holes, thus joining the hides and discovering what grew into sewing. If your imagination has gone along this far, now visualize him fiddling absent-mindedly with one of these leather strips and discovering that he had made a loop and had been pulling successive loops thru the first one. Don't laugh—it could have happened exactly that way.

Granted this may have been his only contribution, but it was an important one. Without the chain there would never have been crochet—for crochet is entirely based on a series of loops. Without making any effort to pinpoint the exact time in history of the further developments in crochet, let's see if we can continue from this point and develop each step as it must have happened.

Crochet hooks come in many sizes. Steel hooks are numbered from 00 (the largest) to 14 (the smallest). Aluminum and Plastic hooks are lettered from E (smallest) to K (largest). With a very fine crochet thread you would use one of the finer or smaller hooks; with a heavy yarn, you would use one of the larger aluminum or plastic size hook. This is a book of pattern stitches only—not an instruction book for making any specific article. The patterns have been worked with yarn, so that the stitch detail can be seen in more detail. The finer yarns were worked with a No. 2 steel hook, medium weights with F or G aluminum hooks and the heavier weight with an H hook. The appearance of any pattern can be greatly changed by substituting other weight yarns or crochet threads and by changing to another size hook. These changes can prove to be one of the greatest fascinations of crochet.

No effort has been made to use specific names for specific patterns. Many patterns included here have been found in old, old books under one name, and in later books, although the pattern is the same, the name of the pattern is entirely different. Our patterns have been divided into certain descriptive classifications, with some poetic license taken. A pattern placed under one heading might very well be just as aptly placed under another one. Many patterns are combinations of a variety of stitches and might fit into three or four separate classifications.

There are many familiar crochet patterns that must be worked in one continuous direction, and the thread must be cut at the end of every row. These patterns have not been included in this collection for the simple reason that the crocheter today dislikes the tediousness of weaving in a multitude of loose ends. Another complaint often expressed is that the side edges of crochet are uneven. To solve this problem, end (or selvedge) stitches have been added to the original instructions. To maintain the straight edge, all shaping by increasing and decreasing should be done inside these end stitches.

This book is geared to neither the expert nor the beginner, but can be used by both. All a beginner need do is learn the basic stitches or refer to them when in doubt and when following written instructions, to work from comma to comma and never try to read and remember more than one step at a time.

The only innovation in the entire book is the use of the word triple as opposed to the traditional word treble. This may cause some consternation among the old time crocheters, but the dictionary considers the word treble as primarily a musical term, whereas the definition of triple is more in line with our usage of the words single and double.

Our terms for the basic stitches (single, double, triple, etc.) apply to the number of times pairs of stitches are worked off: in single crochet, 2 loops are worked off once—double crochet, 2 loops are worked off twice, etc. Literal translations of European instructions may prove confusing, since they have no slip stitch as we use it and have named their basic stitches by the number of loops on the hook before the next stitch is made. Our slip stitch thus is their single crochet, our single crochet is their double crochet, etc. If this sounds confusing to you, don't give it another thought, but always be sure to check the glossary of terms and abbreviations given in any instruction book.

THE LOWLY SLIP STITCH

To continue our imaginative recreation of the development of crochet, it would seem that the single crochet, being the first real stitch, must have been the next step. But old European books prove us wrong. The slip stitch must have come first because even now the slip stitch, as we know it, is called a single crochet in modern European crochet. Along the way, perhaps in translation or perhaps for simplification, our method of doing the basic stitches is "one loop removed" from foreign patterns. So we'll consider the slip stitch first and ponder on how it came about. Our guess is that the chain remained the one and only discovery for a long time. If you have ever seen a youngster sit and make a chain of string, over and over again, you realize that, over a certain length of time, it can be fascinating—at least to the child. Making a chain could be the very first hobby of man! And there were many things this chain might be used for—pulling things, tying things, etc. The chain alone may have lasted centuries, with no further progress along the lines of handcraft, until thread and strings were produced. The early history of mankind was on the bloodthirsty side, so it seems highly probable that our early ancestors saw more possibilities in the chain for things other than personal adornment—as chain mail and iron links to fetter human beings! So let's leave our very early ancestor, surrounded by coils of chains and jump ahead to a later time in civilization. One day someone made a chain and decided to see what would happen by pulling new loops thru those already formed. We have no idea of just when the crochet hook came into existence, but are convinced that the earliest experimentation was done with just the fingers. Since a finger is only so long, the obvious thing to do with a new loop would be to pull it thru the previous loop and right there is the first slip stitch. A creative mind, then and there, might have seen that this loop through loop idea could also be used to form a circle. However, the creative mind could have stopped right then, holding the development of crochet back for some time, because the slip stitch is certainly a bit more interesting than a chain, but it is also a method that shows little progress of getting any place—hence we have named it the "lowly" stitch—since that is just what it is. A slip stitch is the shortest (or lowest) crochet stitch among the basic stitches.

THE BASIC CROCHET STITCHES

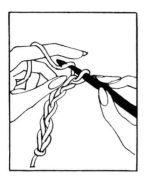

1

1. All crochet begins with a chain. In working any stitch, ALWAYS INSERT HOOK UNDER THE 2 TOP STRANDS unless otherwise specified.

A **SLIP STITCH** is worked by (2) inserting the hook into a stitch and then drawing the yarn thru **BOTH** stitch and loop on hook. It is used to carry the yarn to a specified position without breaking the yarn and it adds no height to the work. (3) It is always used to form a ring, as shown.

2

3

A **SINGLE CROCHET** is the shortest of the basic stitches.

4. Insert hook in stitch and draw yarn thru. (2 loops on hook).

5. Draw yarn thru both loops, completing 1 single crochet. Always chain 1 to start a new row or round.

SINGLE CROCHET

DOUBLE CROCHET

4

5

A **DOUBLE CROCHET** is one step longer than a single crochet.

6. Yarn over hook once and insert hook thru stitch. Draw yarn thru stitch. (3 loops on hook).

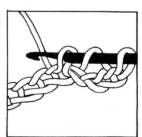

6

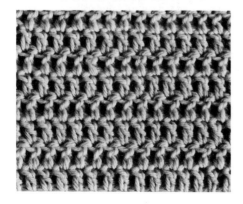

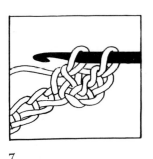

7

8

A *HALF DOUBLE CROCHET* is longer than a single crochet and shorter than a double crochet.

9. Yarn over hook once and insert hook thru stitch. Draw yarn thru stitch. (3 loops on hook).

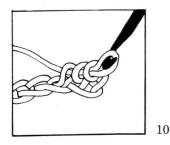

10

7. Draw yarn thru 2 loops. (2 loops on hook).

8. Draw yarn thru both loops, completing 1 double crochet. Always chain 2 or 3 (as specified) to start a new row or round.

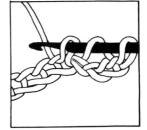

9

10. Draw yarn thru all 3 loops, completing 1 half double crochet. Always chain 2 to start a new row or round.

HALF DOUBLE CROCHET

TRIPLE CROCHET

The following basic stitches are all worked similar to a double crochet, with the addition of extra yarn overs, forming longer stitches.

A *TRIPLE CROCHET* is one step longer than a double crochet. Yarn over hook twice and insert hook thru stitch. Draw yarn thru. (4 loops on hook). (Draw yarn thru 2 loops) 3 times. Always chain 3 to start a new row or round.

A *DOUBLE TRIPLE CROCHET* is one step longer than a triple crochet. Yarn over hook 3 times and insert hook thru stitch. Draw yarn thru. (5 loops on hook). (Draw yarn thru 2 loops) 4 times. Always chain 4 to start a new row or round.

A *TRIPLE TRIPLE CROCHET* is one step longer than a double triple crochet. Yarn over hook 4 times and insert hook thru stitch. Draw yarn thru. (6 loops on hook). (Draw yarn thru 2 loops) 5 times. Always chain 5 to start a new row or round.

BASIC AFGHAN STITCH

All afghan stitch patterns start with a chain.
One row of afghan stitch is worked in two steps, right to left, then left to right.
In instructions this is always considered as one row only.

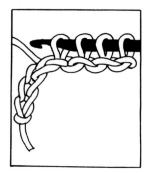

1. *Row 1—First Half:* Skip first chain from hook. * Insert hook thru top loop only of next ch and draw yarn thru, forming loop on hook. Retain loop on hook and repeat from * to end of chain. There will be the same number of loops on hook as the number of chains.

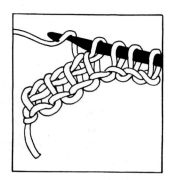

2. *Row 1—Second Half:* Yarn over hook and draw thru first loop. * Yarn over hook and draw thru 2 loops; repeat from * to end. There is 1 loop on hook and this is the first stitch for the next row.

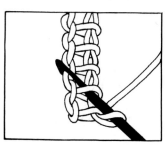

3. *Row 2—First Half:* Insert hook in 2nd upright stitch (called a bar) and draw yarn thru, forming loop on hook. Draw up a loop in each bar to end. There will be the same number of loops on hook as the number of chains.
Row 2—Second Half: Same as 2nd half of Row 1. Repeat Row 2 for Basic Afghan Stitch.

Afghan Stitch is the only crochet stitch that must be bound-off to complete.
To Bind Off: Skip first bar, * draw yarn thru both next bar AND thru loop on hook; repeat from * to end. Break yarn and draw thru last loop to fasten off.

The Single Crochet Patterns

Once the single crochet was discovered, things must have moved at a much faster pace. Here was a stitch that really got some place, whether back and forth in rows or around and around in rounds. Each row added to the last much more rapidly than the slip stitch. Single crochet is the shortest of the basic stitches and it would seem there was little to do with it except working row after row. Boredom is not confined to the present generation and is probably entirely responsible for the development of just about everything when combined with curiosity. So, being bored by the tediousness of single crochet, the first crochet patterns were worked out by our prototype. And in a rather amazing way, for it seems almost ridiculous that so many entirely different patterns could come from one single stitch. The twenty different ones shown here show what can be done. Many of the first lace patterns could have developed from an early combination of just the single crochet and a chain. But sooner or later, even with a variety of patterns, single crochet must have lost its charm—simply because it grew so slowly. So once again, boredom and experimentation obviously led to the first of the yarn over (or wrap yarn around hook) stitches.

It's hard to decide which came first—the half double crochet or the double crochet. Perhaps it is the name of the half double that creates the doubt—for logically this had to precede the double crochet. So we must remember that the terms we use have come about through translations and have possibly been changed many times. A half double crochet, if originally termed a single and a half crochet, would come first. For that is almost as descriptive a term as half double. The poor half double is certainly a stitch in its own right, but is rather like a stepchild—it is more than a single, yet less than a double. As such, it proves an attractive stitch and is widely used but still does not grow in length very rapidly. So the moment those 3 loops were worked off 2 at a time, the whole aspect of crochet became clear. Stitches could be made taller and taller and taller, simply with the addition of more yarn overs.

No. 1

Chain an uneven number.

Foundation Row: Work 1 sc in 2nd ch from hook and in each ch to end. Ch 1, turn.

Row 1: Working thru back loop only, work 1 sc in first and each sc to end. Ch 1, turn.

Repeat Row 1 for pattern.

No. 2

Chain an even number.

Foundation Row: Work 1 sc in 2nd ch from hook and in each ch to end. Ch 1, turn.

Row 1: Sc in first sc, * ch 1, skip 1 sc, sc in next sc; rep from * to end. Ch 1, turn.

Row 2: Sc in first sc, * sc under next ch-1, ch 1, skip next sc; rep from *, ending sc under ch-1, sc in last sc. Ch 1, turn.

Row 3: Sc in first sc, * ch 1, skip next sc, sc under next ch-1; rep from *, ending ch 1, skip 1 sc, sc in last sc. Ch 1, turn.

Repeat Rows 2 and 3 for pattern.

No. 3

Chain an uneven number.

Foundation Row: Work 1 sc in 2nd ch from hook and in each ch to end. Ch 1, turn.

Row 1: Working thru front loop only, work 1 sc in first and each sc to end. Ch 1, turn.

Repeat Row 1 for pattern.

No. 4

Chain a multiple of 4 plus 9 to turn.

Row 1: Work 1 sc in 9th ch from hook, * ch 5, skip 3 ch, sc in next ch; rep from * to end. Ch 5, turn.

Row 2: * Sc in center ch of ch-5, ch 5; rep from *, ending sc in 6th ch of turning ch. Ch 5, turn.

Row 3: * Sc in center ch of ch-5, ch 5; rep from * to end. Ch 5, turn.

Repeat Row 3 for pattern. (To finish with a straight edge, on last row ch 3 between each sc.)

No. 5

Chain an even number.

Row 1: 2 sc in 2nd ch from hook, * skip 1 ch, 2 sc in next ch; rep from * to end. Ch 2, turn.

Row 2: * Skip first sc, 2 sc in next sc; rep from *, ending 1 sc in last sc, 1 sc in top of turning ch. Ch 2, turn.

Repeat Row 2 for pattern.

No. 6

Chain an even number.

Row 1: Sc in 2nd ch from hook, * (sc, ch 1, sc) in next ch, skip 1 ch; rep from *, ending (sc, ch 1, sc) in next to last ch, 1 sc in last ch. Ch 2, turn.

Row 2: Work (1 sc, ch 1, 1 sc) under each ch-1 across, ending 1 sc in top of turning ch. Ch 2, turn.

Repeat Row 2 for pattern.

No. 7

Chain a multiple of 6 plus 4.

Foundation Row: Work 1 sc in 2nd ch from hook and in each ch to end. Ch 1, turn.

Row 1: Working thru back loop only, 1 sc in each of first 3 sc, * thru front loop only, 1 sc in each of next 3 sc; thru back loop only, 1 sc in each of next 3 sc; rep from * to end. Ch 1, turn.

Row 2: Thru front loops work 1 sc in each of first 3 sc, * thru back loops work 1 sc in each of next 3 sc, thru front loops work 1 sc in each of next 3 sc; rep from * to end. Ch 1, turn.

Repeat Rows 1 and 2 for pattern.

No. 8

Chain an even number.

Foundation Row: Work 1 sc in 2nd ch from hook and in each ch to end. Ch 1, turn.

Row 1: 1 sc in first sc, * 1 sc thru back loop of next sc, 1 sc in next sc; rep from *, ending sc in last sc. Ch 1, turn.

Row 2: 1 sc in first sc, * 1 sc thru front loop of next sc, 1 sc in next sc; rep from *, ending sc in last sc. Ch 1, turn.

Repeat Rows 1 and 2 for pattern.

No. 9

Chain a multiple of 4.

Row 1: 1 sc in 2nd ch from hook and in each ch to end. Ch 1, turn.

Row 2: Thru back loop only, work 1 sc in first and each sc to end. Ch 1, turn.

Row 3: * 1 sc in back loop of each of next 3 sc, insert hook into next st in row below, draw up a long loop, yo and thru 2 loops (long sc), skip sc behind long sc; rep from *, ending sc in back loop of each of last 3 sc. Ch 1, turn.

Row 4: Work same as Row 2.

Row 5: 1 sc in back loop of first sc, long sc in next st in row below; rep from * of Row 3, ending with a long sc, sc in back loop of last sc.

Repeat from Row 2 for pattern.

No. 10

Chain a multiple of 4.

Foundation Row: Sc in 2nd ch from hook and in each ch to end. Ch 1, turn.

Rows 1 and 2: 1 sc in first and each sc to end. Ch 1, turn.

Row 3: * 1 sc in each of next 3 sc, insert hook into next st 2 rows below, draw up a long loop, yo and thru 2 loops (long sc), skip sc behind long sc; rep from * to end. Ch 1, turn.

Row 4: 1 sc in first and each sc to end. Ch 1, turn.

Row 5: 1 sc in first sc, long sc in next sc 2 rows below, skip sc behind long sc; rep from * of Row 3, ending long sc, sc in last sc. Ch 1, turn.

Repeat from Row 2 for pattern.

No. 11

Chain an even number.

Row 1: Draw up loop in 3rd ch from hook, * yo and thru 1 loop, yo and thru 2 loops, draw up loop in next ch; rep from * to end. Ch 2, turn.

Row 2: Skip first st, * draw up loop in next st, yo and thru 1 loop, yo and thru 2 loops; rep from *, ending last st in top of turning ch. Ch 2, turn.
Repeat Row 2 for pattern.

No. 12

Chain an uneven number.

Row 1: Draw up loop in 3rd ch from hook, * yo and thru 1 loop, yo and thru 2 loops, * ch 1, skip 1 ch, draw up loop in next ch, yo and thru 1 loop, yo and thru 2 loops; rep from * to end. Ch 2, turn.

Row 2: Under each ch-1, draw up loop, yo and thru 1 loop, yo and thru 2 loops, ch 1, ending with last st under turning ch. Ch 2, turn.
Repeat Row 2 for pattern.

No. 13

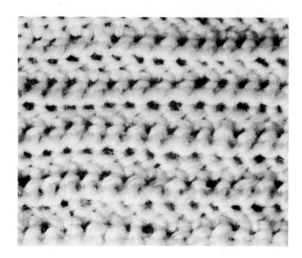

Chain an uneven number.

Foundation Row: 1 sc in 2nd ch from hook and in each ch to end. Ch 1, turn.
Row 1: Keeping yarn at front and holding with thumb under hook, work 1 sc in first and each sc to end. Ch 1, turn.
Repeat Row 1 for pattern.

No. 14

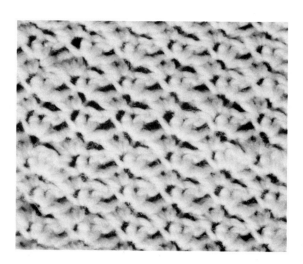

Chain an even number.

Foundation Row: 1 sc in 2nd ch from hook and in each ch to end. Ch 1, turn.
Row 1: 1 sc in first sc, ch 1, * skip next sc, 2 sc in next sc, ch 1; rep from *, ending ch 1, skip 1 sc, 1 sc in last sc. Ch 1, turn.
Row 2: 1 sc in first sc, ch 1, * skip ch-1 and next sc, 2 sc in next sc, ch 1; rep from *, ending ch 1, 1 sc in last sc. Ch 1, turn.
Repeat Row 2 for pattern.

No. 15

Chain an even number.

Row 1: 1 sc in 2nd ch from hook, 1 hdc in same ch, * skip next ch, 1 sc in next ch, 1 hdc in same ch (group); rep from * to end. Ch 1, turn.
Row 2: 1 sc in each hdc and in each sc to end. Ch 1, turn.
Row 3: * Skip 1 sc, group in next sc; rep from * to end. Ch 1, turn.
Repeat Rows 2 and 3 for pattern.

No. 16

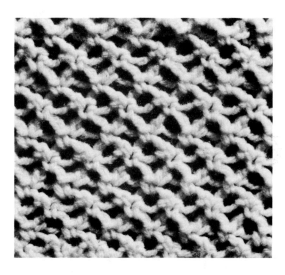

Chain a multiple of 3 plus 1.

Foundation Row: 1 sc in 2nd ch from hook and in each ch to end. Turn.
Row 1: * Draw up loop to about ½ inch, draw yarn thru loop, insert hook between loop and single strand and work 1 sc (to complete knot), skip first 2 sc, 1 sc in next sc, * draw up loop and complete knot, skip next 2 sc, 1 sc in next sc; rep from * to end. Turn.
Row 2: * Draw loop up and complete knot, 1 sc under 2 top strands of next loop; rep from *, ending 1 sc under 2 top strands of last loop. Turn.
Repeat Row 2 for pattern.

No. 17

Chain a multiple of 3 plus 1.

Row 1: 1 sc in 2nd ch from hook, * ch 1, skip 1 ch, 1 sc in each of next 2 ch; rep from *, ending 1 sc in last ch. Ch 1, turn.

Row 2: 1 sc in first sc, * ch 1, skip 2 sc, 2 sc in sp under next ch-1; rep from *, ending 1 sc in last sc. Ch 1, turn.

Repeat Row 2 for pattern.

No. 18

Chain a multiple of 4 plus 3.

Foundation Row: 1 sc in 2nd ch from hook and in each ch to end. Ch 1, turn.

Row 1: 1 sc in first sc, * ch 4, 1 sc in each of next 4 sc; rep from *, ending ch 4, 1 sc in last sc. Ch 1, turn.

Row 2: Holding ch-4 at back (right side), work 1 sc in each sc to end. Ch 1, turn.

Row 3: 1 sc in each of first 3 sc, * ch 4, 1 sc in each of next 4 sc; rep from *, ending ch 4, 1 sc in each of last 3 sc. Ch 1, turn.

Row 4: Same as Row 2.

Repeat from Row 1 for pattern.

No. 19

Chain an even number.

Row 1: 1 sc in 2nd ch from hook, in next ch work 1 sc and 1 hdc (cluster), * skip next ch, cluster in next ch; rep from *, ending 1 sc in last ch. Ch 1, turn.

Row 2: Working in front loops only, 1 sc in first sc, work 1 cluster in each hdc across, ending 1 sc in last sc. Ch 1, turn.

Repeat Row 2 for pattern.

No. 20

Chain an even number.

Row 1: 1 hdc in 3rd ch from hook and in each ch to end. Ch 2, turn.

Row 2: 1 hdc in first hdc and in each hdc to end. Ch 1, turn.

Row 3: 1 sc in first hdc, * skip next hdc, 1 sc in next hdc, 1 sc in skipped hdc; rep from *, ending 1 sc in last hdc. Ch 2, turn.

Row 4: 1 hdc in first sc and in each sc to end. Ch 1, turn.

Row 5: Rep Row 3. Ch 2, turn.

Row 6: 1 hdc in first sc and in each sc to end. Ch 2, turn.

Row 7: 1 hdc in first hdc and in each hdc to end. Ch 1, turn.

Repeat from Row 3 for pattern.

Double Crochet

Without any doubt, this is the most widely used of the basic stitches and is the first yarn over stitch. It is very hard to decide just how to classify double crochet patterns since this stitch is used in practically all of the classifications chosen for this book. Filet Crochet, for example, is worked primarily with double crochet, yet Filet has come to mean a stitch in itself. In fact, you will find double crochet stitches cropping up in every following classification. One very specific double crochet pattern that fits in no other group is the "V-Stitch"—probably the first stitch that led our early experimenter on to the shell patterns and then to the more complicated ones. The double crochet certainly led to the triple crochet—if a yarn over the hook once is interesting, why not a yarn over twice? Happily our early designers seem to have stopped with the triple triple stitch, but if you are enjoying our imaginative trip back into history, can't you almost see someone getting carried away with yarn over stitches—each one taller than the one before. Who knows why today's stitches stop where they do—maybe at that particular time in history counting was unknown and our crocheter may have well been the originator of one of our better known adages—"Let well enough alone."

No. 1

Chain a multiple of 5.

Row 1: Dc in 3rd ch from hook, 1 dc in each of next 2 ch, * ch 1, skip 1 ch, 1 dc in each of next 4 ch; rep from * to end. Ch 4, turn.

Row 2: * Sc under next ch-1 sp, ch 4; rep from *, ending sc in top of turning ch. Ch 2, turn.

Row 3: 3 dc under first ch-4 loop, * ch 1, skip next sc, 4 dc under next ch-4 loop; rep from * to last ch-4 loop, 3 dc under loop, 1 dc in first ch of turning ch. Ch 4, turn. Repeat Rows 2 and 3 for pattern.

No. 2

Chain a multiple of 6 plus 2.

Row 1: 1 dc in 3rd ch from hook, 1 dc in next ch, * ch 3, skip 3 ch, 1 dc in each of next 3 ch; rep from *, ending skip 3 ch, 1 dc in last ch. Ch 2, turn.

Row 2: 2 dc under first ch-3, * ch 3, 3 dc under next ch-3; rep from *, ending ch 3, 1 dc in top of turning ch. Ch 2, turn. Repeat Row 2 for pattern.

No. 3

Chain a multiple of 3.

Row 1: 3 dc in 5th ch from hook, * skip 2 ch, 3 dc (group) in next ch; rep from *, ending 1 dc in last ch. Ch 2, turn.

Row 2: * In each of the 3 group sts work (yo, draw up loop, yo and thru 2 loops), yo and thru 4 loops, ch 1; rep from *, ending 1 dc in top of turning ch. Ch 2, turn.

Row 3: Work a 3-dc group in each ch-1, ending with 1 dc in top of turning ch. Ch 2, turn.

Repeat Row 2 and 3 for pattern.

No. 4

Chain a multiple of 8.

Row 1: Sc in 8th ch from hook, * ch 3, skip 3 ch, 1 sc in next ch, rep from * to end. Ch 2, turn.

Row 2: Work 4 dc under first ch-3, * ch 1, 1 dc under next ch-3, ch 1, 4 dc under next ch-3; rep from *, ending 4 dc under last ch-3, 1 dc in 6th ch of turning ch. Ch 4, turn.

Row 3: * Skip next 4 dc, sc under next ch-1, ch 3, skip 1 dc, sc under next ch-1, ch 3; rep from *, ending skip last 4 dc, 1 sc in top of turning ch. Ch 3, turn.

Row 4: 1 dc under first ch-3, ch 1, * 4 dc under next ch-3, ch 1, 1 dc under next ch 3, ch 1; rep from *, ending 1 dc under last ch-3, ch 1, 1 dc in first ch of turning ch. Ch 1, turn.

Row 5: 1 sc in first dc, * ch 3, skip next dc, sc under next ch-1, ch 3, skip 4 dc, sc under next ch-1; rep from *, ending skip last dc and 1 ch, sc in 2nd ch of turning ch. Ch 2, turn.

Repeat from Row 2 for pattern.

No. 5

Chain an even number.

Row 1: In 2nd ch from hook work 1 sc and 1 dc, * skip next ch, in next ch work 1 sc and 1 dc; rep from *, ending skip next ch, sc in last ch. Ch 1, turn.

Row 2: 1 sc in first sc, * work 1 sc and 1 dc in next dc, skip next sc; rep from *, ending 1 sc in last sc. Ch 1, turn.

Repeat Row 2 for pattern.

No. 6

Chain an uneven number.

Row 1: Work 1 dc in 4th ch from hook, keeping hook in back of last dc, work 1 dc in 3rd ch from hook * skip 1 ch, 1 dc in next ch, from back work 1 dc in skipped st (crossed dc), rep from * to last ch, 1 dc in last ch. Ch 2, turn.

Row 2: Skip first dc, * work crossed dc over next 2 dc; rep from *, ending 1 dc in top of turning ch. Ch 2, turn.

Repeat Row 2 for pattern.

No. 7

Chain an uneven number.

Foundation Row: 1 sc in 2nd ch from hook and in each ch to end. Ch 2, turn.

Row 1: Yo, insert hook in first sc and draw up loop, yo and thru 1 loop, insert hook in next sc and draw up loop, yo and thru 3 loops, yo and thru 2 loops, * yo, draw up loop in last sc worked, yo and thru 1 loop, draw up loop in next sc, yo and thru 3 loops, yo and thru 2 loops; rep from *, ending 1 dc in last sc. Ch 1, turn.

Row 2: 1 sc in first dc and in each st across, ending 1 sc in turning ch. Ch 2, turn. Repeat Rows 1 and 2 for pattern.

No. 8

Chain an uneven number.

Row 1: Skip first ch from hook, * 1 sc in next ch, 1 dc in next ch; rep from *, ending 1 dc in last ch. Ch 1, turn.

Row 2: * I sc in dc, 1 dc in sc; rep from *, ending with 1 dc in last sc. Ch 1, turn. Repeat Row 2 for pattern.

No. 1

No. 2

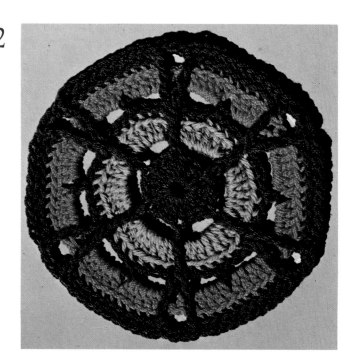

No. 1

Worked in 3 colors, A, B, and C.

With A, ch 4. Join with sl st to form a ring.

Rnd 1: * 1 sc in ring, ch 10; rep from * 7 times more. Join with sl st to first sc. Break A.

Rnd 2: Join B at top of any ch-10 loop, ch 3, 2 dc under same loop, * under next loop work (3 dc, ch 2, 3 dc) for corner, 3 dc under next loop; rep from * around, ending with a corner. Join with sl st in top of ch-3. Break B.

Rnd 3: Join C in ch-2 of any corner, ch 2, work 2 dc under same ch-2, * 1 dc in each dc to ch-2 of next corner, 3 dc under ch-2; rep from * around. Join and fasten off.

No. 2

Worked with 3 colors, A, B, and C.

With A, ch 4. Join with sl st to form a ring.

Rnd 1: Ch 3 (count as 1 dc), work 17 dc in ring. Join with sl st to top of ch-3.

Rnd 2: Ch 1, 1 sc in same place with joining, * ch 5, skip 2 dc, 1 sc in next dc; rep from * around, ending ch 5. Join with sl st to first sc. (6 loops). Drop A, draw B thru loop on hook.

Rnd 3: Work sl st under first ch-5 loop, ch 3 (count as 1 dc), 6 dc under same ch-5, * 7 dc under next ch-5; rep from * around. Join with sl st in top of ch-3. Draw A thru loop on hook. Tighten B, break and fasten off.

Rnd 4: * Yo twice, insert hook from right to left behind next sc of Rnd 2, yo and draw up loop to height of dc of Rnd 3, (yo and thru 2 loops) 3 times; thru back loops work 1 sc in each of next 7 dc; rep from * around. Join with sl st to top of first tr, ch 1.

Rnd 5: 1 sc in same st with sl st, * ch 5, skip 3 sts, 1 sc in next st; rep from * around. Join with sl st to first sc. (12 loops). Drop A, draw C thru loop on hook.

Rnd 6: Sl st under first ch-5, ch 3, 5 dc under same ch-5, * 6 dc under next ch-5; rep from * around. Join with sl st, draw A thru loop on hook, tighten C and fasten off.

Rnd 7: Ch 1, yo 3 times, insert hook under tr of Rnd 4, yo and draw up long loop, (yo and thru 2 loops) 4 times (dtr worked around tr), ch 2, dtr around same tr, skip 1 st, * thru back loops, 1 sc in each of next 10 sts, dtr around next tr, ch 2, dtr around same tr, skip 2 sts; rep from * around, ending 1 sc thru back loop of each of 10 sts. Skip last st, join with sl st to first dtr.

Rnd 8: Ch 1, yo, insert hook behind first dtr, yo and draw up loop, yo and thru 3 loops on hook (hdc worked around dtr), 3 sc under ch-2, hdc around next dtr, 1 sc in back loop of each of next 10 sts; rep from * around. Join with sl st to first hdc and fasten off.

No. 3

Worked with 2 colors, A and B.

With A, chain 4. Join with sl st to form a ring.

Rnd 1: Ch 2, work 9 dc in ring. Join with sl st to top of ch-2.

Rnd 2: Ch 1, 1 sc in joining, 2 sc in next dc, * 1 sc in next dc, 2 sc in next dc; rep from * around. Join with sl st to first sc.

Rnd 3: Ch 1, 1 sc in joining, 1 sc in next sc, 2 sc in next sc, * 1 sc in each of next 2 sc, 2 sc in next sc; rep from * around. Join with sl st to first sc. (20 sc).

Rnd 4: * Ch 7, 1 sc in 2nd ch from hook and in each of next 5 ch, sl st in next sc, 1 sc in next sc; rep from * around. Join and turn.

Rnd 5: * Skip sc and sl st, 1 sc in back loop of each of next 6 sc, in top of point work (1 sc, ch 1, 1 sc), 6 sc on other side of ch; rep from * around, ending sl st in joining sl st. Draw B thru loop, break A. Turn.

Rnd 6: Skip first sc, * 1 sc in back loop of each of 6 sc, in ch-1 of point work (1 sc, ch 2, 1 sc), 1 sc in back loop of each of next 6 sc, skip next 2 sc; rep from * around, ending skip next sc, sl st in sl st. Turn.

Rnds 7, 8 and 9: Work as Rnd 6, thru back loops of 6 sts at each side of points with (1 sc, ch 2, 1 sc) under ch at each point. Fasten off.

No. 4

Worked in 3 colors, A, B, and C.

With A, ch 6. Join with sl st to form a ring.

Rnd 1: Ch 1, in ring work (3 sc, ch 4) 4 times. Join with sl st.

Rnd 2: Ch 1, * 1 sc in each of 3 sc, sl st under ch-3, ch 9, sl st under same ch-3; rep from * 3 times. Join with sl st, break and fasten off.

Rnd 3: Holding ch-9 loop to front, join B in sp. * In sp behind ch-9 loop work (2 dc, ch 2, 2 dc), 1 dc in each of next 3 sc; rep from * around. Join with sl st to top of first dc.

Rnd 4: Ch 3, 1 dc in next dc, * 2 dc under next ch-2, 1 dc in ch-9 loop, ch 9, sl st in top of last dc made, 2 dc under same ch-2, 1 dc in each of next 2 dc, ch 3, skip 3 dc, 1 dc in each of next 2 dc; rep from * around. Join with sl st to top of first ch-2. Draw C thru loop, tighten B, break and fasten off.

Rnd 5: Ch 3, 1 dc in each of next 3 dc, * holding ch-9 to front, in dc where ch-9 was started work (2 dc, ch 1, 2 dc), I dc in each of next 4 dc, work 1 tr around post of each of next 3 dc of Rnd 3, 1 dc in each of next 4 dc; rep from * around. Join with sl st to top of first ch-3.

Rnd 6: Ch 1, * 1 sc in each st to corner ch-1 sp, ch 1, 1 sc in ch-9 loop, ch 1; rep from * around. Join with sl st to first ch-1 and fasten off.

No. 3

No. 4

No. 5

No. 6

No. 5

Worked with 4 colors, A, B, C, and D.

With A, chain 5. Join with sl st to form a ring.

Rnd 1: * In next ch work (1 sc, 1 dc, 1 sc); rep from * 3 times. (4 petals).

Rnd 2: * Ch 2, from wrong side sl st to base of 2nd sc of next petal; rep from * 3 times.

Rnd 3: * 4 dc and 1 sl st under next ch-2; rep from * 3 times. Draw B thru loop on hook, tighten and fasten off A.

Rnd 4: * Ch 3, sl st in base of next sl st of previous row; rep from * 3 times.

Rnd 5: * 8 dc and 1 sl st under next ch; rep from * 3 times.

Rnd 6: Rep Rnd 4.

Rnd 7: * 10 dc and 1 sl st under next ch; rep from * 3 times. Draw C thru loop, tighten and fasten off B.

Rnd 8: 3 dc in sl st just made, * ch 2, 3 dc in 5th dc of next petal, ch 1, 3 dc in same dc, ch 2, 3 dc in sp before next petal; rep from *, ending ch 2, sl st in top of first dc. Fasten off C.

Rnd 9: Attach D in any corner ch (between two 3-dc groups). Ch 3 and in same sp work (2 dc, ch 1, 3 dc), ch 2, *(3 dc in next sp, ch 2) twice, in next sp work (3 ch, ch 1, 3 dc), ch 2; rep from * around. Join with sl st to top of first dc and fasten off.

No. 6

Worked with 2 colors, A and B.

With A, chain a multiple of 8 plus 6.

Foundation Row: 1 sc in 2nd ch from hook and in each ch to end. Ch 1, turn.

Row 1: 1 sc in first sc, ch 5, * skip 3 sc, 1 sc in next sc; rep from * to end. Drop A. Draw B thru loop, ch 2, turn.

Row 2: With B work 4 dc under first ch-5, * ch 3, 1 sc under next ch-5, ch 3, 5 dc under next ch-5; rep from *, ending 4 dc under last ch-5, 1 dc in last sc. Pull up loop, drop B. Do not turn.

Row 3: At opposite end draw A thru top of first dc, ch 1, 1 sc in same dc, * ch 5, 1 sc under next ch-3; rep from *, ending ch 5, 1 sc in last dc. Drop A, pull B thru, turn.

Row 4: With B ch 5, 1 sc under first ch-5, * ch 3, 5 dc under next ch-5, ch 3, 1 sc under next ch-5; rep from *, ending 1 sc under last ch-5, ch 3, 1 dc in last sc. Pull up long loop, drop B. Do not turn.

Row 5: At opposite end draw A thru 2nd ch, ch 1, 1 sc in same ch, * ch 5, 1 sc under next ch-3; rep from *, ending 1 sc in last dc. Drop A, draw B thru loop, ch 2, turn. Repeat from Row 2 for pattern.

No. 7

Worked with 2 colors, A and B.

With A, ch 4. Join with sl st to form a ring.

Rnd 1: Ch 3 (count as 1 dc), work 15 dc in ring, join with sl st to top of ch-3 (16 dc in ring).

Rnd 2: Ch 4, * 1 dc in next dc, ch 1; rep from *, ending sl st in 3rd ch of ch-4. Draw B thru loop on hook, tighten A, break and fasten off.

Rnd 3: Ch 3, 4 dc in first sp, drop loop from hook, insert hook from front to back thru top of ch-3 and thru dropped loop, draw loop thru (popcorn), ch 2, * 5 dc in next sp, drop loop from hook, insert hook in top of first of 5-dc group and thru dropped loop, draw loop thru (popcorn), ch 2; rep from * around. Join with sl st to top of ch-3 of first popcorn. Draw A thru loop on hook, tighten B, break and fasten off.

Rnd 4: Ch 3, 2 dc in last ch-2 sp of last row, * (3 dc in next ch-2 sp) 3 times, in next sp work (3 dc, ch 2, 3 dc) for corner; rep from *, ending 3 dc in same sp as first 3 dc, ch 2, join with sl st to top of first ch-3. Draw B thru loop on hook, tighten A, break and fasten off.

Rnd 5: Thru back loops, work 1 sc in same st with sl and in each dc, working 3 sc under each ch-2 at corners. Join and fasten off.

No. 8

Worked with 2 colors, A and B.

With A, chain a multiple of 6 plus 2.

Row 1: 1 sc in 2nd ch from hook, * ch 2, skip next 2 ch, in next ch work (1 dc, ch 2, 1 dc) V st, ch 2, skip next 2 ch, 1 sc in next ch; rep from *, ending with 1 sc in last ch. Draw up a long loop and drop from hook.

Row 2: Join B to first sc at beg of last row, ch 3, 2 dc in same sc, * 1 sc under next ch-2 of V st, 5 dc in next sc; rep from *, ending 3 dc in last sc. Pull A thru loop, drop and tighten B. Ch 1, turn.

Row 3: 1 sc in first dc, * ch 2, V-st in next sc, ch 2, 1 sc in center dc of next 5-dc group; rep from *, ending with 1 sc in top of turning ch. Draw up a long loop and drop from hook.

Row 4: Pull B thru first sc at beg of last row and work same as Row 2.

Repeat Rows 3 and 4 for pattern.

No. 7

No. 8

No. 9

No. 10

No. 9

Worked with 5 colors, A, B, C, D, and E.

With A, chain 4. Join with sl st to form a ring.

   Rnd 1: Ch 3, 2 dc in ring, * ch 3, 3 dc in ring; rep from * twice more, ch 3, join with sl st to top of ch-3. Fasten off.

   Rnd 2: Join B in any ch-3 sp, ch 3, 2 dc in same sp, * ch 2, in next sp work (3 dc, ch 3, 3 dc); rep from * twice more, ch 2, 3 dc in same sp as first ch-3, ch 3, join with sl st to top of ch-3. Fasten off.

   Rnd 3: Join C in any ch-3 corner sp, ch 3, 2 dc in same sp, * ch 2, 3 dc in next sp, ch 2, in corner sp work (3 dc, ch 3, 3 dc); rep from *, ending ch 2, 3 dc in same sp as first ch-3, ch 3, join with sl st to top of ch-3. Fasten off.

   Rnd 4: Join D as in Rnd 3 and work the same, having 2 groups of 3 dc between corners. Fasten off.

   Rnd 5: Join D and work as Rnd 3, having 3 groups of 3 dc between corners. Fasten off.

No. 10

Worked with 2 colors, A and B.

With A, chain a multiple of 4 plus 3.

   Row 1: 1 dc in 3rd ch from hook and in each ch to end. Drop A.

   Row 2: Join B to top of turning ch at beg of last row, ch 2, * 1 dc worked from front around post of next dc, 1 dc worked from back around post of next dc; rep from *, ending with a front post dc around last dc, pull A thru loop, drawing to height of last row. Drop and tighten B. Ch 2, turn.

   Row 3: Skip first dc, * back post dc around next dc, front post dc around next dc; rep from *, ending with back post dc around turning ch. Pull up long loop and drop from hook.

   Row 4: Draw B thru top of ch-2 at other end, ch 2, * front post dc around next dc, back post dc around next dc; rep from *, ending front post dc around last st. Pull A thru loop, drop and tighten B. Ch. 2, turn.

Repeat Rows 3 and 4 for pattern.

No. 11

Worked with 4 colors, A, B, C, and D.

With A, chain 6. Join with sl st to form a ring.

Rnd 1: Ch 3, * (yo, draw up loop in ring, yo and thru 2 loops) 3 times, yo and thru 4 loops (petal), ch 3; rep from * 5 times more, ending ch 3. Join with sl st to top of first petal. Break A.

Rnd 2: Attach B in any ch-3 loop, ch 3, 1 dc in same loop, ch 2, 2 dc in same loop, ch 1, * Under next ch-3 work (2 dc, ch 2, 2 dc), ch 1; rep from *, ending ch 1, join with sl st to top of first ch-3. Break B.

Rnd 3: Attach C in any ch-1 sp, ch 4, * under next ch-2 work (petal, ch 2, petal), ch 1, 1 dc in next ch-1 sp, ch 1; rep from *, ending ch 1, join with sl st to 3rd ch of ch-4. Break C.

Rnd 4: Join D in any ch-2 sp, 2 sc in same sp, * 1 sc in petal, 1 sc in next ch-1, 1 sc in dc, 1 sc in ch-1, 1 sc in petal, 3 sc under ch-2; rep from * around, ending 1 sc under first ch-2, join with sl st to first sc. Fasten off.

No. 12

Worked with 3 colors, A, B, and C.

With A, chain a multiple of 11 plus 10.

Row 1: 1 sc in 2nd ch from hook and in each of next 3 ch, 3 sc in next ch, * 1 sc in each of next 4 ch, skip next 2 ch, 1 sc in each of next 4 ch, 3 sc in next ch; rep from *, ending 1 sc in each of last 4 ch. Ch 1, turn.

Row 2: Skip first sc, 1 sc in each of next 4 sc, 3 sc in next sc, * 1 sc in each of next 4 sc, skip next 2 sc, 1 sc in each of next 4 sc, 3 sc in next sc; rep from * ending 1 sc in each of next 3 sc, skip next sc, 1 sc in last sc. Ch 1, turn.

Repeat Row 2 for pattern, changing colors every 4 rows.

No. 11

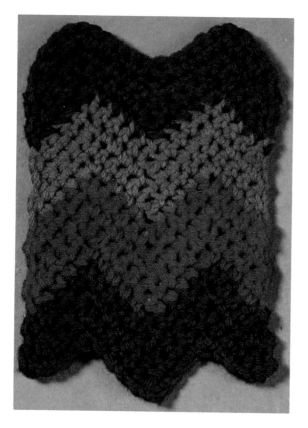

No. 12

No. 13

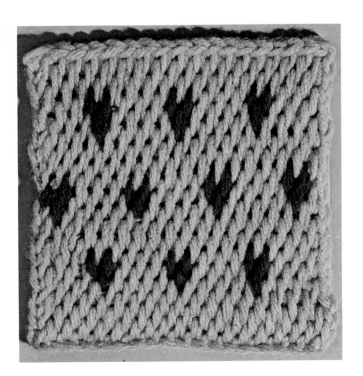

No. 14

No. 13

Worked in 2 colors, A and B.
With A, chain a multiple of 5 plus 4.

Row 1: Basic afghan st.

Rows 2 and 4—First Half: Draw up loop in sp between first and 2nd bars and in each sp to last 2 bars, skip last sp, draw up loop in last bar.

Rows 2 and 4—Second Half: Work off loops in basic afghan st.

Row 3—First Half: Skip sp between first 2 bars, draw up loop in each remaining sp, draw up loop in last bar.

Row 3—Second Half: Work off loops in basic afghan st.

Row 5—First Half: Skip sp between first 2 bars, draw up loop in each of next 3 sps, * drop A; with B draw up loop in next sp, drop B; pick up A, draw up loop in each of next 4 sps; rep from *, (always carry color not in use loosely across wrong side), ending with 3 A loops in last 3 sps, draw up loop in last bar. Break B.

Row 5—Second Half: Work off loops with A in basic afghan st.

Row 6—First Half: Draw up loop in sp between first 2 bars and in each of next 2 sps; * drop A, with B draw up loop in each of next 2 sps; drop B; with A draw up loop in each of next 3 sps; rep from *, ending with 2 A loops, skip last sp, draw up loop in last bar. Break B.

Row 6—Second Half: Work off loops with A.

Rows 7, 8 and 9: Rep Rows 3, 2 and 3.

Row 10—First Half: In first sp draw up 1 A loop, * drop A, with B draw up loop in next sp, drop B; draw up A loops in each of next 4 sps; rep from *, ending skip last sp, draw up A loop in last bar. Break B.

Row 10—Second Half: Work off loops with A.

Row 11—First Half: Skip first sp, * with B draw up loop in each of next 2 sps, drop B; A loops in each of next 3 sps; rep from *, ending 2 B loops, drop B, with A draw up loop in last bar.

Row 11—Second Half: Work off loops with A.
Repeat from Row 2 for pattern.

No. 14

Worked with 2 colors, A and B.
With A, chain a multiple of 8 plus 4.

Row 1: 1 sc in 4th ch from hook, * ch 1, skip next ch, 1 sc in next ch; rep from * to end. Ch 2, turn.

Row 2: * 1 sc in next ch-1 sp, ch 1; rep from *, ending 1 sc under turning ch. Draw B thru loop, drop A. Ch 2, turn.
Repeat Row 2 for pattern, alternating colors every 2 rows.

No. 15

Worked with 5 colors, A, B, C, D, and E.

With A, ch 4. Join with sl st to form a ring.

Rnd 1: Ch 3, 2 dc in ring, * ch 1, 3 dc in ring; rep from * twice more, ch 1, join with sl st to top of ch-3. Fasten off.

Rnd 2: Join B to any ch-1 sp, ch 3, in same sp work (2 dc, ch 2, 3 dc), * ch 2, in next sp work (3 dc, ch 2, 3 dc); rep from * twice more, ch 2, join with sl st to top of ch-3. Fasten off.

Rnd 3: Join C to any ch-2 corner sp, ch 2, 1 hdc in same sp, * 1 hdc after each of next 2 dc, 2 hdc under next ch-2; rep from * around, join with sl st to top of ch-2. Draw D thru loop, tighten C, and fasten off.

Rnd 4: With D, * 1 hdc in each of next 3 sts, 2 hdc in next st; rep from * around, join with sl st to first st. Draw E thru loop, tighten D and fasten off.

Rnd 5: With E, * 1 hdc in each of next 4 sts, 2 hdc in next st; rep from * around, join with sl st. Fasten off.

No. 16

Worked with 2 colors, A and B.

With A, chain an even number.

Row 1—First Half: Basic afghan st. Drop A.

Row 1—Second Half: With B, work off loops.

Row 2—First Half: Insert hook under 2nd and 3rd bars and draw up loop, * yo, draw up loop under next 2 bars; rep from *, ending yo, draw up loop in last bar. Drop B.

Row 2—Second Half: With A, work off loops.

Row 3—First Half: Rep first half of Row 2, inserting hook under bar and slanted st of same color. Drop A.

Row 3—Second Half: With B, work off loops.

Repeat Rows 2 and 3 for pattern.

No. 15

No. 16

No. 9

Chain an even number.

Row 1: 2 dc in 3rd ch from hook, * skip 1 ch, 2 dc in next ch (group); rep from *, ending 1 dc in last ch. Ch 2, turn.

Row 2: Work 2 dc in sp between the dc's of each 2-dc group of Row 1, ending 1 dc in top of turning ch. Ch 2, turn.

Repeat Row 2 for pattern.

No. 10

Chain a multiple of 6 plus 4.

Row 1: In 3rd ch from hook work 1 dc, ch 1, 1 dc (V st), * skip 2 ch, 3 dc in next ch, skip 2 ch, V st in next ch; rep from *, ending 1 dc in last ch. Ch 2, turn.

Row 2: * Work V st under ch-1 of V st, 3 dc in center dc of 3-dc group; rep from *, ending V st, 1 dc in top of turning ch. Ch 2, turn.

Repeat Row 2 for pattern.

No. 11

Chain a multiple of 3.

Row 1: 2 dc in 3rd ch from hook, * skip 2 ch, 1 sc and 2 dc in next ch; rep from *, ending skip 2 ch, 1 sc in last ch. Ch 2, turn.

Row 2: 2 dc in first sc, * skip 2 dc, 1 sc and 2 dc in next sc; rep from *, ending 1 sc in top of turning ch. Ch 2, turn.

Repeat Row 2 for pattern.

No. 12

Chain a multiple of 3.

Row 1: 1 dc in 3rd ch from hook, ch 2, 1 dc in same ch, * skip 2 ch, (2 dc, ch 2, 1 dc) in next ch; rep from * to end. Ch 2, turn.

Row 2: Work (2 dc, ch 2, 1 dc) under first and each ch-2 across, ending 1 dc in top of turning ch. Ch 2, turn.

Repeat Row 2 for pattern.

No. 13

Chain a multiple of 6 plus 5.

Row 1: 1 dc in 3rd ch from hook, * ch 1, 1 dc in each of next 3 ch, ch 2, 1 dc in each of next 3 ch; rep from *, ending ch 1, 1 dc in each of last 2 ch. Ch 3, turn.

Row 2: Under first ch-1 work (1 dc, ch 2, 1 dc), * under next ch-2 work (2 dc, ch 1, 2 dc), under next ch-1 work (1 dc, ch 2, 1 dc); rep from *, ending pat under last ch-1, 1 dc in top of turning ch. Ch 3, turn.

Row 3: * (2 dc, ch 1, 2 dc) under next ch 2, (1 dc, ch 2, 1 dc) under next ch-1; rep from *, ending pat under last ch-2, 1 dc in top of turning ch. Ch 3, turn.

Repeat Rows 2 and 3 for pattern.

No. 14

Chain a multiple of 6 plus 1.

Row 1: 1 dc in 4th ch from hook, * ch 1, skip 2 ch, 1 sc in next ch, ch 1, skip 2 ch, in next ch work (1 dc, ch 2, 2 dc) group; rep from *, ending skip 2 ch, 1 sc in last ch. Ch 2, turn.

Row 2: 1 dc in first sc, * ch 1, 1 sc under the ch-2 of next group, ch 1, work group in next sc; rep from *, ending ch 1, sc in top of turning ch. Ch 2, turn.

Repeat Row 2 for pattern.

No. 15

Chain a multiple of 4 plus 2.

Row 1: Work 3 dc in 4th ch from hook, * skip 1 ch, 1 sc in next ch, skip 1 ch, 3 dc in next ch; rep from *, ending skip 1 ch, 1 dc in last ch. Ch 2, turn.

Row 2: 1 sc in center dc of first 3-dc group, * 3 dc in next sc, 1 sc in center dc of next group; rep from * ending 1 dc in top of turning ch. Ch 2, turn.

Row 3: In first sc work (2 dc, ch 1, 1 dc), * skip 3 dc, in next sc work (2 dc, ch 1, 1 dc); rep from *, ending pat in last sc, 1 dc in top of turning ch. Ch 2, turn.

Row 4: Under first and each ch-1 work (2 dc, ch 1, 1 dc), ending with 1 dc in top of turning ch. Ch 2, turn.

Row 5: 3 dc under next ch-1, * skip next dc, sc in next dc, skip next dc, 3 dc under next ch-1; rep from *, ending skip 2 dc, dc in top of turning ch. Ch 2, turn.
Repeat from Row 2 for pattern.

No. 16

Chain a multiple of 4 plus 3.

Row 1: In 4th ch from hook work (2 dc, ch 1, 1 dc), * skip 3 ch, in next ch work (3 dc, ch 1, 1 dc); rep from *, ending skip 2 ch, 1 dc in last ch. Ch 3, turn.

Row 2: Under first ch-1 work (2 dc, ch 1, 1 dc), * under next ch-1 work (3 dc, ch 1, 1 dc); rep from *, ending pat under last ch-1, 1 dc in 2nd ch of turning ch. Ch 3, turn.
Repeat Row 2 for pattern.

No. 17

Chain a multiple of 3 plus 2.

Row 1: 1 dc in 5th ch from hook, * skip 2 ch, in next ch work (1 dc, ch 2, 1 dc); rep from * to end. Ch 5, turn.

Row 2: 1 dc under first ch-2, * under next ch-2 work (1 dc, ch 2, 1 dc); rep from *, ending with pat under turning ch. Ch 5, turn.
Repeat Row 2 for pattern.

No. 18

Chain a multiple of 10 plus 4.

Row 1: 1 dc in 3rd ch from hook, 1 dc in next ch, * skip 3 ch, in next ch work (2 dc, ch 2, 2 dc) group, skip 3 ch, 1 dc in each of next 3 ch; rep from * to end. Ch 2, turn.

Row 2: Skip first dc, 1 dc in each of next 2 dc, * work group under ch-2 of group, 1 dc in each of 3 single dc; rep from *, ending 1 dc in each of last 2 dc, 1 dc in top of turning ch. Ch 2, turn.
Repeat Row 2 for pattern.

No. 19

Chain a multiple of 6 plus 2.

Row 1: 1 sc in 2nd ch from hook, * skip 2 ch, in next ch work 1 dc, ch 3, 1 dc (V st), skip 2 ch, sc in next ch; rep from * to end. Ch 4, turn.

Row 2: 1 dc in first sc (½ V st), * sc under ch-3 of next V st, V st in next sc; rep from *, ending 1 dc, ch 1 and 1 dc (½ V st) in last sc. Ch 1, turn.

Row 3: 1 sc in first ch-1 space, * V st in next sc, sc under ch-3 of next V st; rep from *, ending 1 sc in top of turning ch. Ch 4, turn.
Repeat Rows 2 and 3 for pattern.

No. 20

Chain an even number.

Foundation Row: 1 dc in 3rd ch from hook and in each ch to end. Ch 3, turn.

Row 1: Skip next dc, * 1 dc in next dc, ch 1, skip 1 dc; rep from *, ending skip last dc, 1 dc in top of turning ch. Ch 3, turn.

Row 2: Yo, draw up loop in first ch-1 sp, * yo and thru 2 loops, yo and draw up loop in next ch-1 sp, yo and thru 2 loops, yo and thru 3 loops, ch 1; yo and draw up loop in same ch-1 sp; rep from *, ending draw up loop in last ch-1 sp, yo and thru 2 loops, yo and draw up loop under turning ch, yo and thru 2 loops, yo and thru 3 loops, ch 1, 1 dc in 2nd ch of turning ch. Ch 3, turn.

Row 3: * Skip ch-1, 1 dc in next st, ch 1; rep from *, ending 1 dc in 2nd ch of turning ch. Ch 3, turn.
Repeat Rows 2 and 3 for pattern.

No. 21

Chain a multiple of 4.

Foundation Row: 1 dc in 3rd ch from hook and in each ch to end. Ch 3, turn.

Row 1: Skip next dc, 1 dc in next dc, * ch 1, skip 1 dc, 1 dc in next dc; rep from *, ending skip last dc, 1 dc in top of turning ch. Ch 3, turn.

Row 2: * Dc in next ch-1 sp, 1 dc in next dc; rep from *, ending 1 dc under turning ch, 1 dc in 2nd ch of turning ch. Ch 2, turn.

Row 3: 1 dc in each of next 2 dc, * ch 1, skip 1 dc, 1 dc in each of next 3 dc; rep from *, ending with last dc in top of turning ch. Ch 2, turn.

Row 4: Work 1 dc in each dc and in each ch-1 sp, ending 1 dc in top of turning ch. Ch 3, turn.

Repeat from Row 1 for pattern.

No. 22

Chain a multiple of 9 plus 4.

Foundation Row: Skip 3 ch, 1 dc in each of next 2 ch, ch 3, skip 2 ch, 1 sc in next ch, * ch 3, skip 2 ch, 1 dc in each of next 4 ch, ch 3, skip 2 ch, 1 sc in next ch; rep from *, ending 1 dc in each of last 3 ch. Ch 3, turn.

Row 1: Skip first dc, 1 dc in each of next 2 dc, ch 3, 1 sc in sc, ch 3, * 1 dc in each of next 4 dc, ch 3, 1 sc in sc, ch 3; rep from *, ending 1 dc in each of last 2 dc, 1 dc in top of turning ch. Ch 1, turn.

Row 2: 1 sc in first dc, ch 2, skip next dc, 1 sc in next dc, * ch 4, 1 sc in first dc of 4-dc group, ch 4, 1 dc in last dc of same group; rep from *, ending ch 4, 1 sc in first dc of last 3-dc group, ch 2, skip last dc, 1 dc in top of turning ch. Ch 1, turn.

Row 3: 1 sc in first sc, ch 3, 4 dc under first ch-4 loop, * ch 3, 1 sc under next ch-4 loop, ch 3, 4 dc under next ch-4 loop; rep from *, ending ch 3, 1 sc in last sc. Ch 1, turn.

Row 4: 1 sc in first sc, ch 3, 1 dc in each dc of 4-dc group, * ch 3, 1 sc in next sc, ch 3, dc in each dc of next group; rep from *, ending ch 3, 1 sc in last sc. Ch 1, turn.

Row 5: 1 sc in first sc, ch 2, 1 sc in first dc of group, ch 4, 1 dc in last dc of same group, * ch 4, 1 sc in first dc of next group, ch 4, 1 sc in last dc of same group; rep from *, ending ch 2, 1 sc in last sc. Ch 3, turn.

Row 6: 2 dc under ch-2 loop, ch 3, 1 sc under next ch-4 loop, ch 3, * 4 dc under next ch-4 loop, ch 3, 1 sc under next ch-4 loop, ch 3; rep from *, ending 2 dc under last ch-2 loop, 1 dc in last sc. Ch 3, turn.
Repeat from Row 1 for pattern.

No. 23

Chain a multiple of 6 plus 5.

Foundation Row: 1 sc in 2nd ch from hook and in each ch to end. Ch 3, turn.

Row 1: Skip first 2 sc, * 5 dc in next sc, skip 3 sc; rep from *, ending skip 2 sc, 1 dc in last sc. Ch 1, turn.

Row 2: 1 sc in first dc, ch 2, 1 sc in center dc of 5-dc group, * ch 3, 1 sc in center dc of next group; rep from *, ending ch 2, 1 sc in top of turning ch. Ch 3, turn.

Row 3: * 5 dc in next sc; rep from *, ending 1 dc in last sc. Ch 1, turn.
Repeat Rows 2 and 3 for pattern.

No. 24

Chain a multiple of 6.

Row 1: Work 3 hdc in 3rd ch from hook, * skip 2 ch, 3 hdc in next ch; rep from * to end. Ch 2, turn.

Row 2: Skip first hdc, * 3 hdc in next hdc (center hdc of 3-hdc group), skip 2 hdc; rep from *, ending skip last hdc, 1 dc in top of turning ch. Ch 2, turn.

Repeat Row 2 for pattern.

No. 25

Chain a multiple of 4.

Foundation Row: Work 1 dc in 3rd ch from hook and in each ch to end. Ch 1, turn.

Row 1: 1 sc in each of first 2 dc, * ch 2, skip 2 dc, 1 sc in each of next 2 dc; rep from *, ending 1 sc in last dc, 1 sc in top of turning ch. Ch 2, turn.

Row 2: Skip first sc, 1 dc in next sc, * 2 dc under ch-2, 1 dc in each of next 2 sc; rep from * to end. Ch 1, turn.

Repeat Rows 1 and 2 for pattern.

No. 26

Chain an even number.

Foundation Row: Work 1 sc in 2nd ch from hook and in each ch to end. Ch 4, turn.

Row 1: Skip first 2 sc, 1 dc in next sc, * ch 1, skip next sc, 1 dc in next sc; rep from * to end. Ch 1, turn.

Row 2: Working thru front loop only, work 1 sc in first and in each dc and in each ch ending 1 sc under turning ch, 1 sc in top of turning ch. Ch 4, turn.

Repeat Rows 1 and 2 for pattern.

No. 27

Chain a multiple of 3.

Row 1: Work 3 dc in 6th ch from hook, ch 1, * skip 2 ch, 3 dc in next ch, ch 1; rep from *, ending 1 dc in last ch. Ch 5, turn.

Row 2: 1 dc under first ch-1, * (1 dc, ch 3, 1 dc) under next ch-1; rep from *, ending 1 dc under turning ch, ch 3, 1 dc in 3rd ch of turning ch. Ch 2, turn.

Row 3: 2 dc in first ch-3 sp, * ch 1, 3 dc in next ch-3 sp; rep from *, ending 2 dc under turning ch, 1 dc in 3rd ch of turning ch. Ch 3, turn.

Row 4: (1 dc, ch 3, 1 dc) under first ch-1, * (1 dc, ch 3, 1 dc) under next ch-1; rep from *, ending 1 dc in top of turning ch. Ch 4, turn.

Row 5: 3 dc in first ch-3 sp, * ch 1, 3 dc in next ch-3 sp; rep from *, ending ch 1, 1 dc in top of turning ch. Ch 5, turn.

Repeat from Row 2 for pattern.

No. 28

Chain a multiple of 6 plus 2.

Row 1: 1 dc in 5th ch from hook, ch 3, 1 dc in same ch, * skip 2 ch, 3 dc in next ch, skip 2 ch, (1 dc, ch 3, 1 dc) in next ch; rep from *, ending skip 2 ch, 1 dc in last ch. Ch 3, turn.

Row 2: * 3 dc under next ch-3, in center dc of next 3-dc group work (1 dc, ch 3, 1 dc); rep from *, ending 3 dc under last ch-3, 1 dc under turning ch. Ch 3, turn.

Row 3: * (1 dc, ch 3, 1 dc) in center dc of next group, 3 dc under next ch-3; rep from *, ending (1 dc, ch 3, 1 dc) in last group, 1 dc under turning ch. Ch 3, turn. Repeat Rows 2 and 3 for pattern.

No. 29

Chain a multiple of 6 plus 3.

Foundation Row: 1 sc in 2nd ch from hook and in each ch to end. Turn.

Row 1: Ch 3 (count as first dc), * skip next sc, 1 dc in each of next 2 sc, 1 dc in skipped sc; rep from *, ending 1 dc in last sc. Ch 1, turn.

Row 2: 1 sc in first and in each dc, ending 1 sc in top of turning ch. Turn. Repeat Rows for 1 and 2 for pattern.

No. 30

Chain a multiple of 6 plus 5.

Foundation Row: 1 sc in 2nd ch from hook and in each ch to end. Ch 1, turn.

Row 1: 1 sc in first sc, * ch 3, skip 2 sc, 1 sc in next sc; rep from * to end. Ch 3, turn.

Row 2: 3 dc under first ch-3, * ch 2, 1 sc under next ch-3, ch 2, 3 dc under next ch-3; rep from * ending 1 dc in last sc. Ch 1, turn.

Row 3: 1 sc in first dc, * ch 3, skip 3 dc, 1 sc under next ch-2, ch 3, skip next sc, 1 sc under next ch-2; rep from *, ending ch 3, skip 3 dc, 1 sc in top of turning ch. Ch 5, turn.

Row 4: 1 sc under first ch-3, ch 2, * 3 dc under next ch-3, ch 2, 1 sc under next ch-3, ch 2; rep from *, ending 1 dc in last sc. Ch 1, turn.

Row 5: 1 sc in first dc, ch 3, skip ch-2 and sc, 1 sc under next ch-2, * ch 3, skip 3 dc, 1 sc under next ch-2, ch 3, skip next sc, 1 sc under next ch-2, rep from *, ending ch 3, skip last sc, 1 sc in 3rd ch of turning ch. Ch 3, turn.

Repeat from Row 2 for pattern.

No. 31

Chain a multiple of 8 plus 2.

Foundation Row: 1 sc in 2nd ch from hook and in each ch to end. Ch 4, turn.

Row 1: Skip first sc, 1 dc in next sc, * ch 1, skip 2 sc, in next sc work 1 dc, ch 3, 1 dc (V st), ch 1, skip 2 sc, 1 dc in each of next 3 sc (group); rep from *, ending 1 dc in each of last 2 sc. Ch 4, turn.

Row 2: 1 dc in first dc, * ch 1, under ch-3 of next V st work 7 dc (shell), ch 1, 1 dc in center dc of next group; rep from *, ending 1 dc under turning ch, ch 1, 1 dc in 3rd ch of turning ch. Ch 4, turn.

Row 3: 1 dc in first dc, * ch 1, skip first 2 dc of shell and work 1 dc in each of next 3 dc, ch 1, work V st in next single dc; rep from *, ending 1 dc under turning ch, ch 1, 1 dc in 3rd ch of turning ch. Ch 4, turn.

Row 4: 3 dc in first dc, * ch 1, 1 dc in center dc of next group, ch 1, 7-dc shell under ch-3 of next V st; rep from *, ending 3 dc under turning ch, 1 dc in 3rd ch of turning ch. Ch 3, turn.

Row 5: 1 dc in next dc, ch 1, V st in next single dc, * ch 1, 3-dc group in center 3-dc of next shell, ch 1, V st in next single dc; rep from *, ending 1 dc in last dc, 1 dc in 3rd ch of turning ch. Ch 4, turn.

Repeat from Row 2 for pattern.

No. 32

Chain a multiple of 5 plus 3.

Row 1: 1 dc in 4th ch from hook, * ch 3, 1 sc in 3rd ch from hook (picot), skip next 2 ch, 1 dc in each of next 3 ch; rep from *, ending picot, skip next 2 ch, 1 dc in each of last 2 ch. Ch 3, turn.

Row 2: Skip first dc, 1 dc in next dc, * ch 3, 1 sc in 3rd ch from hook (picot), skip picot of row below, 1 dc in each of next 3 dc; rep from *, ending with picot, 1 dc in last dc, 1 dc in top of turning ch.

Repeat Row 2 for pattern.

No. 33

Chain a multiple of 4.

Row 1: 1 dc in 4th ch from hook, * 1 sc in each of next 2 ch, 1 dc in each of next 2 ch; rep from * to end. Ch 1, turn.

Row 2: 1 sc in each of first 2 dc, * 1 dc in each of next 2 sc, 1 sc in each of next 2 dc; rep from *, ending 1 sc in last dc, 1 sc in top of turning ch. Ch 2, turn.

Row 3: Skip first sc, 1 dc in next sc, * 1 sc in each of next 2 dc, 1 dc in each of next 2 sc; rep from * to end. Ch 1, turn.
Repeat Rows 2 and 3 for pattern.

No. 34

Chain an even number.

Row 1: 1 dc in 6th ch from hook, * ch 1, skip 1 ch, 1 dc in next ch; rep from * to end. Ch 3, turn.

Row 2: Skip first dc, * 2 dc in next dc; rep from *, ending 2 dc in last dc, skip next ch of turning ch, 1 dc in next ch. Ch 3, turn.

Row 3: Skip first 2 dc, 1 dc in next dc, * ch 1, skip 1 dc, 1 dc in next dc; rep from * ending 1 dc in last dc, ch 1, 1 dc in 2nd ch of turning ch. Ch 3, turn.
Repeat Rows 2 and 3 for pattern.

No. 35

Chain an uneven number.

Row 1: 1 sc in 2nd ch from hook, 1 dc in back of sc just worked, * skip 1 ch, 1 sc in next ch, 1 dc in back of sc just worked; rep from * to last ch, 1 sc in last ch. Ch 1, turn.

Row 2: Skip first sc, * in next dc work 1 sc and 1 dc in back of sc just worked, skip next sc; rep from *, ending pat st in last dc, 1 sc in last sc. Ch 1, turn.
Repeat Row 2 for pattern.

No. 36

Chain a multiple of 6 plus 2.

Row 1: 1 sc in 2nd ch from hook, 1 sc in next ch, * skip 1 ch, 3 dc in next ch, skip 1 ch, 1 sc in each of next 3 ch; rep from *, ending 1 sc in each of last 2 ch. Ch 2, turn.

Row 2: 1 dc in first sc, * skip 1 sc, 1 sc in each of next 3 dc, skip 1 sc, 3 dc in next sc; rep from *, ending skip 1 sc, 2 dc in last sc. Ch 1, turn.

Row 3: 1 sc in each of first 2 dc, * skip 1 sc, 3 dc in next sc, skip next sc, 1 sc in each of next 3 dc; rep from *, ending skip 1 sc, 1 sc in top of next dc, 1 sc in top of turning ch. Ch 2, turn.
Repeat Rows 2 and 3 for pattern.

No. 37

Chain a multiple of 6 plus 5.

Foundation Row: 1 sc in 2nd ch from hook and in each ch to end. Ch 1, turn.

Row 1: 1 sc in first sc, * skip 1 sc, 1 dc in next sc, 1 dc in skipped sc, 1 sc in each of next 2 sc; rep from *, ending 1 sc in last sc. Ch 2, turn.

Row 2: Skip first sc, 1 sc in each of next 2 dc, * skip 1 sc, 1 dc in next sc, 1 dc in skipped sc, 1 sc in each of next 2 dc; rep from *, ending 1 dc in last sc. Ch 1, turn.

Row 3: 1 sc in first dc, skip next sc, 1 dc in next sc, 1 dc in skipped sc, * 1 sc in each of next 2 dc, skip 1 sc, 1 dc in next sc, 1 dc in skipped sc; rep from *, ending 1 sc in top of turning ch. Ch 2, turn.

Repeat Rows 2 and 3 for pattern.

No. 38

Chain a multiple of 4.

Row 1: 1 sc in 2nd ch from hook, skip 1 ch, in next ch work (1 dc, ch 1, 1 dc), * skip 1 ch, 1 sc in next ch, skip 1 ch, in next ch work (1 dc, ch 1, 1 dc); rep from * to end. Ch 1, turn.

Row 2: * 1 sc under ch-1, in next sc work (1 dc, ch 1, 1 dc); rep from * to end. Ch 1, turn.

Repeat Row 2 for pattern.

No. 39

Chain a multiple of 3 plus 2.

Foundation Row: 1 sc in 2nd ch from hook and in each ch to end. Ch 1, turn.

Row 1: 1 sc in first sc, * skip 1 sc, 1 dc in next sc, 1 dc in skipped sc, 1 sc in next sc; rep from *, ending 1 sc in last sc. Ch 2, turn.

Row 2 (right side): * 1 sc in each of next 2 dc, 1 dc in next sc; rep from *, ending 1 dc in last sc. Ch 1, turn.

Row 3: 1 sc in first dc, * skip 1 sc, 1 dc in next sc, 1 dc in skipped sc, 1 sc in next dc; rep from *, ending 1 sc in top of turning ch. Ch 2, turn.

Repeat Rows 2 and 3 for pattern.

No. 40

Chain an uneven number.

Foundation Row: 1 sc in 2nd ch from hook and in each ch to end. Ch 1, turn.

Row 1: Skip first sc, * in next sc work (1 sc, ch 1, 1 dc), skip next sc; rep from * to end. Ch 1, turn.

Row 2: In each sc of last row work (1 sc, ch 1, 1 dc). Ch 1, turn.

Repeat Row 2 for pattern.

No. 41

Chain a multiple of 4 plus 3.

Row 1: 2 dc in 3rd ch from hook, skip 3 ch, * in next ch work (1 sc, ch 3, 2 dc), skip next 3 ch; rep from *, ending skip 3 ch, 1 sc in last ch. Ch 2, turn.

Row 2: 2 dc in first sc, * in next ch-3 work (1 sc, ch 3, 2 dc); rep from *, ending 1 sc in top of turning ch. Ch 2, turn.

Repeat Row 2 for pattern.

No. 42

Chain an even number.

Foundation Row: 1 dc in 4th ch from hook and in each ch to end. Ch 1, turn.

Row 1: 1 sc in first dc, ch 2, 1 sc in sp between 2nd and 3rd dc, * ch 2, 1 sc in sp after next 2 dc; rep from *, ending ch 2, 1 sc in top of turning ch. Ch 2, turn.

Row 2: 1 dc under first ch-2, * 2 dc under next ch-2; rep from *, ending 1 dc under last ch-2, 1 dc in last sc. Ch 1, turn.

Repeat Rows 1 and 2 for pattern.

No. 43

Chain an even number.

Row 1: 1 sc and 1 dc in 2nd ch from hook, * skip 1 ch, 1 sc and 1 dc in next ch; rep from * to end. Ch 1, turn.

Row 2: Skip first dc, * 1 sc and 1 dc in next sc, skip next dc; rep from *, ending 1 sc and 1 dc in last sc. Ch 1, turn.

Repeat Row 2 for pattern.

No. 44

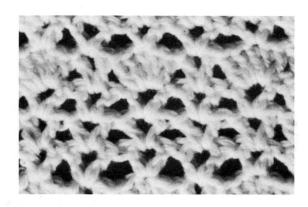

Chain a multiple of 6 plus 2.

Foundation Row: 1 sc in 2nd ch from hook and in each ch to end. Ch 2, turn.

Row 1: 1 dc in first sc, * skip next 2 sc, in next sc work (1 dc, ch 1, 1 dc) V st; rep from *, ending skip 2 sc, 2 dc in last sc. Ch 2, turn.

Row 2: 1 dc in first dc, 5 dc under ch-1 of next V, * V under ch-1 of next V, 5 dc under ch-1 of next V; rep from *, ending skip last dc, 2 dc in top of turning ch. Ch 2, turn.

Row 3: 1 dc in first dc, * V in center dc of 5-dc group, V under ch-1 of next V; rep from *, ending V in last group, 2 dc in top of turning ch. Ch 2, turn.

Rows 4 and 5: 1 dc in first dc, * V under ch-1 of next V; rep from *, ending 2 dc in top of turning ch. Ch 2, turn.

Repeat from Row 2 for pattern.

No. 45

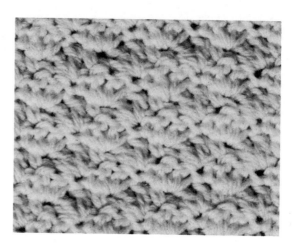

Chain a multiple of 6 plus 2.

Row 1: 1 dc in 4th ch from hook, 1 sc in next ch, * skip 1 ch, 2 dc in next ch, 1 sc in next ch; rep from * to end. Ch 2, turn.

Row 2: 1 dc in first sc, skip 1 dc, 1 sc in next dc, * 2 dc in next sc, skip 1 dc, 1 sc in next dc; rep from *, ending 1 sc in top of turning ch. Ch 2, turn.
Repeat Row 2 for pattern.

No. 46

Chain a multiple of 9 plus 2.

Foundation Row: 1 dc in 4th ch from hook, skip 2 ch, in next ch work (1 dc, ch 1, 1 tr, ch 1, 1 tr, ch 1, 1 dc) shell, * skip 2 ch, 1 dc in each of next 4 ch, skip 2 ch, shell in next ch; rep from *, ending 1 dc in each of last 2 ch. Ch 2, turn.

Row 1: Skip first dc, 1 dc in next dc, * ch 2, in center sp of shell work (1 sc, ch 3, 1 sc), ch 2, 1 dc in each of next 4 dc; rep from *, ending ch 2, 1 dc in last dc, 1 dc in top of turning ch. Ch 2, turn.

Row 2: Skip first dc, 1 dc in next dc, * shell under next ch-3, 1 dc in each of next 4 dc; rep from *, ending 1 dc in last dc, 1 dc in top of turning ch. Ch 2, turn.
Repeat Rows 1 and 2 for pattern.

No. 47

Chain an even number.

Row 1: 1 hdc in 3rd ch from hook and in each ch to end. Ch 2, turn.

Row 2: Skip first hdc, * skip next hdc, 1 dc in next hdc, 1 sc loosely in skipped hdc; rep from *, ending 1 hdc in top of turning ch. Ch 2, turn.

Row 3: Skip first hdc, 1 hdc in each st, ending 1 hdc in top of turning ch. Ch 2, turn.

Repeat Rows 2 and 3 for pattern.

No. 48

Chain a multiple of 10 plus 7.

Row 1: 1 dc in 4th ch from hook, 1 dc in each of next 3 ch, * ch 3, skip 2 ch, 1 sc in next ch, ch 3, skip 2 ch, 1 dc in each of next 5 ch; rep from * to end. Ch 2, turn.

Row 2: Skip first dc, 1 dc in each of next 4 dc, * ch 4, 1 dc in each of next 5 dc; rep from *, ending 1 dc in each of last 4 dc, 1 dc in top of turning ch. Ch 6, turn.

Row 3: 1 sc in center dc of 5-dc group, * ch 3, 5 dc under ch-4, ch 3, 1 sc in center dc of next 5-dc group; rep from *, ending ch 3, 1 dc in top of turning ch. Ch 6, turn.

Row 4: Skip sc, * 1 dc in each of next 5 dc, ch 5; rep from *, ending ch 4, 1 dc in 3rd ch of turning ch. Ch 3, turn.

Row 5: 4 dc under first ch, * ch 3, 1 sc in center dc of 5-dc group, ch 3, 5 dc under next ch-5; rep from *, ending 4 dc under turning ch, 1 dc in 3rd ch of turning ch. Ch 3, turn.

Repeat from Row 2 for pattern.

Loop Patterns

This classification is somewhat of a catch-all for all the patterns that are made with none of the basic stitches. They are simply interesting combinations of loops—few or many, with or without yarn overs (or a combination of both) and then worked off in many different ways. These patterns aren't shells and they aren't clusters. They seem to be the "hit or miss" variety, and, as such, are extremely creative. They must have developed as a real form of experimentation. Another mental picture of our early crocheter—bored with the simple basic stitches. "I'll draw up a loop here, another one there—wonder what would happen if I went down a few rows—let's see what a yarn over will do. Now what shall I do with all these loops . . . etc." Not so crazy as it sounds because somewhere and at some time, someone certainly went thru just such a process or we wouldn't have the great variety of patterns that we do.

No. 1

Chain an even number.

Row 1: * Yo, skip 2 ch, insert hook in next ch and draw up loop, yo and draw up loop in next ch, yo and thru 5 loops, ch 1 (group); rep from * to end. Ch 3, turn.

Row 2: Yo, draw up loop in ch-1 of first group, yo and draw up loop under next ch-1, yo and thru 5 loops, * yo and draw up loop under same ch-1, yo and draw up loop under next ch-1, yo and thru 5 loops; rep from *, ending yo and draw up loop under same (last) ch-1, yo and draw up loop in top of turning ch, yo and thru 5 loops. Ch 3, turn.

Repeat Row 2 for pattern.

No. 2

Chain an uneven number.

Row 1: Yo and draw up loop in 4th ch from hook, * yo and thru 2 loops, yo, skip next ch, draw up loop in next ch, yo and thru 2 loops, yo and thru 3 loops, ch 1, yo, draw up loop in same ch; rep from *, ending ch 1, dc in last ch. Ch 3, turn.

Row 2: Yo, draw up loop under first ch-1, * yo and thru 2 loops, yo, draw up loop under next ch-1, yo and thru 2 loops, yo and thru 3 loops, ch 1, draw up loop under same ch-1; rep from *, ending draw up loop under turning ch, yo and thru 2 loops, yo and thru 3 loops, ch 1, 1 dc in 2nd ch of turning ch. Ch 3, turn.

Repeat Row 2 for pattern.

No. 3

Chain an even number.

Row 1: 1 sc in 2nd ch from hook and in each ch to end. Ch 1, turn.

Row 2: 1 sc in first and each sc to end. Ch 3, turn.

Row 3: Yo, draw up loop in first sc, draw up loop in next sc, yo and thru 4 loops, * ch 1, yo, draw up loop in next sc, draw up loop in next sc, yo and thru all loops; rep from * to last sc, ch 1, 1 dc in last sc. Ch 3, turn.

Row 4: Working thru back loops only, yo and draw up loop in first ch-1, draw up loop in next ch-1, yo and thru all loops, * ch 1, yo and draw up loop in same ch-1, draw up loop in next ch-1, yo and thru all loops; rep from *, ending yo and draw up loop in same ch-1, draw up loop under turning ch, yo and thru all loops ch 1, dc in top of turning ch. Ch 3, turn.

Row 5: Rep Row 4, working under ch-1 sp.

Row 6: Rep Row 4, working thru back loops of ch-1's. Ch 1, turn.

Row 7: Work 1 sc under turning ch-1, * 2 sc in each ch-1 sp; rep from *, ending 1 sc under turning ch, 1 sc in top of turning ch. Ch 1, turn.

Row 8: Work 1 sc in each sc. Ch 3, turn.

Repeat from Row 3 for pattern.

No. 4

Chain an even number.

Row 1: Skip 1 ch, * draw up loop in each of next 2 ch, yo and thru 2 loops, yo and thru 2 loops (group), ch 1; rep from *, ending group in next to last 2 ch, ch 1, sc in last ch. Ch 1, turn.

Row 2: 1 sc in first sc, then work 1 sc under each ch-1 and in each group across row, ending with sc under turning ch. Ch 2, turn.

Row 3: Group in first 2 sc, ch 1, * group in next 2 sc, ch 1; rep from *, ending group in last 2 sc, ch 1, sc in last sc. Ch 1, turn.

Repeat Rows 2 and 3 for pattern.

No. 5

Chain an even number.

Row 1: Skip 1 ch, draw up loop in each of next 2 ch, yo and thru 3 loops, ch 1, * draw up loop in each of next 2 ch, yo and thru 3 loops, ch 1; rep from *, ending 1 sc in last ch, ch 1, turn.

Row 2: * Draw up loop in each of next 2 sts, yo and thru 3 loops, ch 1; rep from *, ending 1 sc in last st, ch 1, turn.

Repeat Row 2 for pattern.

No. 6

Chain an even number.

Foundation Row: Sc in 2nd ch from hook and in each ch to end. Ch 1, turn.

Row 1: Draw up loop in each of first 2 sc, yo and thru 3 loops, ch 1, * draw up loop in each of next 2 sc, yo and thru 3 loops, ch 1; rep from *, ending 1 sc in last sc. Ch 1, turn.

Row 2: Draw up loop in first sc, draw up loop in next ch-1, yo and thru 3 loops, * ch 1, draw up loop in next sc, draw up loop in next ch-1, yo and thru 3 loops; rep from *, ending 1 sc in last sc. Ch 1, turn.

Repeat Row 2 for pattern.

No. 7

Chain an even number.

Foundation Row: Work 1 sc in 2nd ch from hook and in each ch to end. Ch 2, turn.

Row 1: Skip first sc, * yo, insert hook in next sc, draw yarn thru, yo, insert hook in next sc, draw yarn thru, yo hook and draw thru 5 loops, ch 1; rep from * to end. Ch 1, turn.

Row 2: * 1 sc in top of first st, 1 sc under ch 1; rep from *, ending 1 sc under turning ch, 1 sc in top of turning ch. Ch 2, turn.

Repeat Rows 1 and 2 for pattern.

No. 8

Chain an even number.

Foundation Row: Work 1 sc in 2nd ch from hook and in each ch to end. Ch 1, turn.

Row 1: Draw up a loop in each of first 2 sc, yo and thru 3 loops, ch 1 (eye), * draw up loop thru eye, thru last worked sc and thru each of next 2 sc, yo and thru 5 loops, ch 1; rep from *, ending 1 sc in last sc. Ch 1, turn.

Row 2: Work 1 sc in first and in each st across row. Ch 1, turn.

Repeat Rows 1 and 2 for pattern.

No. 9

Chain an even number.

Foundation Row: 1 sc in 2nd ch from hook and in each ch to end. Ch 2, turn.

Row 1: Draw up a loop in each of first 2 sc, yo and thru 3 loops, 1 dc in same sc as last loop, * draw up a loop in each of next 2 sc, yo and thru 3 loops (cluster), 1 dc in same sc as last loop; rep from *, ending 1 dc in last sc. Ch 2, turn.

Row 2: Skip first (single) dc, * draw up loop in next dc and in next cluster, yo and thru 3 loops, 1 dc in same cluster; rep from *, ending 1 dc in top of turning ch. Ch 2, turn.

Repeat Row 2 for pattern.

No. 10

Chain an uneven number.

Foundation Row: 1 sc in 2nd ch from hook and in each ch to end. Ch 2, turn.

Row 1: Skip first sc, * draw up loop in next sc, yo, draw up loop in next sc, yo and thru 4 loops, ch 1; rep from *, ending ch 1, 1 sc in last sc. Ch 2, turn.

Row 2: Draw up loop in first sc, yo and draw up loop in sp to left of single strand, yo and thru 4 loops, ch 1, * draw up loop in sp to right of next single strand, yo, draw up loop in sp to left of same single strand, yo and thru 4 loops, ch 1; rep from *, ending ch 1, 1 sc in top of turning ch. Ch 2, turn.

Repeat Row 2 for pattern.

No. 11

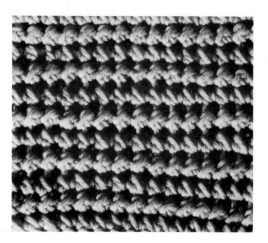

Chain an uneven number.

Foundation Row: 1 sc in 2nd ch from hook and in each ch to end. Ch 2, turn.

Row 1: 1 sc in first sc * draw up loop in same sc, yo, draw up loop in next sc, yo and thru 4 loops; rep from * to end. Ch 2, turn.

Row 2: 1 sc under both loops of first st, * draw up loop under both strands of same st, yo, draw up loop under both strands of next st, yo and thru 4 loops; rep from * to end. Ch 2, turn.

Repeat Row 2 for pattern.

No. 12

Chain an uneven number.

Row 1: Draw up loop in 2nd and each of next 4 ch (6 loops on hook), yo and thru all loops, ch 1 for eye (star), * draw up loop in eye, draw up loop thru back of last loop of last star, draw up loop thru same ch as last loop of last star, draw up loop in each of next 2 ch, yo and thru all 6 loops, ch 1; rep from *, ending 1 hdc in last ch. Ch 1, turn.

Row 2: 1 sc in hdc, 1 sc in first eye, then 2 sc in each eye across row, ending with 1 sc in end ch of last row. Ch 2, turn.

Row 3: Draw up loop in front strand of 2nd ch from hook, then draw up loop in back strand of same ch, draw up loop in each of next 3 sc, yo and thru all 6 loops, ch 1, * draw up loop in eye, draw up loop in back of last loop of star, draw up loop in same sc as last loop of star, draw up loop in each of next 2 sc, yo and thru all 6 loops, ch 1; rep from *, ending with 1 hdc in side of same sc as last loop of star. Ch 1, turn.

Repeat Rows 2 and 3 for pattern.

No. 13

Chain an even number.

Foundation Row: 1 hdc in 3rd ch from hook and in each ch to end. Ch 2, turn.

Row 1: Yo, draw up loop at base of ch-2, * yo, skip 1 st, draw up loop in next st, yo and thru 4 loops, yo and thru last 2 loops, ch 1, yo, draw up loop in same st as last loop; rep from *, ending ch 1, 1 dc in same st as last loop. Ch 3, turn.

Row 2: * 1 hdc in next st, 1 hdc in next ch-1 sp; rep from *, ending 1 hdc in last st, 1 dc under turning ch. Ch 2, turn.

Row 3: Same as Row 1, ending last st under turning ch, 1 dc in 2nd ch of turning ch.

Repeat Rows 2 and 3 for pattern.

No. 14

Chain an uneven number.

Row 1: 1 sc in 3rd ch from hook, * ch 1, skip 1 ch, 1 sc in next ch; rep from * to end. Ch 3, turn.

Row 2: Draw up loop under first ch-1, draw up loop under next ch-1, yo and thru 3 loops, * ch 1, draw up loop under same ch-1 as last loop, draw up loop under next ch-1, yo and thru 3 loops; rep from *, ending draw up loop under same ch-1 as last loop, draw up loop under turning ch, yo and thru 3 loops. Ch 3, turn.
Repeat Row 2 for pattern.

No. 15

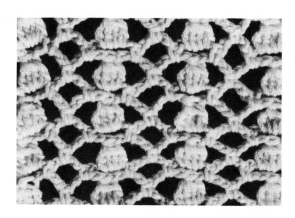

Chain a multiple of 8.

Row 1: 1 sc in 8th ch from hook, * ch 4, skip 3 ch, 1 sc in next ch; rep from * to end. Ch 4, turn.

Row 2: (Yo, draw up loop under first ch-4 loop, yo and thru 2 loops) 4 times, yo and thru 4 loops, yo and thru 2 loops (cluster), * ch 4, 1 sc under next loop, ch 4, cluster under next loop; rep from *, ending cluster under turning ch, tr in 5th ch of turning ch. Ch 4, turn.

Row 3: * 1 sc under next ch-4 loop, ch 4; rep from *, ending ch 4, 1 sc under turning ch. Ch 4, turn.

Row 4: * Cluster under next loop, ch 4, 1 sc under next loop, ch 4, rep from *, ending cluster under turning ch, 1 tr in top of tr of last cluster row. Ch 4, turn.
Repeat Rows 3 and 4 for pattern.

Cluster Patterns

A cluster is a group of 2 or more individual stitches that are partially worked (to the last step) and then all worked together to form what will be a single stitch in the following row. A cluster can be worked with one stitch as a common base, as in shell patterns, or each individual stitch in the cluster can be worked in a separate stitch. Regardless of how it is worked and regardless of the number of stitches in it, that final step that unites the stitches into one makes it a cluster. In the following pages you will find single clusters, multiple clusters, all-over cluster patterns and even sideways clusters. Not to mention both fat clusters and skinny clusters. Imagination plus a combination of guesswork and logic might give us the correct position of the cluster in our historical saga. Logic places it at least after the double crochet, since, to be unfinished in at least one step, there has to be a minimum of 2 steps in the stitch—requiring at least one yarn over. Also, logically, the other yarn over stitches probably pre-dated the cluster. It's the imagination that is much more interesting—to place the cluster before the shell. Picture some early crocheter fooling around with yarn over stitches worked under a chain or each with an individual base and discovering that by drawing them all together at the top, a new pattern had developed. Certainly one interesting enough to pursue further. An accomplishment deserves admiration, so suppose our proud designer picked the work up to admire—and it was upside down. Right then and there must have been born the first glimmer of shell patterns to come. Far fetched? Yes— but still probable.

No. 1

Chain an even number.

Row 1: In 4th ch from hook work (yo, draw up loop, yo and thru 1 loop, yo and thru 2 loops) 3 times, yo and thru 4 loops, ch 1 (cluster made), * skip 1 ch, cluster in next ch; rep from *, ending skip 1 ch, tr in last ch. Ch 3, turn.

Row 2: Work a cluster under first and each ch-1, ending with tr in 3rd ch of turning ch. Ch 3, turn.

Repeat Row 2 for pattern.

No. 2

Chain an even number.

Row 1: In 4th ch from hook work (yo, draw up loop, yo and thru 1 loop, yo and thru 2 loops) 3 times, yo and thru 4 loops, ch 1 (cluster made), * skip 1 ch, cluster in next ch; rep from *, ending skip 1 ch, tr in last ch. Ch 1, turn.

Row 2: * 1 sc in ch-1, 1 sc in top of cluster; rep from *, ending 1 sc in 3rd ch of turning ch. Ch 3, turn.

Row 3: * Skip 1 sc, cluster in next sc; rep from *, ending tr in last sc. Ch 1, turn.

Repeat Rows 2 and 3 for pattern.

No. 3

Chain an even number.

Row 1: Yo and insert hook in 3rd ch from hook, * (yo, draw up long loop) 4 times in same ch, yo and thru 8 loops, yo and thru 2 loops (cluster), ch 1, skip 1 ch, yo, insert hook in next ch; rep from *, ending ch 1, 1 dc in last ch. Ch 2, turn.

Row 2: Work a cluster and ch 1 under first and each ch-1, ending with 1 dc in top of turning ch. Ch 2, turn.
Repeat Row 2 for pattern.

No. 4

Chain a multiple of 3 plus 2.

Foundation Row: Work 1 sc in 2nd ch from hook and in each ch to end. Ch 1, turn.

Row 1: 1 sc in first sc, * in next sc (yo, draw up loop, yo and thru 2 loops) 5 times, yo and thru 6 loops, ch 1, 1 sc in each of next 2 sc; rep from *, ending 1 sc in each of last 2 sc. Ch 1, turn.

Row 2: 1 sc in each sc and in each ch-1, ending 1 sc in last sc. Ch 1, turn.

Row 3: 1 sc in each of first 2 sc, rep from * of Row 2, ending 1 sc in last sc. Ch 1, turn.

Row 4: Same as Row 2.
Repeat from Row 1 for pattern.

No. 5

Chain a multiple of 4.

Foundation Row: Work 1 sc in 2nd ch from hook and in each ch to end. Ch 1, turn.

Rows 1 and 2: Work 1 sc in each sc. Ch 1, turn.

Row 3: 1 sc in first sc, * yo, draw up loop around next sc 2 rows below, yo, draw up loop around same sc (5 loops on hook), yo and thru 3 loops, yo and thru 3 loops (cluster), skip 1 sc, 1 sc in each of next 3 sc; rep from *, ending 1 sc in last sc. Ch 1, turn.

Row 4: 1 sc in first and each st to end. Ch 1, turn.

Row 5: * 1 sc in each of 3 sc, work a cluster around center sc between clusters 2 rows below, skip 1 sc; rep from *, ending 1 sc in each of last 3 sc. Ch 1, turn.

Row 6: Same as Row 4.

Repeat from Row 3 for pattern.

No. 6

Chain a multiple of 8 plus 5.

Foundation Row: 1 dc in 5th ch from hook, * ch 1, skip 1 ch, 1 dc in next ch; rep from * to end. Ch 3, turn.

Row 1: Skip first ch-1, * 1 dc in next dc, (1 dc in next sp, 1 dc in next dc) 3 times, ch 1; rep from *, ending 1 dc in 3rd ch of turning ch. Ch 3, turn.

Row 2: Skip first ch-1, * 1 dc in each of next 3 dc, draw up loop in next dc (yo, draw up loop in same dc) 4 times, yo and thru all 10 loops (popcorn), ch 1 to fasten, 1 dc in each of next 3 dc, ch 1; rep from *, ending 1 dc in 2nd ch of turning ch. Ch 3, turn.

Row 3: Skip first ch-1, * 1 dc in each of next 3 dc, 1 dc in ch-1 of popcorn, 1 dc in each of next 3 dc, ch 1; rep from *, ending 1 dc in 2nd ch of turning ch. Ch 3, turn.

Row 4: Skip first ch-1, * 1 dc in next dc, (ch 1, skip 1 dc, 1 dc in next dc) 3 times ch 1; rep from *, ending 1 dc in 2nd ch of turning ch. Ch 3, turn.

Repeat from Row 1 for pattern.

No. 7

Chain a multiple of 10 plus 4.

Foundation Row: Work 1 sc in 2nd ch from hook and in each ch to end. Ch 2, turn.

Row 1: Skip first sc, 5 dc in next sc, drop loop from hook, insert hook thru top of first dc, catch loop and pull thru dc (popcorn), * skip 4 sc, 9 tr in next sc, skip 4 sc, popcorn in next sc; rep from *, ending 1 dc in last sc. Ch 1, turn.

Row 2: 1 sc in dc, * 1 sc in joining st of popcorn, 1 sc in each tr; rep from *, ending 1 sc in popcorn, 1 sc in top of turning ch. Ch 2, turn.

Repeat Rows 1 and 2 for pattern.

No. 8

Chain a multiple of 3 plus 2.

Row 1: (Yo, draw up loop in 4th ch from hook) twice, yo and thru 5 loops, ch 1 to form eye (½ pat), ch 1, skip 1 ch, in next ch (yo, draw up loop) twice, * skip 2 ch, in next ch (yo, draw up loop) twice, yo and thru 9 loops, ch 1 to form eye (1 pat), ch 2, (yo, draw up loop in same ch as last half of last pat) twice; rep from *, ending (yo, draw up loop in same ch as last half of last pat) twice, yo and thru 5 loops, ch 1 to form eye, ch 1, skip 1 ch, 1 dc in last ch. Ch 2, turn.

Row 2: (Yo, draw up loop in first eye) twice, yo and thru 5 loops, ch 1, * ch 2, (yo, draw up loop in same eye as last half pat) twice, skip ch-2, (yo, draw up loop in next eye) twice, yo and thru 9 loops, ch 1; rep from *, ending ch 1, 1 dc under turning ch. Ch 2, turn.

Row 3: Work ½ pat in ch-1 sp, ch 2, (yo, draw up loop in first eye) twice, (yo, draw up loop in next eye) twice, yo and thru 9 loops, ch 1; rep from * of Row 2, ending yo and thru 9 loops, ch 1 to form eye, ch 1, 1 dc under turning ch. Ch 2, turn.
Repeat Rows 2 and 3 for pattern.

No. 9

Chain a multiple of 8 plus 4.

Row 1: 1 sc in 2nd ch from hook and in each ch to end. Ch 3, turn.

Row 2: * Skip next sc, 1 dc in next sc, ch 1; rep from *, ending 1 dc in last sc. Ch 1, turn.

Row 3: 1 sc in first dc, * 1 sc under ch-1, 1 sc in next dc; rep from *, ending 1 sc under turning ch, 1 sc in 2nd ch of turning ch. Ch 3, turn.

Row 4: * In next sc (yo, draw up loop, yo and thru 2 loops) 4 times, yo and thru 5 loops, ch 1 to fasten (cluster), 1 dc in next sc, (ch 1, skip 1 sc, 1 dc in next sc) 3 times; rep from *, ending cluster in next to last sc, 1 dc in last sc. Ch 1, turn.

Row 5: I sc in first dc, * 1 sc in ch-1 of cluster, 1 sc in next dc, (1 sc under next ch-1, 1 sc in next dc) 3 times; rep from *, ending 1 sc in cluster, 1 sc in top of turning ch. Ch 3, turn.

Row 6: Repeat Row 2.

Row 7: Repeat Row 3.

Row 8: Skip next sc, 1 dc in next sc, ch 1, skip next sc, 1 dc in next sc, * cluster in next sc, 1 dc in next sc, (ch 1, skip 1 sc, 1 dc in next sc) 3 times; rep from *, ending (ch 1, skip 1 sc, 1 dc in next sc) twice. Ch 2, turn.

Row 9: Work 1 sc under each ch-1, in each dc and in top of each cluster, ending 1 sc under turning ch, 1 sc in 2nd ch of turning ch. Ch 3, turn.

Repeat from Row 2 for pattern.

No. 10

Chain a multiple of 6 plus 5.

Foundation Row: Work 1 dc in 3rd ch from hook and in each ch to end. Ch 3 and count as first dc of next row. Turn.

Row 1: 1 dc in each of next 2 dc, * ch 1, skip 1 dc, 1 dc in next dc, (yo, draw up loop around post of last dc worked, yo and thru 2 loops) 5 times, yo and thru 6 loops (cluster), ch 1, skip next dc, 1 dc in each of next 3 dc; rep from * to end. Ch 3 and count as first dc of next row. Turn.

Row 2: 1 dc in each of next 2 dc, * 1 dc under ch-1, 1 dc in top of cluster, 1 dc under next ch-1, 1 dc in each of next 2 dc; rep from *, ending 1 dc in top of turning ch. Ch 3, turn.

Repeat Rows 1 and 2 for pattern.

No. 11

Chain a multiple of 6 plus 1.

Foundation Row: Work 1 sc in 2nd ch from hook and in each ch to end. Ch 6, turn.

Row 1: Skip first 2 sc, 1 sc in next sc, * ch 3, skip 2 sc, in next st work (yo, draw up loop, yo and thru 2 loops) twice, yo and thru 3 loops (cluster), ch 3, skip 2 sc, 1 sc in next sc; rep from * to last 3 sc, ch 3, 1 dc in last sc. Ch 1, turn.

Row 2: 1 sc in first dc, * ch 3, cluster in next sc, ch 3, 1 sc in top of next cluster; rep from *, ending 1 sc in 3rd ch of turning ch-6. Ch 6, turn.

Row 3: 1 sc in top of first cluster, * ch 3, cluster in next sc, ch 3, 1 sc in top of next cluster; rep from *, ending ch 3, 1 dc in last sc. Ch 1, turn.

Repeat Rows 2 and 3 for pattern.

No. 12

Chain an even number.

Foundation Row: Work 1 sc in 2nd ch from hook and in each ch to end. Ch 1, turn.

Row 1: (Draw up loop in first sc, skip next sc, draw up loop in next sc) 3 times in the same 2 sc, yo and thru 7 loops, ch 1 (Puff st—P st), * (draw up loop in last sc worked, skip next sc, draw up loop in next sc) 3 times in same 2 sc, yo and thru 7 loops, ch 1 (P st); rep from * to end. Ch 1, turn.

Row 2: (Draw up loop in ch-1 of first P st, then in ch-1 between first and 2nd P sts) 3 times in same 2 sts, yo and thru 7 loops, ch 1, * (draw up loop in last ch-1 worked, then in ch-1 between next 2 P sts) 3 times in same 2 ch-1, yo and thru 7 loops, ch 1; rep from *, working under turning ch to complete last P st. Ch 1, turn.
Repeat Row 2 for pattern. There will be same number P sts in each row.

No. 13

Chain a multiple of 8 plus 4.

Row 1: 1 dc in 4th ch from hook, 1 dc in next ch, * ch 2, skip 2 ch, in next ch work (1 sc, ch 3, 1 sc), ch 2, skip 2 ch, 1 dc in next ch, 3 dc in next ch, 1 dc in next ch; rep from *, ending ch 2, skip 2 ch, (1 sc, ch 3, 1 sc) in next ch, ch 2, skip 2 ch, 1 dc in next ch, 2 dc in last ch. Ch 3, turn.

Row 2: 1 dc in each of first 2 dc, * skip next dc and ch-2, 1 dc under ch-3 loop, ch 2, (yo and draw up a ½ inch loop under same ch-3) twice, yo and thru 5 loops (cluster), ch 2, 1 dc under same ch-3, skip ch 2 and next dc, 1 dc in next dc, 3 dc in next dc, 1 dc in next dc; rep from *, ending skip next dc, 1 dc in last dc, 2 dc in top of turning ch. Ch 3, turn.

Row 3: 1 dc in each of first 2 dc, * ch 2, 1 sc under ch-2 before next cluster, ch 3, 1 sc under ch-2 after same cluster, ch 2, skip next 2 dc, 1 dc in next dc, 3 dc in next dc, 1 dc in next dc; rep from *, ending ch 2, skip 2 dc, 1 dc in last dc, 2 dc in top of turning ch. Ch 3, turn.
Repeat Rows 2 and 3 for pattern.

No. 14

Chain an uneven number.

Row 1: 1 sc in 2nd ch from hook, 1 sc in next ch, * ch 4, sl st in 4th ch from hook (picot), 1 sc in each of next 2 ch; rep from *, ending 1 sc in each of last 2 ch. Ch 1, turn.

Row 2: 1 sc in first sc, * 1 sc in next sc at base of picot (holding picot to front of work and keeping yarn in back of picot), 1 sc in next sc; rep from *, ending 1 sc in each of last 2 sc. Ch 1, turn.

Row 3: 1 sc in first sc, * ch 4, sl st in 4th ch from hook, 1 sc in each of next 2 sc; rep from *, ending picot, 1 sc in last sc. Ch 1, turn.

Row 4: * 1 sc in sc at base of picot, 1 sc in next sc; rep from * to end. Ch 1, turn.

Row 5: 1 sc in each of first 2 sc, * ch 4, sl st in 4th ch from hook, 1 sc in each of next 2 sc; rep from *, ending 1 sc in each of last 2 sc. Ch 1, turn.
Repeat from Row 2 for pattern.

No. 15

Chain a multiple of 6 plus 4.

Row 1: Holding back on hook the last loop of each dc, work 2 dc in 4th ch from hook, yo and thru all loops (cluster), * skip 2 ch, 5 dc (shell) in next ch, skip 2 ch, 3-dc cluster in next ch; rep from * to end. Ch 2, turn.

Row 2: 2 dc in back loop of first cluster, * 1 sc in center dc of next shell, shell in back loop of next cluster; rep from *, ending 3 dc in back loop of last cluster. Ch 2, turn.

Row 3: 2-dc cluster in first dc, * shell in back loop of next sc, 3-dc cluster in center dc of next shell; rep from *, ending 3-dc cluster in top of turning ch. Ch 2, turn. Repeat Rows 2 and 3 for pattern.

No. 16

Chain a multiple of 6 plus 4.

Row 1: Holding back on hook the last loop of each dc, work 2 dc in 4th ch from hook, yo and thru 3 loops (2-dc cluster), * ch 2, skip 2 ch, holding back on hook the last loop of each dc, work 3 dc in next ch, yo and thru 4 loops (cluster); rep from *, ending cluster in last ch. Ch 2, turn.

Row 2: 2-dc cluster under first ch-2, * ch 2, cluster under next ch-2; rep from *, ending cluster under last ch-2, ch 2, 1 dc in top of turning ch. Ch 2, turn. Repeat Row 2 for pattern.

No. 17

Chain a multiple of 8 plus 2.

Row 1: 1 dc in 6th ch from hook, * ch 1, skip 1 ch, 1 dc in next ch; rep from * to end. Ch 4, turn.

Row 2: 1 dc in 2nd dc, * under next ch-1 work (yo and draw up loop) 5 times, yo and thru 10 loops, yo and thru last 2 loops (cluster), 1 dc in next dc, (ch 1, 1 dc in next dc) 3 times; rep from *, ending 1 dc in last dc, ch 1, 1 dc in 4th ch of turning ch. Ch 4, turn.

Row 3: 1 dc in 2nd dc, * ch 1, 1 dc in next dc; rep from *, ending ch 1, 1 dc in 3rd ch of turning ch. Ch 4, turn.

Row 4: 1 dc in 2nd dc, (ch 1, 1 dc in next dc) twice; rep from * of Row 2, ending with ch 1, 1 dc in 3rd ch of turning ch. Ch 4, turn.

Row 5: Same as Row 3.

Repeat from Row 2 for pattern.

No. 18

Chain a multiple of 3.

Row 1: Skip first ch, * yo and draw up loop in next ch, draw up loop in next ch, yo and thru 3 loops, yo and thru last 2 loops, ch 2, skip next ch; rep from * to end. Ch 2, turn.

Row 2: * (Yo, draw up loop under next ch-2) 4 times, yo and thru all 9 loops (cluster), ch 2; rep from *, ending ch 2, 1 dc in top of turning ch. Ch 4, turn.

Row 3: Yo and draw up loop in first dc, draw up loop under next ch-2, yo and thru 3 loops, yo and thru 2 loops, * ch 2, yo and draw up loop under same ch-2, draw up loop under next ch-2, yo and thru 3 loops, yo and thru 2 loops; rep from *, ending draw up loop in same ch-2, draw up loop under turning ch, yo and thru 3 loops, yo and thru 2 loops, 1 dc in 2nd ch of turning ch. Ch 2, turn.

Repeat Rows 2 and 3 for pattern.

No. 19

Chain a multiple of 6 plus 1.

Row 1: Holding back on hook last loop of each dc, work 2 dc in 4th ch from hook, yo and thru 3 loops (2-dc cluster), * skip 2 ch, 1 sc in next ch, skip 2 ch, holding back on hook last loop of each dc, work 3 dc in next ch, yo and thru 4 loops (3-dc cluster), ch 4, 2-dc cluster in 4th ch from hook, 3-dc cluster in same ch as last 3-dc cluster (completing cluster group); rep from *, ending 1 sc in last ch. Ch 4, turn.

Row 2: 2-dc cluster in 4th ch from hook, * 1 sc in 2nd ch in top of next cluster group, cluster group in next sc; rep from *, ending 1 sc in top of turning ch. Ch 4, turn. Repeat Row 2 for pattern.

No. 20

Chain a multiple of 4 plus 2.

Foundation Row: 1 sc in 2nd ch from hook and in each ch to end. Ch 3, turn.

Row 1: Skip first 3 sc, * in next sc work (yo, draw up loop) twice, yo and thru 4 loops, yo and thru 2 loops (cluster), ch 1, skip sc to right of cluster, work a cluster in next sc to right (crossed cluster—Cr Cl), ch 1, skip next 3 sc; rep from *, ending with Cr Cl, ch 1, 1 dc in last sc. Ch 3, turn.

Row 2: Skip first dc and ch-1, * work cluster under ch-1 between Cr Cl, ch 1, work cluster under skipped ch-1, ch 1; rep from *, ending Cr Cl in last cluster and ch-1, ch 1, 1 dc in 2nd ch of turning ch. Ch 3, turn. Repeat Row 2 for pattern.

No. 21

Chain a multiple of 12 plus 4.

Row 1: 1 sc in 8th ch from hook, * ch 4, skip 3 ch, 1 sc in next ch; rep from * to end. Ch 5, turn. (No. of loops must be multiple of 3).

Row 2: Under first ch-4 loop work (1 sc, ch 2, 1 sc) group, * ch 4, group under next loop; rep from *, ending ch 4, 1 sc under last loop. Ch 5, turn.

Row 3: Group under first loop, * ch 4, skip next group, 1 sc under next loop; under ch-2 of next group work (yo and draw up a long loop) 4 times, yo and thru 8 loops, yo and thru remaining 2 loops (cluster), ch 2, work another cluster under same ch-2; 1 sc under next loop, ch 4, skip next group, group under next loop; rep from *, ending with 2 clusters, 1 sc under turning ch. Ch 5, turn.

Row 4: Work 3 clusters with ch-2 between in sp between clusters, * ch 3, 1 sc under next loop, ch 4, skip group, 1 sc under next loop, ch 3; work 5 clusters with ch-2 between in sp between clusters; rep from *, ending ch 4, skip last group, 1 sc under turning ch. Ch 5, turn.

Row 5: Group under first loop, * ch 4, 1 sc between next 2 clusters, (ch 3, 1 sc between next 2 clusters) 3 times; ch 4, skip ch-3, group under next ch-4 loop; rep from *, ending ch 4, 1 sc between next 2 clusters, ch 3, 1 sc between next 2 clusters, ch 3, 1 sc under turning ch. Ch 5, turn.

Row 6: Group under ch-3, * ch 4, skip next ch-3, group under next loop, ch 4, skip group, ch 4, group under next loop, ch 4, group in ch-3 over center of 5 clusters; rep from *, ending ch 4, skip last group, 1 sc under turning ch. Ch 5, turn.

Row 7: * Group under next ch-4 loop, ch 4, skip group; rep from *, ending ch 4, 1 sc under turning ch. Ch 5, turn.

Row 8: Group under first ch-4 loop, * ch 4, skip next group, 1 sc under next loop, under ch-2 of next group work cluster, ch 2, cluster, 1 sc under next loop, ch 4, skip next group, group under next loop; rep from *, ending 2 clusters under ch-2 of last group, 1 sc under turning ch. Ch 5, turn.

Rows 9, 10, 11: Same as Rows 4, 5, 6.
Repeat from Row 2 for pattern.

No. 22

Chain a multiple of 8 plus 2.

Foundation Row: 1 sc in 2nd ch from hook and in each ch to end. Ch 3, turn.

Row 1: 1 dc in 2nd sc and in each sc to end. Ch 4, turn.

Row 2: Skip first 2 dc, 1 dc in each of next 2 dc, ch 1, skip next dc, 1 dc in each of next 2 dc, * ch 1, skip next dc; 1 dc in next dc, around post of last dc worked (yo, insert hook from front around dc and draw up loop) 4 times, yo and thru all 9 loops (cluster); skip next dc, 1 dc in each of next 2 dc, ch 1, skip next dc, 1 dc in each of next 2 dc; rep from *, ending ch 1, skip last dc, 1 dc in top of turning ch. Ch 3, turn.

Row 3: 1 dc in first ch-1 sp, * 1 dc in each of next 2 dc, 1 dc in next ch-1 sp, 1 dc in each of next 2 dc, 1 dc in each of next 2 sts (top of cluster), 1 dc in next ch-1 sp; rep from *, ending 1 dc under turning ch, 1 dc in 3rd ch of turning ch. Ch 4, turn.

Row 4: Skip first 2 dc, 1 dc in next dc, * ch 1, skip next dc, 1 dc in next dc; rep from *, ending ch 1, 1 dc in top of turning ch. Ch 3, turn.

Row 5: 1 dc in first ch-1 sp, 1 dc in next dc, * 1 dc in next ch-1 sp, 1 dc in next dc; rep from *, ending 1 dc under turning ch, 1 dc in 3rd ch of turning ch.
Repeat from Row 2 for pattern.

No. 23

Chain a multiple of 20 plus 4.

Row 1: 1 dc in 7th ch from hook, * ch 2, skip 2 ch, 1 dc in next ch; rep from * to end. Ch 5, turn.

Row 2: Skip first dc, 1 dc in next dc, (ch 2, 1 dc in next dc) twice, yo, draw up loop under next ch, (yo, draw up loop under same ch) 3 times, yo and thru all loops (cluster), ch 1, 1 dc in next dc, * (ch 2, 1 dc in next dc) 5 times, work cluster under next ch, ch 1, 1 dc in next dc; rep from *, ending (ch 2, 1 dc in next dc) twice, ch 2, 1 dc in 3rd ch of turning ch. Ch 5, turn.

Row 3: Skip first dc, 1 dc in next dc, ch 2, 1 dc in next dc, * cluster under next ch, ch 1, 1 dc in next dc, ch 2, 1 dc in next dc, cluster under next ch, ch 1, 1 dc in next dc, (ch 2, 1 dc in next dc) 3 times; rep from *, ending ch 2, 1 dc in last dc, ch 2, 1 dc in 3rd ch of turning ch. Ch 5, turn.

Row 4: Skip first dc, * 1 dc in next dc, cluster under next ch, ch 1, 1 dc in next dc, ch 2; rep from *, ending 1 dc in 3rd ch of turning ch. Ch 5, turn.

Row 5: Same as Row 3.

Row 6: Same as Row 2.

Row 7: Skip first dc, 1 dc in next dc, * ch 2, 1 dc in next dc; rep from *, ending ch 2, 1 dc in 3rd ch of turning ch. Ch 5, turn.

Repeat from Row 2 for pattern.

No. 24

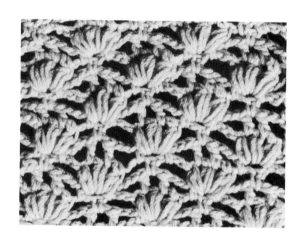

Chain a multiple of 10 plus 2.

Row 1: 1 sc in 7th ch from hook, ch 1, skip 1 ch, 1 sc in next ch, * ch 2, skip 2 ch, 1 dc in next ch, ch 1, skip next ch, 1 dc in next ch, ch 2, skip next 2 ch, 1 sc in next ch, ch 1, skip 1 ch, 1 sc in next ch; rep from *, ending ch 2, 1 dc in last ch. Ch 1, turn.

Row 2: 1 sc in first sc, ch 3, in ch-1 sp (between 2 sc) work (yo and draw up loop) 3 times, yo and thru 7 loops on hook (1 cluster), (ch 2, work cluster in same sp) twice, * ch 3, 1 sc in next ch-1 sp (between 2 dc), ch 3, in next ch-1 sp work 3-cluster group; rep from *, ending ch 3, skip 2 ch, 1 sc in next ch of turning ch. Ch 1, turn.

Row 3: 1 sc in first sc, * ch 3, 1 dc in sp after first cluster, ch 1, 1 dc in sp after next cluster, ch 3, 1 sc under next ch-3 loop; ch 1, 1 sc under next ch-3 loop; rep from *, ending ch 3, skip last ch-3 loop, 1 sc in last sc. Ch 5, turn.

Row 4: * 1 sc in next ch-1 sp (between 2 dc), ch 3, 3-cluster group in next ch-1 sp (between 2 sc), ch 3; rep from *, ending ch 3, 1 dc in last sc. Ch 5, turn.

Row 5: 1 sc under first ch-3, * ch 1, 1 sc under next ch-3, ch 3, 1 dc in sp after first cluster, ch 1, 1 dc in sp after next cluster, ch 3, 1 sc under next ch-3; rep from *, ending 1 sc under last ch-3, ch 1, 1 sc under turning ch, ch 3, 1 dc in 3rd ch of turning ch. Ch 1, turn.
Repeat from Row 2 for pattern.

No. 25

Chain a multiple of 5 plus 4.

Foundation Row: 1 dc in 4th ch from hook, * ch 3, skip 3 ch, 1 dc in each of next 2 ch; rep from * to end. Ch 5, turn.

Row 1: Skip first dc, holding back the last loop of each dc on hook, work 2 dc in next dc, yo and thru all loops (cluster), * cluster in next dc, ch 3, cluster in next dc; rep from *, ending cluster in last dc, ch 2, 1 dc in top of turning ch. Ch 3, turn.

Row 2: * Cluster in next cluster, ch 3, cluster in next cluster; rep from *, ending 1 dc in 3rd ch of turning ch. Ch 3, turn.

Row 3: 1 dc in first cluster, * ch 3, 1 dc in each of next 2 clusters; rep from *, ending 1 dc in last cluster, 1 dc in top of turning ch. Ch 5, turn.
Repeat from Row 1 for pattern.

No. 26

Chain a multiple of 5 plus 13 to turn.

Row 1: 1 tr in 13th ch from hook, * ch 5, skip 4 ch, 1 tr in next ch; rep from * to end. Ch 6, turn.

Row 2: Holding back on hook the last loop of each tr work 1 tr in next tr, 7 tr under ch-5, 1 tr in next tr, yo and thru all loops on hook (cluster), * ch 5, work cluster as before in same tr as last cluster, next ch-5 and next tr; rep from * ending by working last tr of last cluster in 4th ch of turning ch, ch 2, 1 tr in same ch as last tr. Ch 9, turn.

Row 3: 1 tr in loop between next 2 tr, * ch 5, 1 tr in next loop; rep from * to end. Ch 6, turn.

Repeat Rows 2 and 3 for pattern.

No. 27

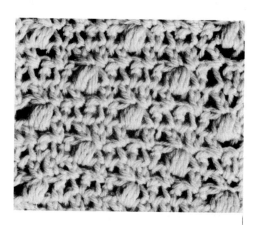

Chain a multiple of 8 plus 7.

Foundation Row: Draw up loop in 5th ch from hook, yo and thru 1 loop, yo and thru 2 loops (long sc), * ch 1, skip 1 ch, 1 long sc in next ch; rep from * to end. Ch 3, turn.

Row 1: Yo, draw up loop in 2nd long sc, yo and draw up loop in same st 3 times (9 loops on hook), yo and thru all loops, ch 1 (popcorn—PC), * 1 long sc in each of next 3 long sc with ch-1 between, PC in next long sc; rep from *, ending skip 2 ch of turning ch, 1 long sc in next ch. Ch 3, turn.

Row 2: * 1 long sc in PC, (ch 1, 1 long sc in next long sc), 3 times, ch 1; rep from *, ending skip 2 ch of turning ch, 1 long sc in next ch. Ch 3, turn.

Row 3: 1 long sc in 2nd long sc, ch 1, 1 long sc in next long sc, * PC in next long sc, 1 long sc in each of next 3 long sc with ch-1 between; rep from *, ending same as before. Ch 3, turn.

Row 4: 1 long sc, ch-1 in 2nd long sc and in each long sc and in each PC, ending as before.

Repeat from Row 1 for pattern.

Afghan Stitch
(Tunisian)

In very old books crochet has only two divisions or stitches. The first is called ordinary or plain or simple crochet and includes every basic stitch. The second is Afghan Stitch. Now we have given names of their own to combinations of stitches. We refer to Shell Stitch, to Popcorn Stitch, etc. But these really are not stitches—they are patterns made of basic stitches. Afghan stitch, too, has its pattern stitches, but the original name of the stitch has held its own and you will seldom see a reference to an afghan pattern stitch. Regardless of what you do and how you maneuver your hook and what results, you are still doing good old afghan stitch. Take a small survey among your friends who crochet by asking them how many afghan stitch patterns they know. There are many crocheters today who will look at you in surprise and answer "Don't be silly—there's only one." Which certainly proves how distinctive this stitch has grown to be. When you receive the above answer, you can be very impressive when you point out that you know of at least 33 different ones! For this is the number of those that we have so far run to earth. The stitch itself became so prominent that its name carried right into its best known use—the afghan as we know it today. Afghan stitch was an open invitation to further embellishment, with its neat lines forming squares, and certainly led to the creation of the utterly gorgeous cross-stitched afghans. These are among treasured heirlooms, can be found in many collections and remain as popular today as they must have been in the beginning. There are very old embroidered afghans that could almost be classed as tapestry, leading us to believe that they might very well have been developed first as wall hangings. Basic afghan stitch must have remained the only stitch for quite some time, until once again, an active mind and agile fingers created the many variations of a most intriguing stitch.

71

BASIC AFGHAN STITCH P

Make a chain of specified length.

    Row 1—First Half: Skip first ch from hook. * Insert hook thru top loop of next ch, yo and draw yarn thru ch forming loop on hook. Retain loop on hook. Rep from * to end. There will be the same number of loops on hook as the number of chains.

    Row 1—Second Half: Yo and draw yarn thru first loop. * Yo and draw yarn thru 2 loops; rep from * across row until there is one loop on hook. This is the first st for next row.

    Row 2—First Half: Insert hook in 2nd upright st (called a bar), yo and draw yarn thru bar, forming loop on hook. Retain loop on hook. Continue drawing up a loop thru each bar across row. There will be the same number of loops on hook as number of chains.

    Row 2—Second Half: Same as 2nd half of Row 1.
Repeat Row 2 for pattern.

TO WORK A PURL (P) AFGHAN STITCH P

Bring yarn forward and hold with left thumb below bar to be worked. Insert hook under this bar and draw up loop.

No. 1

Chain an uneven number.

Row 1: Basic afghan st.

Row 2—First Half: Skip first bar, * bring yarn forward and work a P st in next bar, with yarn at back, insert hook in center of next upright st below ch, draw up loop; rep from * to last bar, draw up loop in last bar.

Row 2—Second Half: Work off loops in basic afghan st.

Repeat Row 2 for pattern.

No. 2

Chain a multiple of 4.

Row 1: Basic afghan st.

Row 2—First Half: Skip first bar, draw up loop in each of next 3 bars; * yo, skip next bar, draw up loop in each of next 3 bars; rep from *, ending draw up loop in each of last 3 bars.

Row 2—Second Half: Yo and thru 2 loops, * ch 3, (yo and thru 2 loops) 4 times; rep from *, ending (yo and thru 2 loops) 6 times.

Row 3—First Half: Skip first bar, draw up loop in each of next 3 bars, in slanted bar (yo of row below) and in next bar; * hold ch at **front**, draw up loop in each of next 2 bars, in slanted bar and in next bar; rep from *, ending draw up loop in each of last 2 bars.

Row 3—Second Half: Work off loops in basic afghan st.

Row 4—First Half: Skip first bar, draw up loop in next bar, * yo, skip 1 bar, draw up loop in each of next 3 bars; rep from *, ending yo, skip 1 bar, draw up loop in each of last 5 bars.

    Row 4—Second Half: (Yo and draw thru 2 loops) 3 times. * ch 3, (yo and draw thru 2 loops) 4 times; rep from * to end.

    Row 5—First Half: Skip first bar, draw up loop in next bar, in slanted bar and in next bar, * hold ch at **front**, draw up loop in each of next 2 bars, in slanted bar and in next bar; rep from *, ending draw up loop in each of last 4 bars.

    Row 5—Second Half: Work off loops in basic afghan st.

Repeat from Row 2 for pattern.

No. 3

Chain a multiple of 4 plus 2.

    Row 1: Basic afghan st.

    Row 2—First Half: Skip first bar, draw up loop in next bar, * bring yarn forward and work a P st in each of next 2 bars, with yarn at back, draw up loop in each of next 2 bars; rep from * to end.

    Row 2—Second Half: Work off loops in basic afghan st.

Repeat Row 2 for pattern.

No. 4

Chain an even number.

Work a row of basic afghan st.

Row 1—First Half: Skip first bar, draw up loop in next bar, * yo, skip next bar, draw up loop in next bar; rep from * to end.

Row 1—Second Half: Work off loops in basic afghan st, counting each yo as a loop.

Row 2—First Half: Skip first bar, * yo, skip next bar, draw up loop in next slanted st (yo of previous row); rep from *, ending draw up loop in yo of previous row, draw up loop in last bar.

Row 2—Second Half: Work off loops in basic afghan st, counting each yo as a loop.

Row 3—First Half: Skip first bar, draw up loop in yo of previous row, * yo, skip next bar, draw up loop in yo of previous row; rep from *, ending yo, skip next to last bar, draw up loop in last bar.

Row 3—Second Half: Work off loops as before.

Repeat Rows 2 and 3 for pattern.

No. 5

Chain a multiple of 6 plus 5.

Work a row of basic afghan stitch.

Row 1—First Half: Skip first bar, draw up loop in each of next 3 bars, * bring yarn forward and work a P st in each of next 3 bars, with yarn at back, draw up loop in each of next 3 bars; rep from *, ending draw up loop in each of last 4 bars.

Row 1—Second Half: Work off loops in basic afghan st.

Rep Row 1 twice.

Row 4—First Half: Skip first bar, * bring yarn forward and work a P st in each of next 3 bars, with yarn at back, draw up loop in each of next 3 bars; rep from *, ending with 3 P sts, yarn at back, draw up loop in last bar.

Row 4—Second Half: Work off loops in basic afghan st.

Repeat Row 4 twice.

Repeat these 6 rows for pattern.

No. 6

Chain an even number.

Work a row of basic afghan st.

Row 1—First Half: Skip first bar, * bring yarn forward, insert hook under next 2 bars and work a P st (P 2 tog), insert hook from front to back in space (below ch) between last st worked and next st and draw up loop; rep from *, ending draw up loop in space before last bar, draw up loop in last bar.

Row 1—Second Half: Work off loops in basic afghan st.

Repeat Row 1 for pattern.

No. 7

Chain a multiple of 8 plus 4.

Row 1 (shells): 4 dc in 4th ch from hook, * skip 3 ch, 1 sc in next ch, skip 3 ch, 9 dc in next ch; rep from * to last 4 ch, skip 3 ch, 5 dc in last ch. Ch 1, turn.

Row 2 (afghan st): 1 sc in first dc, * (draw up loop in next st and retain loop on hook) 5 times (6 loops on hook), draw up loop in next st and draw this loop thru first loop on hook forming an upright st or bar, (yo and thru 2 loops) 5 times *. There are 6 bars and 1 loop on hook. ** Retain loops on hook and draw up loop in each of next 5 bars (6 loops on hook), draw up loop in next st and thru first loop on hook, (yo and thru 2 loops) 5 times. Rep from ** twice. Insert hook in 2nd bar, yo and thru bar and loop on hook (1 st bound off), bind off 4 more sts, 1 sc in next st. Rep from *, ending bind off 5 sts, sl st in top of turning ch. Ch 1, turn.

Row 3: Skip first st, 1 sc in each st across, sl st in last st. Ch 3, turn.

Row 4 (shells): Yo, draw up loop in 2nd sc, yo and thru 2 loops on hook, (yo and draw up loop in next st, yo and thru 2 loops) 3 times, yo and thru 5 loops on hook, ch 1 tightly to form eye of ½ shell, * ch 3, 1 sc in next st, ch 3, (yo and draw up loop in next st, yo and thru 2 loops) 9 times, yo and thru 10 loops on hook, ch 1 tightly to form eye of full shell; rep from *, ending last rep (yo and draw up loop in next st, yo and thru 2 loops) 4 times, yo and thru 5 loops, ch 1 tightly to form eye. Ch 3, turn.

Row 5 (shells): 4 dc in eye of first ½ shell, 1 sc in first sc, * 9 dc in eye of next shell, 1 sc in next sc; rep from *, ending 5 dc in eye of last shell, Ch 1, turn.
Repeat Rows 2 thru 5 for pattern.

No. 8

Chain an uneven number.

Row 1: Basic afghan st.

Row 2—First Half: Yo, insert hook from front to back between first 2 sts and draw up loop, * insert hook between next 2 sts, draw up loop, yo, draw up loop in same sp; rep from *, ending draw up loop between last 2 sts, yo, draw up loop in same sp, draw up loop under last bar.

Row 2—Second Half: Yo and thru 1 loop, * yo and thru 4 loops (cluster); rep from * to end.

Row 3—First Half: Draw up loop in sp between first 2 clusters, * yo, draw up loop in same sp, draw up loop in sp between next 2 clusters; rep from *, ending skip sp after last cluster, draw up loop in last bar.

Row 3—Second Half: Yo and thru 1 loop, * yo and thru 4 loops; rep from *, ending yo and thru last 2 loops.

Row 4—First Half: Yo, draw up loop in sp between first st and first cluster, * draw up loop between next 2 clusters, yo, draw up loop in same sp; rep from *, ending draw up loop in sp between last cluster and last st, yo, draw up loop in same sp, draw up loop in last bar.

Row 4—Second Half: Yo and thru 1 loop, * yo and thru 4 loops; rep from * to end. Repeat Rows 3 and 4 for pattern.

No. 9

Chain an even number.

Row 1: Basic afghan st.

Row 2—First Half: Skip first bar, * insert hook thru to back under next loop (below ch) and draw up loop; rep from * to last bar, draw up loop in last bar.

Row 2—Second Half: Work off loops in basic afghan st. Repeat Row 2 for pattern.

No. 10

Chain an even number.

Work a row in basic afghan st.

Row 1—First Half: Skip first bar, draw up loop in next bar, * bring yarn forward and work a P st in next bar, take yarn back and draw up loop in next bar; rep from * to end.

Row 1—Second Half: Work off loops in basic afghan st.

Row 2—First Half: Skip first bar, * bring yarn forward and work a P st in next bar, take yarn back and draw up loop in next bar; rep from *, ending draw up loops in last 2 bars.

    Row 2—Second Half: Work off loops in basic afghan st.

Repeat Rows 1 and 2 for pattern.

No. 11

Chain an even number.

Work a row in basic afghan st.

    Row 1—First Half: Skip first bar, * skip next bar and draw up loop in next bar, draw up loop in skipped bar to right; rep from *, ending draw up loop in last bar.

    Row 1—Second Half: Work off loops in basic afghan st.

Repeat Row 1 for pattern.

No. 12

Chain an even number.

Work a row in basic afghan st.

    Row 1—First Half: Skip first bar, * skip next bar and draw up loop in next bar, draw up loop in skipped bar to right; rep from *, ending draw up loop in last bar.

    Row 1—Second Half: Work off loops in basic afghan st.

    Row 2—First Half: Skip first bar, draw up loop in next bar, * skip next bar and draw up loop in next bar, draw up loop in skipped bar to right; rep from *, ending draw up loop in each of last 2 bars.

    Row 2—Second Half: Work off loops in basic afghan st.

Repeat Rows 1 and 2 for pattern.

No. 13

Chain an even number.

 Row 1: Basic afghan st.
 Row 2—First Half: Skip first bar, bring yarn forward and work a P st in each bar. to last bar, with yarn at back, draw up loop in last bar.
 Row 2—Second Half: Work off loops in basic afghan st.
Repeat Rows 1 and 2 for pattern.

No. 14

Chain an even number.

Work a row in basic afghan st.
 Row 1—First Half: Skip first bar, * from back insert hook in back loop of next bar and draw up loop; rep from * to last bar, ending draw up loop in front loop of last bar.
 Row 1—Second Half: Work off loops in basic afghan st.
Repeat Row 1 for pattern.

No. 15

Chain a multiple of 4 plus 2.

Work a row in basic afghan st.

Row 1—First Half: Skip first bar, draw up loop in next bar, * draw up loop thru back of each of next 2 bars, draw up loop in each of next 2 bars; rep from * to end.

Row 1—Second Half: Work off loops in basic afghan st.

Repeat Row 1 for pattern.

No. 16

Chain an even number.

Work a row in basic afghan st.

Row 1—First Half: Insert hook under ch in sp after first bar and draw up loop, * draw up loop under ch in sp after next bar; rep from *, ending skip last sp, draw up loop in last bar.

Row 1—Second Half: Work off loops in basic afghan st.

Row 2—First Half: Skip first sp, * draw up loop under ch in next sp; rep from *, ending draw up loop in last sp, draw up loop in last bar.

Row 2—Second Half: Work off loops in basic afghan st.

Repeat Rows 1 and 2 for pattern.

No. 17

Chain an even number.

Work a row in basic afghan st.
    Row 1—First Half: Ch 1, * draw up loop in next bar, ch 1; rep from * to end.
    Row 1—Second Half: Work off loops in basic afghan st.
Repeat Row 1 for pattern.

No. 18

Chain a multiple of 6 plus 5.

Work a row in basic afghan st.
    Row 1—First Half: Skip first bar, * with yarn at front work a P st in each of next 3 bars, yarn at back draw up loop in each of next 3 bars; rep from *, ending with 3 P sts, draw up loop in last bar.
    Row 1—Second Half: Work off loops in basic afghan st.
    Row 2: Rep Row 1.
    Row 3—First Half: Skip first bar, * draw up loop in each of next 3 bars, work a P st in each of next 3 bars; rep from *, ending draw up loop in each of last 4 bars.
    Row 3—Second Half: Work off loops in basic afghan st.
    Row 4: Rep Row 3.
Repeat from Row 1 for pattern.

No. 19

Chain a multiple of 4 plus 1.

Row 1—First Half: Skip first ch from hook, draw up loop in each ch to end.

Row 1—Second Half: * Ch 3, yo and draw thru 5 loops, ch 1 for eye; rep from * to end.

Row 2—First Half: * Draw up loop in eye, draw up loop in each ch of ch-3; rep from *, ending draw up loop in each ch of last ch-3.

Row 2—Second Half: Same as second half of Row 1.

Repeat Row 2 for pattern.

No. 20

Chain a multiple of 6 plus 2.

Work a row in basic afghan st.

Row 1—First Half: Skip first bar, * draw up a loop in each of next 3 bars, with yarn at front work a P st in each of next 3 bars; rep from *, ending draw up loop in last bar.

Row 1—Second Half: Work off loops in basic afghan st.

Row 2—First Half: Skip first bar, work a P st in next bar, * draw up loop in each of next 3 bars, work a P st in each of next 3 bars; rep from *, ending P st in each of next 2 sts, draw up loop in last bar.

Row 2—Second Half: Work off loops in basic afghan st.

Row 3—First Half: Skip first bar, work a P st in each of next 2 bars, * draw up loop in each of next 3 bars, work a P st in each of next 3 bars; rep from *, ending with 1 P st, draw up loop in last bar.

Row 3—Second Half: Work off loops in basic afghan st.

Row 4—First Half: Skip first bar, * work a P st in each of next 3 bars, draw up loop in each of next 3 bars; rep from *, ending draw up loop in each of last 4 bars.

Row 4—Second Half: Work off loops in basic afghan st.

Row 5—First Half: Skip first bar, draw up loop in next bar, * work a P st in each of next 3 bars, draw up loop in each of next 3 bars; rep from * to end.

Row 5—Second Half: Work off loops in basic afghan st.

Row 6—First Half: Skip first bar, draw up loop in each of next 2 bars * work a P st in each of next 3 bars, draw up loop in each of next 3 bars; rep from *, ending draw up loop in each of last 2 bars.

Row 6—Second Half: Work off loops in basic afghan st.

Repeat from Row 1 for pattern.

No. 21

Chain a multiple of 4 plus 1.

Work a row of basic afghan st.

Row 1—First Half: Draw up loop in sp between first and 2nd bars, * draw up loop in next bar, draw up loop in sp after bar; rep from *, ending draw up loop under last bar.

Row 1—Second Half: Yo and thru first loop, * yo and thru 4 loops, yo and thru 2 loops; rep from * to end.

Row 2—First Half: Draw up loop between first bar and 3-bar cluster, draw up loop under 3-bar cluster, draw up loop in sp after cluster, draw up loop in next bar, * draw up loop in sp before cluster, draw up loop under cluster, draw up loop in sp after cluster, draw up loop in next bar; rep from * to end.

Row 2—Second Half: Yo and thru first loop, * yo and thru 4 loops, yo and thru 2 loops; rep from * to end.

Repeat Row 2 for pattern.

No. 22

Chain a multiple of 5 plus 1.

Work a row of basic afghan st.

Row 1—First Half: Skip first bar, * with yarn at front, work a P st in next bar, skip next bar, draw up loop in next bar, draw up loop in skipped bar, work a P st in next bar, draw up loop in next bar; rep from *, ending draw up loop in last bar.

Row 1—Second Half: Work off loops in basic afghan st.
Repeat Row 1 for pattern.

No. 23

Chain an even number.

Work a row of basic afghan st.

Row 1—First Half: * Skip next bar, draw up loop in next bar, draw up loop in skipped bar; repeat from *, ending draw up loop in last bar.

Row 1—Second Half: Work off loops in basic afghan st.

Row 2—First Half: Skip first bar, work a P st in next bar, * skip next bar, draw up loop in next bar, draw up loop in skipped bar; rep from * to last 2 bars, work a P st in next bar, draw up loop in last bar.

Row 2—Second Half: Work off loops in basic afghan st.

Row 3—First Half: Skip first bar, * keeping yarn at front, work a P st in each bar to last bar, draw up loop in last bar.

Row 3—Second Half: Work off loops in basic afghan st.
Repeat from Row 1 for pattern.

No. 24

Chain a multiple of 6 plus 5.

Work a row of basic afghan st.

Row 1—First Half: * Skip next bar, draw up loop in next bar, draw up loop in skipped bar, with yarn at front work a P st in next bar; rep from *, ending draw up loop in last bar.

Row 1—Second Half: Work off loops in basic afghan st.

Row 2—First Half: * Work a P st in each of next 2 bars, yarn back and draw up loop in next bar; rep from *, ending draw up loop in last bar.

Row 2—Second Half: Work off loops in basic afghan st.

Repeat Rows 1 and 2 for pattern.

No. 25

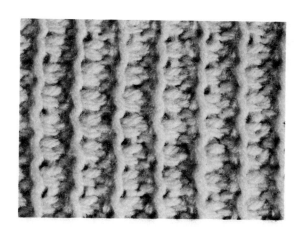

Chain an uneven number.

Work a row of basic afghan st.

Row 1—First Half: Skip first bar, * with yarn at front work a P st in next bar, yarn back and draw up loop in next bar; rep from * to end.

Row 1—Second Half: Work off loops in basic afghan st.

Repeat Row 1 for pattern.

No. 17

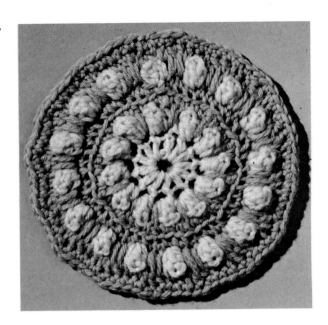

No. 18

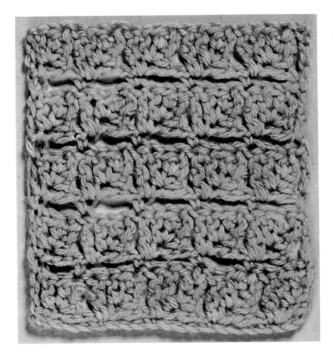

No. 17

Worked with 2 colors, A and B.

With A, chain 5. Join with sl st to form a ring.

Rnd 1: Ch 2, 12 dc in ring. Join with sl st to first dc (not in ch-2).

Rnd 2: Ch 2, 3 dc in joining, drop loop from hook and insert hook before the first of these 3 dc and pick up dropped loop, tighten and draw loop thru, ch 1 (popcorn), * ch 2, popcorn in next dc; rep from * around, ending ch 2 (12 popcorns), draw B thru and join with sl st in back loop of first popcorn.

Rnd 3: Ch 1, 1 sc in joining, * 1 sc in ch-2 sp, 1 long dc in base of next popcorn, 1 sc in same sp, 1 sc in back loop of next popcorn; rep from * around, ending with 1 sc, 1 long dc and 1 sc before last popcorn. Join with sl st in back loop of first sc.

Rnd 4: Ch 1, 1 sc in back loop of each st around. Join with sl st in first sc. Drop B, draw A thru loop.

Rnd 5: Skipping 2 sc between popcorns, rep Rnd 2. (16 popcorns). Draw B thru loop. Break A.

Rnd 6: Ch 1, 1 sc in joining, * 1 sc in next ch-2 sp, 1 long dc in each of 2 sc between popcorns, 1 sc in same ch-2 sp; rep from * around and join.

Rnd 7: Ch 1, 1 sc in each st around. Join and fasten off.

No. 18

Worked with 2 colors, A and B.

With A, chain a multiple of 4.

Row 1: * 1 sc in 2nd ch from hook, 1 hdc in next ch, 1 dc in next ch (point worked), skip 3 ch, 1 sc in next ch, ch 4; rep from *, ending with 1 sc in last ch. Draw B thru loop, ch 2, turn.

Row 2: * 1 dc in next dc, 1 hdc in next hdc, 1 sc in next sc, 1 tr in next sc; rep from *, ending 1 sc in last sc. Ch 4, turn.

Row 3: * 1 sc in 2nd ch from hook, 1 hdc in next ch, 1 dc in next ch, skip 3 sts, 1 sc in next st, ch 4; rep from *, ending 1 sc in top of turning ch. Draw A thru loop, ch 2, turn.

Repeat Rows 2 and 3 for pattern, alternating colors every 2 rows.

No. 19

Worked with 2 colors, A and B.

With A, chain 8. Join with sl st to form a ring.

Rnd 1: Ch 1, work 18 sc in ring. Join with sl st to first sc.

Rnd 2: Working thru front loops only, 1 sc in joining, * ch 3, 1 sc in next sc; rep from * around, ending with ch 3. Join with sl st to first sc and fasten off.

Rnd 3: Attach B behind A to any sc on Rnd 1. Work thru back loops only of each sc in Rnd 1, holding the ch-3 loops forward. Ch 4, * 1 dc in next sc, ch 1; rep from * around. Join with sl st to 3rd ch of ch-4.

Rnd 4: Ch 3, holding back on hook the last loop of each dc, work 1 dc in first ch-1 sp and following dc, yo and thru all loops (2-dc cluster), * ch 5, 3 dc cluster in same dc last worked, next sp and following dc; ch 3, 3 dc cluster in last dc, next sp and following dc; ch 5, 3 dc cluster in last dc, next sp and following dc; rep from * around, ending with ch 5, 3 dc cluster in last dc, in next sp and following dc; ch 3, 3 dc cluster in last dc, next sp and first st used at beg of rnd; ch 5, join with sl st to tip of first cluster. Fasten off.

No. 20

Worked with 2 colors, A and B.

With A, chain a multiple of 10 plus 7.

Row 1: 1 dc in 4th ch from hook and in each ch to end. Draw B thru loop, break and tighten A. Ch 1, turn.

Row 2: * 1 sc around post of each of first 5 dc, (1 dc in next dc, 1 sc in next dc) twice, 1 dc in next dc; rep from *, ending 1 sc around post of each of last 5 dc. Draw A thru loop, break and tighten B. Ch 3, turn.

Row 3: Skip first sc, 1 dc in each st to end. Draw B thru loop, break and tighten A. Ch 2, turn.

Row 4: Skip first sc, 1 sc in first dc, (1 sc in next dc, 1 dc in next dc) twice, * 1 sc around post of each of next 5 dc, (1 dc in next dc, 1 sc in next dc) twice, 1 dc in next dc; rep from *, ending (dc in next dc, 1 sc in next dc) twice, 1 dc in top of turning ch. Draw A thru loop, break and tighten B. Ch 3, turn.

Row 5: Same as Row 3.

Repeat from Row 2 for pattern.

No. 19

No. 20

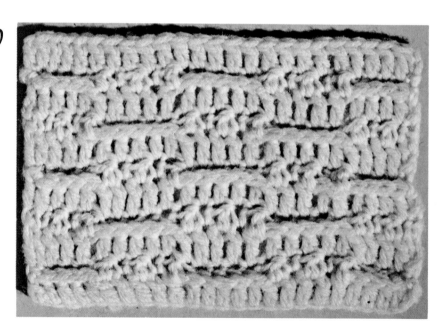

No. 21

No. 22

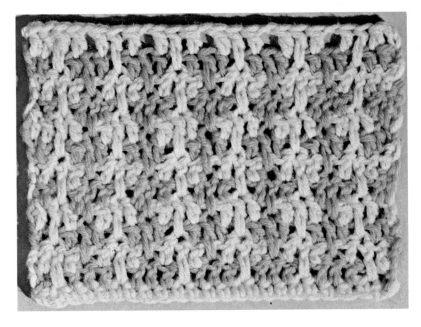

No. 21

Worked with 3 colors, A, B, and C.
With A, chain 4. Join with sl st to form a ring.

Rnd 1: Ch 1, 8 sc in ring. Join with sl st to first sc. Draw B thru loop on hook, break A and fasten off.

Rnd 2: Draw B loop to 1-inch, (yo and draw up 1-inch loop in same place as joining) 4 times, yo and thru 9 loops on hook, ch 3, * in next sc (yo and draw up 1-inch loop) 4 times, yo and thru 9 loops, ch 3; rep from * 6 times. Join with sl st to top of first cluster. Fasten off.

Rnd 3: Attach C in any ch-3 loop. Ch 2, 4 dc in same loop, * 4 dc in next loop, 5 dc in next loop; rep from * around, ending 4 dc in last loop, join with sl st to top of ch-2.

Rnd 4: Ch 2, 1 dc in next sc, * 3 dc in next dc, 1 dc in each of next 8 dc; rep from * around, ending 3 dc in next dc, 1 dc in each of last 6 dc. Join with sl st to top of ch-2.

Rnd 5: Ch 2, 1 dc in each of next 2 dc, * 3 dc in next dc, 1 dc in each of next 10 dc; rep from * around, ending 3 dc in next dc, 1 dc in each of last 7 dc. Join with sl st to top of ch-2 and fasten off.

No. 22

Worked with 2 colors, A and B.
With A, chain a multiple of 4.

Foundation Row: 1 sc in 2nd ch from hook and in each ch to end, draw B thru loop, drop A, ch 3, turn.

Row 1: 1 dc in first sc, * ch 1, skip 1 sc, 1 dc in each of next 3 sc; rep from *, ending ch 1, skip 1 sc, 1 dc in last sc. Ch 2, do not turn. Pull up a long loop and drop B.

Row 2: Working from same side as last row, pull A thru top of ch-3, ch 2, 1 dc in first dc, yo, insert hook in A sc 2 rows below (directly under ch-1 of Row 1), draw up a long loop, (yo and thru 2 loops) twice (long dc), 1 dc in next dc (3-st group completed), * ch 1, skip next dc, work 3-st group; rep from * to end. Ch 2, turn. Pull up a long loop and drop A.

Row 3: Pick up B, sl st in first ch of A ch-2, ch 2, 1 dc in first dc, * ch 1, skip next dc, 1 dc in next dc, long dc in dc 2 rows below, 1 dc in next dc (3-st group); rep from *, ending ch 1, skip next dc, 1 dc in last dc, ch 2. Draw up loop, drop B, do not turn.

Row 4: Pick up A, join with sl st to top of ch-2 of last row, ch 2, 1 dc in first dc, * long dc in dc 2 rows below, 1 dc in next dc, ch 1, skip next dc, 1 dc in next dc; rep from *, ending with group. Ch 2, turn. Pull up long loop, drop A.
Repeat Rows 3 and 4 for pattern.

No. 23

Worked in 2 colors, A and B.

With A, chain 12. Join with sl st to form a ring.

Rnd 1: Ch 5, (1 tr in ring, ch 1) 15 times. Join with sl st to 4th ch of ch-5. (16 ch-1 sps)

Rnd 2: Ch 4, 3 dc in first ch-1 sp, drop loop from hook, insert hook in 4th ch of ch-4 and thru dropped loop, draw loop thru ch, ch 2, (4 dc in next ch-1 sp, drop loop from hook, insert hook under 2 loops at top of first of the 4-dc and thru dropped loop, draw loop thru dc, ch 2) 15 times. Join with sl st in top of ch-4. Break A.

Rnd 3: Join B in any ch-2 sp, ch 3, 3 dc in same sp with joining, ch 2, 4 dc in same sp (corner), * (ch 3, 1 sc in next ch-2 sp) 3 times, ch 3; in next ch-2 sp work (4 dc, ch 2, 4 dc) for corner; rep from * twice, (ch 3, 1 sc in next ch-2 sp) 3 times, ch 3. Join with sl st in top of ch-3.

Rnd 4: Sl st to first ch-2, sl st under ch-2, ch 3 and under same ch-2 work 3 dc, ch 2, 4 dc), * ch 1, skip next ch-3, (4 dc under next ch-3, ch 1) twice, in corner sp work (4 dc, ch 2, 4 dc); rep from * twice, ch 1, skip next ch-3, (4 dc under next ch-3, ch 1) twice. Join with sl st in top of ch-3. Break B.

Rnd 5: Join A in a corner ch-2 sp, ch 3, in same sp with joining work (3 dc, ch 2, 4 dc), * (4 dc in next ch-1 sp) 3 times, in corner sp work (4 dc, ch 2, 4 dc); rep from * twice, (4 dc in next ch-1 sp) 3 times. Join with sl st in top of ch-3. Fasten off.

No. 24

Worked with 2 colors, A and B.

With A, chain a multiple of 4.

Row 1 (wrong side): Pulling up long loops, in 4th ch from hook work (3 hdc, ch 3, sl st), * skip 3 ch, in next ch work (3 hdc, ch 3, sl st) shell; rep from * to end. Ch 4, pull up long loop and drop from hook. Do not turn.

Row 2: Attach B to turning ch at beg of last row before first shell. Under next ch-3 work (sl st, ch 3, 3 hdc) shell; rep from * to end. Ch 4, draw up a long loop, drop B from hook. Pick up A and tighten. Turn.

Row 3: Under next ch-3 work (sl st, ch 3 and 3 hdc); rep from * to end. Ch 4, draw up long loop, drop A from hook. Do not turn.

Row 4: Pick up B loop and tighten, * under next ch-3 work (3 hdc, ch 3, sl st): rep from * to end. Ch 4, draw up long loop, drop B from hook, pick up A and tighten. Turn.

Row 5: * Under next ch-3 work (3 hdc, ch 3, sl st); rep from * to end. Ch 4, draw up long loop, drop A. Do not turn. Pick up B.

Repeat from Row 2 for pattern.

No. 23

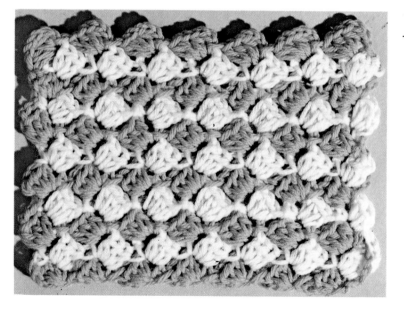

No. 24

No. 25

No. 26

No. 25

Worked with 2 colors, A and B.

With A, chain a multiple of 3 plus 1.

Foundation Row: 1 sc in 2nd ch from hook and in each ch to end. Ch 1, turn.

Row 1: Skip first sc, draw up loop in each of next 3 sc, yo and thru 1 loop, (yo and thru 2 loops) 3 times (4 afghan sts). Draw B thru loop, drop and tighten A; ch 4, skip 1 ch, draw up loop in each of 3 remaining B chs, draw up loop in vertical bar of each of first 3 afghan sts (leaving last afghan st free—7 loops on hook); yo and thru all 7 loops (star), ch 1 for eye; * draw A thru loop, drop and tighten B; draw up loop in eye of star just made, 1 loop in back of last loop of star, 1 loop in vertical bar of last free afghan st, 1 loop in each of next 3 sc (7 loops on hook); yo and thru 1 loop, (yo and thru 2 loops) 6 times (7 afghan sts); draw B thru loop, drop and tighten A; draw up loop in each of first 6 vertical bars of afghan sts, yo and thru all 7 loops, ch 1 for eye; rep from *, ending draw A thru loop, drop and tighten B, draw up loop in eye of star, in back of last star, in bar of free afghan st and in each of last 2 sc (6 loops on hook); yo and thru 1 loop, (yo and thru 2 loops) 5 times (6 afghan sts); draw B thru loop, drop and tighten A; draw up loop in each of last 6 bars of afghan sts, yo and thru 7 loops on hook, ch 1. Draw A thru loop, drop and tighten B.

Row 2: 1 sc in eye of first star, * 1 sc in top loop of same star, 1 sc in top of next afghan st, 1 sc in eye of next star; rep from *, ending 1 sc in top loop of last star, 1 sc in top of B ch.

Repeat Rows 1 and 2 for pattern.

No. 26

Worked with 2 colors, A and B.

With A, chain an even number. Skip first bar in each row. Pick up color by drawing thru loop.

Rows 1, 2 and 3: Basic afghan st. Drop A, draw B thru loop.

Rows 4 and 5: With B, basic afghan st. Drop B, pick up A.

Row 6—First Half: With A, draw up loop in each bar to end.

Row 6—Second Half: Yo and thru 1 loop, yo and thru 3 loops, * ch 1, yo and thru 3 loops; rep from *, ending ch 1, yo and thru 2 loops. Drop A, pick up B.

Row 7—First Half: With B, * draw up loop under ch-1, insert hook under next 2 bars and draw up loop; rep from *, ending draw up loop in last bar.

Row 7—Second Half: Work off loops in basic afghan st.

Row 8: With B, basic afghan st. Drop B, pick up A.

Repeat from Row 1 for pattern.

No. 27

Worked in 3 colors, A, B, and C.

With A chain 5. Join with sl st to form a ring.

Rnd 1: 10 sc in ring. Place marker to indicate end of rnds.

Rnd 2: 1 sc in first sc, 2 sc in next sc, * 1 sc in next sc, 2 sc in next sc; rep from * around. (15 sc)

Rnd 3: * 1 sc in each of first 2 sc, 2 sc in next sc; rep from * around. (20 sc)

Rnd 4: 1 sc in first and in each sc around. Join with sl st to first sc. Draw B thru loop on hook, tighten A, break and fasten off.

Rnd 5: Ch 2, 1 dc in same sc with sl st, 1 sc in each of next 4 sc, * 2 dc in next sc, 1 sc in each of next 4 sc; rep from * around. Join with sl st in sp between ch-2 and next dc.

Rnd 6: Ch 2, 1 dc in same sp with sl st, * 1 sc in next dc, 1 sc in each of next 4 sc, 1 sc in next dc, 2 dc in sp between 2 dc of last rnd; rep from *, ending 1 sc in each of next 5 sts, 1 sc at base of ch-2. Join with sl st to sp between ch-2 and next dc.

Rnd 7: Attach C between 2 dc at any corner. Ch 2, 1 dc in same sp, * 1 sc in each st to next corner, 2 dc between corner dc's; rep from * around. Join with sl st and fasten off.

No. 28

Worked with 2 colors, A and B.

With A, chain a multiple of 3 plus 1.

Row 1: 1 dc in 4th ch from hook and in each ch to end, working off last 2 loops of last dc with B. Drop A. Turn.

Row 2 (worked with B): Ch 1, 1 sc in first dc, 1 sc in sp after first dc, * ch 2, 1 sc in sp after next 3 dc; rep from *, ending 1 sc under tunring ch, 1 sc in 2nd ch of turning ch. Draw up long loop of B (so row will not pull out) and drop from hook.

Row 3 (worked with A, beg at same side as last row): Draw A thru first sc of last row, ch 3, * 3 dc under ch-2; rep from *, ending 1 dc in last sc and pulling B loop thru last 2 loops of last dc. Turn.

Repeat Rows 2 and 3 for pattern.

No. 27

No. 28

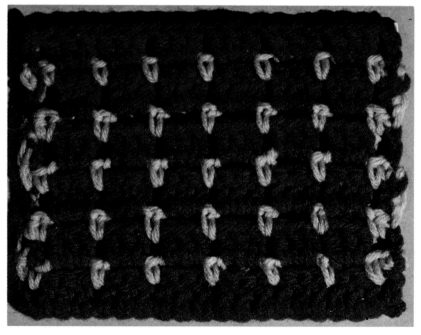

No. 29

No. 30

No. 29

Worked with 3 colors, A, B, and C.
With A, chain 4. Join with sl st to form a ring.

Rnd 1: Ch 3, work 3 dc in ring, drop loop from hook, insert hook in 3rd st of ch, pick up loop and pull thru, ch 1 to tighten (first popcorn), * ch 1, 4 dc in ring, drop loop from hook, insert hook in first of the 4-dc, pick up loop and pull thru, ch 1 (popcorn); rep from * twice, ch 1, join with sl st in first popcorn. Fasten off.

Rnd 2: Attach B in any ch-1 sp, ch 3, in same sp * work 2 popcorns of 5 dc with ch 1 between, ch 1; rep from * in each ch-1 sp. Join and fasten off.

Rnd 3: Attach C in any ch-1 sp between a pair of popcorns. Under same ch work (3 dc, ch 2, 3 dc, sl st), under next ch-1 work (1 sl st, 3 dc, 1 sl st); rep from * around. Join and fasten off.

No. 30

Worked with 3 colors, A, B, and C.
With A, chain a multiple of 5.

Row 1: 1 sc in 2nd ch from hook and in each ch to end. Ch 1, turn.

Rows 2, 3 and 4: 1 sc in first sc and in each sc to end. Ch 1, turn but at end of Row 4, draw B thru last 2 loops of last sc, ch 1, turn.

Row 5: 1 sc in first sc and in each of next 3 sc, * working in row below draw up loop in sc below sc just worked and in each of next 2 sc, insert hook in next sc of Row 5 and draw yarn thru sc and 3 loops, yo and thru remaining 2 loops (cluster), 1 sc in each of next 4 sc; rep from * to end. Ch 1, turn.

Row 6: 1 sc in first sc and in each st to end, drawing A thru 2 loops of last sc. Ch 1, turn.

Repeat from Row 3 for pattern, alternating colors A and B.

No. 31

Worked with 2 colors, A and B.
With A, chain 6. Join with sl st to form a ring.

Rnd 1: Ch 4, (1 dc, ch 1) 11 times in ring. Join with sl st in 3rd ch. Draw B thru loop, drop A.

Rnd 2: (1 sc in next sp, ch 2) 12 times. Join with sl st in first sc. Draw A thru loop, drop B.

Rnd 3: * (1 sc in next sp, ch 2) twice; in next sp work (2 dc, ch 2) twice for corner; rep from * around. Join with sl st in first sc. Draw B thru loop. Fasten off A.

Rnd 4: * 1 sc, ch 3 in each sp to corner; in corner sp work (1 sc, ch 3, 1 sc, ch 3); rep from * around. Join with sl st in first sc. Fasten off.

No. 32

Worked with 2 colors, A and B.
With A, chain a multiple of 4 plus 1.
Note: When changing colors, draw new color thru last 2 loops of last st of previous color. Carry previous color loosely in back of work, continue with new color, working over strand of previous color.

Row 1 (wrong side): Skip first ch, work 1 sc in each ch to end as follows: * 3 A, 1 B; rep from *, ending 1 B. Ch 2 B, turn.

Row 2: Work 1 dc in each sc as follows: Skip first dc, * 1 A, 3 B; rep from *, ending 1 A. Ch 1 A, turn.

Row 3: Work 1 sc in each dc as follows: 1 A, 1 B, * 3 A, 1 B; rep from *, ending 2 A. Ch 1 B, turn.

Row 4: Work 1 sc in each sc as follows: * 1 B, 3 A; rep from *, ending 3 A. Ch 2 B, turn.

Row 5: Work 1 dc in each sc as follows: Skip first dc, 3 B, * 1 A, 3 B; rep from *, ending 3 B, ch 1 A, turn.

Row 6: Work 1 sc in each dc as follows: 2 A, * 1 B, 3 A; rep from *, ending 1 B, 1 A. Ch 1 A, turn.

Row 7: Work 1 sc in each sc as follows: 1 A, 1 B, * 3 A, 1 B; rep from *, ending 1 B, 2 A. Ch 2 B, turn.

Repeat from Row 2 for pattern.

No. 26

Chain a multiple of 6 plus 4.

Work a row in basic afghan st.

Row 1—First Half: Skip first bar, * skip next bar, draw up loop in next bar, draw up loop in skipped bar; rep from *, ending draw up loop in last bar.

Row 1—Second Half: Work off loops in basic afghan st.

Row 2—First Half: Skip first bar, * skip next bar, draw up loop in next bar, draw up loop in skipped bar, with yarn at front work a P st in next bar, yarn back and draw up loop in each of next 2 bars, yarn front and P in next bar; rep from *, ending 2 crossed sts, draw up loop in last bar.

Row 2—Second Half: Work off loops in basic afghan st.

Row 3—First Half: Skip first bar, * skip next bar, draw up loop in next bar, draw up loop in skipped bar, draw up loop in next bar, work a P st in each of next 2 bars, draw up loop under next bar; rep from *, ending 2 crossed sts, draw up loop in last bar.

Row 3—Second Half: Work off loops in basic afghan st.

Repeat Rows 2 and 3 for pattern.

No. 27

Chain a multiple of 4 plus 2.

Work a row of basic afghan st.

Row 1—First Half: Skip first bar, * skip next bar, draw up loop in next bar, draw up loop in skipped bar, with yarn at front work a P st in each of next 2 bars; rep from *, ending draw up loop in last bar.

Row 1—Second Half: Work off loops in basic afghan st.

Row 2—First Half: Skip first bar, * work a P st in each of next 2 bars, skip 1 bar, draw up loop in next bar, draw up loop in skipped bar; rep from *, ending draw up loop in last bar.

Row 2—Second Half: Work off loops in basic afghan st.

Repeat Rows 1 and 2 for pattern.

No. 28

Chain an even number.

Row 1: Basic afghan stitch.

Row 2—First Half: Skip first bar, * skip next bar, draw up loop in next bar, draw up loop in skipped bar; rep from *, ending draw up loop in last bar.

Row 2—Second Half: Work off loops in basic afghan st.

Repeat Rows 1 and 2 for pattern.

No. 29

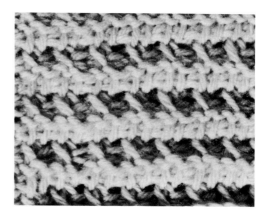

Chain an even number.

Work a row in basic afghan st.

Row 1—First Half: Skip first bar, * with yarn at front, work a P st in each bar to last bar, yarn back, draw up loop in last bar.

Row 1—Second Half: Work off loops in basic afghan st.

Row 2—First Half: Skip first bar, * skip next bar, draw up loop in next bar, draw up loop in skipped bar; rep from *, ending draw up loop in last bar.

Row 2—Second Half: Work off loops in basic afghan st.

Repeat Rows 1 and 2 for pattern.

No. 30

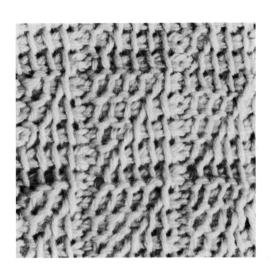

Chain a multiple of 6 plus 5.

Work a row in basic afghan st.

Row 1—First Half: Skip first bar, draw up loop in each of next 4 bars, * yarn at front work a P st in next bar, yarn back and draw up loop in each of next 5 bars; rep from * to end.

Row 1—Second Half: Work off loops in basic afghan st.

Row 2—First Half: Skip first bar, draw up loop in each of next 3 bars, * work a P st in each of next 2 bars, draw up loop in each of next 4 bars; rep from *, ending draw up loop in each of last 5 bars.

Row 2—Second Half: Work off loops in basic afghan st.

Row 3—First Half: Skip first bar, draw up loop in each of next 2 bars, * work a P st in each of next 3 bars, draw up loop in each of next 3 bars; rep from *, ending P 1 bar, draw up loop in last bar.

Row 3—Second Half: Work off loops in basic afghan st.

Row 4—First Half: Skip first bar, draw up loop in next bar, * work a P st in each of next 4 bars, draw up loop in each of next 2 bars; rep from *, ending P 2 bars, draw up loop in last bar.

Row 4—Second Half: Work off loops in basic afghan st.

Row 5—First Half: Skip first bar, work a P st in each of next 5 bars, draw up loop in next bar; rep from *, ending P 3 bars, draw up loop in last bar.

Row 5—Second Half: Work off loops in basic afghan st.

Repeat from Row 1 for pattern.

No. 31

Chain a multiple of 10 plus 4.

Work a row of basic afghan st.

Row 1—First Half: Skip first bar, work a P st in each of next 3 bars, * work a K st (insert hook thru center of st and underneath the ch) in each of the next 6 sts, work a P st in each of the next 4 bars; rep from *, ending with a P st in each of last 3 bars, draw up loop in last bar.

Row 1—Second Half: Work off loops in basic afghan st.

Rows 2 and 3: Same as Row 1.

Row 4—First Half: Same as first half of Row 1.

Row 4—Second Half: Yo and thru 1 loop, (yo and thru 2 loops) 3 times, * pull up loop and drop from needle, slip hook out of the next 6 K loops and twist by inserting hook thru the 3 sts at left, then thru the 3 sts at right (cable), pick up dropped loop, (yo and thru 2 loops) 11 times; rep from * to end.

Repeat from Row 1 for pattern.

No. 32

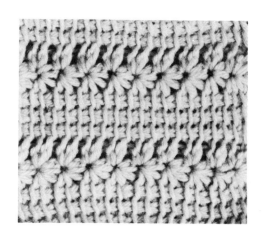

Chain a multiple of 2 plus 1.

Rows 1, 2 and 3: Basic afghan st.

Row 4 (Star St): Ch 2, draw up loop in 2nd ch from hook and in first 3 bars, yo and thru 5 loops, ch 1 (eye), * draw up loop in center of eye, draw up loop in back of last picked up loop of star, draw up loop in each of next 2 bars, yo and thru 5 loops, ch 1 (eye); rep from * to end. Ch 2, turn.

Row 5: Work 2 hdc in eye of each star, ending with 1 hdc in last st. (Same number of hdc as in original ch).

Repeat from Row 1 for pattern, working first row of loops in each hdc.

No. 33

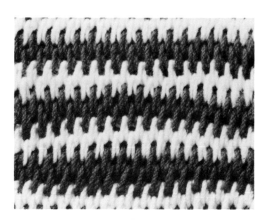

Worked with 2 colors, A and B.

With B, chain an uneven number.

Work a row in basic afghan stitch. Drop B, join A.

Row 1—First Half: With A, draw up loop in first sp (between first 2 bars and in each sp to last sp, skip last sp, draw up loop in last bar.

Row 1—Second Half: Work off loops in basic afghan st. Drop A. Pick up B.

Row 2—First Half: With B, skip first sp, draw up loop in each sp to end, draw up loop in last bar.

Row 2—Second Half: Work off loops in basic afghan st. Drop B, pick up A.

Repeat Rows 1 and 2 for pattern.

Raised Patterns

The word raised was chosen as being a very simple yet descriptive term to include any pattern with an uneven surface as opposed to a smooth and flat one. As you come to realize the great ingenuity of these patterns, a murmured "bravo" to our now familiar early crocheter is well in order. Have you ever tried to create a new crochet stitch? Think of the trial and error involved and be amazed at what emerged. Or perhaps we give too much credit to our forebear—maybe just a slip of the hook in the wrong place created a new pattern stitch!

Consider the Post Stitch Patterns: You learn to work **in** stitches—for a Post Stitch you work **around** a stitch, For a Front Post Stitch, the hook is inserted from front to back, then out to the front on the other side of the stitch. For a Back Post Stitch, the hook is inserted from back to front, then out to the back on the other side of the stitch.

Consider the overlay patterns, where stitches are made through previously worked rows, creating all kinds of interesting effects and designs.

Consider the working of one stitch right **on** top (not **in** the top) of another stitch, one or more times.

Indeed, consider them all, for these are fascinating patterns and stitches that offer a wealth of variety.

No. 1

Chain an even number.

Foundation Row: 1 sc in 2nd ch from hook and in each ch to end. Ch 2, turn.

Row 1: Skip first sc, hdc in next sc, yo and insert hook from front to back to right of hdc, draw up loop, yo and thru 3 loops (double hdc), * skip 1 sc, double hdc in next sc; rep from *, ending 1 hdc in last sc. Ch 1, turn.

Row 2: Working thru single strand at front of st (keeping ch formed by last row on right side), 1 sc in first hdc, * 1 sc in each st of double hdc; rep from *, ending 1 sc in top of turning ch. Ch 2, turn.

Repeat Rows 1 and 2 for pattern.

No. 2

Chain an even number.

Foundation Row: 1 sc in 2nd ch from hook and in each ch to end. Ch 2, turn.

Row 1: 1 dc in first st, * yo, draw up loop thru back loop of next st, yo and thru 1 loop, yo and thru 3 loops; yo, draw up loop thru front loop of next st, yo and thru 1 loop, yo and thru 3 loops; rep from *, ending with working thru back loop, 1 dc in last st. Ch 2, turn. (Do not count turning ch on following rows).

Row 2: Same as Row 1, ending with dc in last dc. Ch 2, turn.

Repeat Row 2 for pattern.

No. 3

Chain a multiple of 8.

Row 1 (wrong side): 1 dc in 3rd ch from hook and in each ch to end. Ch 2, turn.

Row 2: 1 dc in each of next 2 dc, ch 1, skip 1 dc, * 1 dc in each of next 3 dc, 1 dc around post of next dc in row below (raised dc), skip dc behind raised dc, 1 dc in each of next 3 dc, ch 1, skip 1 dc; rep from *, ending 1 dc in each of last 2 dc, 1 dc in top of turning ch. Ch 2, turn.

Row 3: 1 dc in each of next 2 dc, ch 1, * 1 dc in each of next 3 dc, from right side, work 1 dc around raised dc of row below, skip dc behind raised dc, 1 dc in each of next 3 dc, ch 1; rep from *, ending 1 dc in each of last 2 dc, 1 dc in top of turning ch. Ch 2, turn.

Repeat Rows 2 and 3 for pattern.

No. 4

Chain a multiple of 4 plus 3.

Row 1 (right side): 1 dc in 4th ch from hook, 1 dc in each of next 2 ch, yo twice, * skip the 3 dc just worked and with hook in front of work insert from back to front thru next ch at right of first dc, draw up loop, (yo and thru 2 loops) 3 times (a tr, worked across 3 dc), skip 1 ch, 1 dc in each of next 3 ch; rep from *, ending tr across last 3 dc, 1 dc in last ch. Ch 2, turn.

Row 2: Skip first dc and tr, * 1 dc in each of next 3 dc, yo twice, insert hook as before in top of skipped tr, draw up loop and complete tr, skip next tr of row below; rep from *, ending tr across last 3 dc, 1 dc under turning ch. Ch 2, turn.
Repeat Row 2 for pattern.

No. 5

Chain a multiple of 8 plus 3.

Foundation Row: 1 dc in 3rd ch from hook and in each ch to end. Ch 2, turn.

Row 1: Skip first dc, * yo, insert hook from front to back to front around next dc and draw up loop, yo and thru 2 loops twice (front dc), work front dc around next 3 dc; work a back dc in same way (inserting hook from back to front to back) around each of next 4 dc; rep from *, ending 1 hdc in top of turning ch. Ch 2, turn.

Rows 2 and 3: Rep Row 1.

Row 4: Skip hdc, * 1 back dc around each of next 4 dc, 1 front dc around each of next 4 dc; rep from *, ending 1 hdc in top of turning ch. Ch 2, turn.

Rows 5 and 6: Rep Row 4.
Repeat from Row 1 for pattern.

No. 6

Chain an even number.

Row 1: Skip 3 ch, * in next ch draw up a loop, yo and thru 1 loop, yo and thru 2 loops; rep from * to end. Ch 3, turn.

Row 2: Skip first st, * thru **back** loop of next st draw up a loop, yo and thru 1 loop, yo and thru 2 loops; rep from *, ending with last pat st in top of turning ch. Ch 3, turn.

Repeat Row 2 for pattern.

No. 7

Chain an even number.

Foundation Row: Work 1 sc in 2nd ch from hook and in each ch to end. Ch 1, turn.

Row 1: 1 sc in first sc, * ch 1, skip next sc, 1 sc in next sc; rep from * to end. Ch 2, turn.

Row 2: Work 1 dc at base of first sc (working **over** the sc of row below), * 1 sc in ch-1 sp, 1 dc at base of next sc; rep from * to end. Ch 2, turn.

Row 3: 1 sc in first sc, * ch 1, skip dc, 1 sc in next sc; rep from *, ending last sc in top of turning ch. Ch 1, turn.

Row 4: 1 sc in first ch-1 sp, * 1 dc at base of next sc, sc in next ch-1 sp; rep from *, ending sc under turning ch. Ch 1, turn.

Row 5: 1 sc in first sc, * ch 1, skip dc, 1 sc in next sc; rep from * to end. Ch 2, turn.

Repeat from Row 2 for pattern.

No. 8

Chain an even number.

Row 1: 1 hdc in 4th ch from hook and in each ch to end. Ch 2, turn.

Row 2: Working thru **back** loop only, work 1 hdc in first and in each hdc to end. Ch 2, turn.

Repeat Row 2 for pattern.

No. 9

Chain a multiple of 8 plus 6.

Row 1: 1 dc in 3rd ch from hook and in each of next 3 ch, * skip 1 ch, in next ch work (2 dc, ch 2, 2 dc) shell, skip 1 ch, 1 dc in each of next 5 ch; rep from * to end. Ch 2, turn.

Row 2: Skip first dc, 1 dc around post of each of next 4 dc, * shell under center ch-2 of shell, skip 2 dc of shell, 1 dc around post of each of next 5 dc; rep from *, ending 1 dc around post of last 4 dc, 1 dc in top of turning ch. Ch 2, turn.

Repeat Row 2 for pattern.

No. 10

Chain an even number.

Foundation Row: 1 dc in 3rd ch from hook and in each ch to end. Ch 3, turn.

Row 1: Skip first dc, * 1 dc from front around post of next dc, 1 dc from back around post of next dc; rep from *, ending 1 dc from front around post of last dc, 1 dc under turning ch. Ch 3, turn.

Repeat Row 1 for pattern.

No. 11

Chain an uneven number.

Row 1: 1 hdc in 2nd ch from hook and in each ch to end. Ch 1, turn.

Row 2: Working thru single loop (so that the 2 loops of each st of Row 1 forms an unbroken chain on other side) work 1 hdc in each st to end. Ch 1, turn.

Repeat Row 2 for pattern.

No. 12

Chain a multiple of 5 plus 3.

Foundation Row: 1 dc in 3rd ch from hook and in each ch to end. Ch 2, turn.

Row 1: Skip first dc, 1 dc from front around post of each of next 2 dc, 1 dc from back around post of each of next 2 dc, * 1 dc from front around post of each of next 3 dc, 1 dc from back around post of each of next 2 dc; rep from *, ending front post around 2 dc, 1 dc in top of turning ch. Ch 2, turn.

Row 2: Skip first dc, 1 dc from back around post of each of next 2 dc, 1 dc from front around post of each of next 2 dc, * 1 dc from back around post of each of next 3 dc, 1 dc from front around post of each of next 2 dc; rep from *, ending back post around 2 dc, 1 dc in top of turning ch.

Repeat Rows 1 and 2 for pattern.

No. 13

Chain a multiple of 4 plus 2.

Foundation Row: 1 sc in 2nd ch from hook and in each ch to end. Ch 1, turn.

Rows 1, 2, 3 and 4: 1 sc in first sc and in each sc to end. Ch 1, turn.

Row 5: 1 sc in each of first 2 sc, * insert hook in next sc 4 rows below, draw up loop to top of work and complete sc (long sc), skip sc in back of long sc, 1 sc in each of next 3 sc; rep from *, ending 1 sc in each of last 2 sc. Ch 1, turn.

Rows 6, 7, 8 and 9: 1 sc in first and each sc to end. Ch 1, turn.

Row 10: 1 sc in each of first 4 sc, * long sc in next sc 4 rows below, skip sc in back of long sc, 1 sc in each of next 3 sc; rep from *, ending 1 sc in each of last 4 sc. Ch 1, turn.

Repeat from Row 1 for pattern.

No. 14

Chain a multiple of 4 plus 2.

Foundation Row: 1 sc in 2nd ch from hook and in each ch to end. Ch 3, turn.

Row 1: Skip first 2 sc, * in next sc work (1 dc, ch 1, 1 dc) shell, skip 1 sc, 1 dc in next sc, skip next sc; rep from *, ending shell, skip 1 sc, 1 dc in last sc. Ch 3, turn.

Row 2: * Shell under ch-1 of next shell, 1 dc worked from front around post of next dc; rep from *, ending shell in last shell, 1 dc in 2nd ch of turning ch. Ch 3, turn.

Row 3: * Shell under ch-1 of next shell, 1 dc worked from back around post of next dc; rep from *, ending shell in last shell, 1 dc in 2nd ch of turning ch. Ch 3, turn.

Repeat Rows 2 and 3 for pattern.

No. 15

Chain an even number.

Foundation Row: 1 sc in 2nd ch from hook and in each ch to end. Ch 1, turn.

Row 1: 1 sc in first sc, * 1 dc around post of next sc, 1 sc in next sc; rep from * to end. Ch 1, turn.

Row 2: 1 sc in first and in each st to end. Ch 1, turn.

Row 3: 1 sc in first sc, * 1 dc around post of dc in row below, skip sc behind post, 1 sc in next sc, rep from * to end. Ch 1, turn.

Row 4: 1 sc in first and in each st to end. Ch. 1, turn.

Repeat Rows 3 and 4 for pattern.

No. 16

Chain a multiple of 6 plus 2.

Foundation Row: 1 sc in 2nd ch from hook and in each ch to end. Ch 1, turn.

Row 1: 1 sc in each of first 2 sc, skip 2 sc, work 1 dc from front around post of next sc, 1 sc in sc before post st, work 1 dc from front around post of first skipped st (Cable made), skip next sc, 1 sc in each of next 3 sc, * work cable as before over next 3 sc, skip next sc, 1 sc in each of next 3 sc; rep from *, ending 1 sc in each of last 2 sc. Ch 1, turn.

Row 2: 1 sc in first sc and in each st to end. Ch 1, turn.

Row 3: 1 sc in each of first 2 sc, * work 1 dc around 2nd post of cable below, skip next sc, 1 sc in next sc, work 1 dc around first post of cable below, skip next sc, 1 sc in each of next 3 sc; rep from *, ending 1 sc in each of last 2 sc. Ch 1, turn.

Repeat Rows 2 and 3 for pattern.

No. 17

Chain a multiple of 6 plus 2.

Foundation Row: 1 hdc in 3rd ch from hook and in each ch to end. Ch 2, turn.

Row 1: Skip first 2 hdc, work 3 dc from front around post of next hdc; * skip next hdc, 1 hdc from front around post of next hdc, skip next hdc, work 3 dc from front around post of next hdc (shell); rep from *, ending skip last hdc, 1 dc in top of turning ch. Ch 2, turn.

Row 2: * Work 3 dc from back around post of center dc of next shell, 1 hdc from back around post of next hdc; rep from *, ending shell over center dc of last shell, 1 dc in top of turning ch. Ch 2, turn.

Row 3: * Work shell from front around post of center dc of next shell, 1 hdc from front around post of next hdc; rep from * ending shell over center dc of last shell, 1 dc in top of turning ch. Ch 2, turn.

Repeat Rows 2 and 3 for pattern.

No. 18

Chain an uneven number.

Row 1 (right side): 1 sc in 2nd ch from hook and in each ch to end. Ch 1, turn.

Row 2: 1 sc in first sc, * 1 tr in next sc, 1 sc in next sc; rep from *, ending 1 sc in each of last 2 sc. Ch 1, turn.

Row 3: 1 sc in first sc and in each st to end. Ch 1, turn.

Row 4: 1 sc in each of first 2 sc, * 1 tr in next sc, 1 sc in next sc; rep from * to end. Ch 1, turn.

Row 5: 1 sc in first sc and in each st to end. Ch. 1, turn.

Repeat from Row 2 for pattern.

No. 19

Chain a multiple of 4 plus 1.

Row 1: 1 dc in 4th ch from hook and in each ch to end. Ch 3, turn.

Row 2: Skip first dc, 1 dc from front around post of each of next 2 dc, * 1 dc from back around post of next dc, 1 dc from front around post of each of next 3 dc; rep from *, ending 1 dc from front around post of each of last 2 sts, 1 dc in top of turning ch. Ch 3, turn.

Row 3: Skip first dc, 1 dc in each of next 2 dc, * 1 dc from front around post of next dc, 1 dc in each of next 3 dc; rep from *, ending 1 dc in each of last 2 dc, 1 dc in top of turning ch. Ch 3, turn.

Repeat Rows 2 and 3 for pattern.

No. 20

Chain a multiple of 4 plus 3.

Row 1: Skip first ch from hook, 1 sc in each of next 2 ch, ch 2, 2 dc in last sc worked, * skip 2 ch, 1 sc in each of next 2 ch, ch 2, 2 dc in last sc worked; rep from *, ending 1 sc in each of last 2 ch. Ch 1, turn.

Row 2: 1 sc in each of first 2 sc, * ch 2, 2 dc in last sc worked, 1 sc in each of next 2 sc; rep from * to end. Ch 1, turn.

Repeat Row 2 for pattern.

No. 21

Chain a multiple of 3 plus 1.

Foundation Row: 1 sc in 2nd ch from hook and in each ch to end. Ch 1, turn.

Row 1: 1 sc in each of first 2 sc, * draw up loop in next sc and ch 3 on loop, draw yarn thru last ch and loop on hook, 1 sc in each of next 2 sc; rep from *, ending 1 sc in each of last 3 sc. Ch 1, turn.

Rows 2, 3 and 4: 1 sc in first sc and in each st to end. Ch 1, turn.

Row 5: 1 sc in first sc, rep from * of Row 1, ending 1 sc in last sc. Ch 1, turn.

Rows 6, 7 and 8: 1 sc in first sc and in each st to end. Ch 1, turn.

Repeat from Row 2 for pattern.

No. 22

Chain a multiple of 3 plus 1.

Row 1: In 3rd ch from hook work (1 sc, 1 dc, 1 sc) group, * skip 2 ch, group in next ch; rep from * ending 1 dc in last ch. Ch 2, turn.

Row 2: Skip first dc, * group in dc of next group; rep from *, ending group in dc of last group, 1 dc in top of turning ch. Ch 2, turn.

Repeat Row 2 for pattern.

No. 23

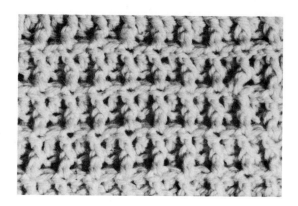

Chain an uneven number.

Foundation Row: 1 dc in 3rd ch from hook and in each ch to end. Ch 2, turn.

Row 1: Skip first dc, * 1 dc from front around post of next dc, 1 dc in top of next dc; rep from *, ending 1 dc in top of turning ch. Ch 2, turn.

Repeat Row 1 for pattern, always working the post dc around the dc that was worked in the top dc of previous row.

No. 24

Chain a multiple of 4.

Foundation Row: 1 sc in 2nd ch from hook and in each ch to end. Ch 1, turn.

Row 1: 1 sc in first sc and in each sc to end. Ch 1, turn.

Row 2: 1 sc in each of first 3 sc, * 1 dc around post of next sc 1 row below, skip next sc (behind post dc), 1 sc in each of next 3 sc; rep from * to end. Ch 1, turn.

Rows 3, 5 and 7: 1 sc in first sc and in each st to end. Ch 1, turn.

Row 4: 1 sc in each of first 4 sc, * 1 dc around post dc below, skip next sc, 1 sc in each of next 3 sc; rep from *, ending skip next sc, 1 sc in each of last 2 sc. Ch 1, turn.

Row 6: 1 sc in first sc, 1 dc around post of next sc in row below, * skip next sc, 1 sc in each of next 3 sc, 1 dc around post dc below; rep from *, ending skip 1 sc, 1 sc in last sc. Ch 1, turn.

Row 8: 1 sc in each of first 2 sc, * 1 dc around post dc below, skip next sc, 1 sc in each of next 3 sc; rep from *, ending skip 1 sc, 1 sc in each of last 4 sc. Ch 1, turn.

Repeat from Row 1 for pattern.

No. 25

Chain an uneven number.

Foundation Row: 1 hdc in 3rd ch from hook and in each ch to end. Ch 2, turn.

Row 1: 1 hdc in back loop of first hdc, * 1 hdc in front loop of next hdc, 1 hdc in back loop of next hdc; rep from * to end. Ch 2, turn.

Row 2: 1 hdc in front loop of first hdc, * 1 hdc in back loop of next hdc, 1 hdc in front loop of next hdc; rep from * to end.

Repeat Rows 1 and 2 for pattern.

No. 26

Chain a multiple of 4 plus 1.

Foundation Row: 1 sc in 2nd ch from hook, * ch 3, skip 2 ch, 1 sc in next ch, ch 3, sl st in last sc made (picot), 1 sc in next ch; rep from *, ending ch 3, skip 2 ch, 1 sc in last ch. Ch 4, turn.

Row 1: Work (1 sc in center ch of first loop, ch 3, sl st in last sc, 1 sc in same st as last sc) picot * ch 3, skip next picot, 1 picot in center ch of next loop; rep from *, ending ch 1, 1 dc in last sc. Ch 1, turn.

Row 2: 1 sc in first dc, ch 3, skip first picot, * 1 picot in center ch of next loop, ch 3, skip next picot; rep from *, ending skip picot and 1 ch of turning ch, 1 sc in next ch. Ch 4, turn.

Repeat Rows 1 and 2 for pattern.

No. 27

Chain a multiple of 10 plus 6.

Row 1: Sl st in 2nd ch from hook and in each of next 4 ch, * 1 hdc in each of next 5 ch, sl st in each of next 5 ch; rep from * to end. Ch 1, turn.
Work all following rows thru back loops only.

Row 2: Work sl st over each sl st, hdc over each hdc. Ch 2, turn.

Row 3: Work hdc over each sl st, sl st over each hdc. Ch 2, turn.

Row 4: Same as Row 2, ending ch 1, turn.

Row 5: Same as Row 3. Ch 1, turn.

Row 6: Same as Row 2.

Repeat last 4 rows for pattern.

Lace Patterns

As with double crochet, every lace pattern shown could well be included in another classification and be well represented in all the other groupings. But these patterns are combinations of so many different stitches that they deserve a heading of their own. The history of lace making of all types is a fascinating one that goes back many generations. Crocheted lace is one of the easiest methods of lacemaking when compared with handmade laces worked with shuttles and needles. At least easy to us in the present day, with the patterns all worked out in days long past. Handmade lace is a constant source of wonder to researchers. The earliest known laces were made of very fine thread and almost bring the imagination to a complete halt—for how could such masterpieces, with the intricacies of their design, ever have been created by human hands? Descendants far removed from our earlier crocheter must have developed the first crocheted lace. These are a far cry from simple basic stitches and were never achieved by simple experimentation. They are patterns obviously planned in advance and then produced. The examples shown here are not intricate patterns. Rather they are a sampling of what can be done with a small hook and a very small number of basic stitches. The art of handwork has never died, but as the tempo of living has continually changed, our thinking, too, has changed. Now we are more prone to be utterly amazed that a machine can make lace—forgetting that long before the machines were invented, living hands did the same thing.

No. 1

Chain a multiple of 7 plus 4.

Row 1: Skip 2 ch, * 1 hdc in each of next 2 ch, ch 3, skip 2 ch, 1 sc in next ch, ch 3, skip 2 ch; rep from *, ending 1 hdc in each of last 2 ch. Ch 2, turn.

Row 2: Skip first hdc, 1 hdc in next hdc, * ch 3, in next sc work (1 sc, ch 3, 1 sc) loop, ch 3, 1 hdc in each of next 2 hdc; rep from *, ending 1 hdc in last hdc, 1 hdc in top of turning ch. Ch 1, turn.

Row 3: 1 sc in each of first 2 hdc, * 1 sc under ch-3, ch 5, skip loop, 1 sc under next ch-3, 1 sc in each of next 2 hdc; rep from * to end. Ch 1, turn.

Row 4: 1 sc in each of first 2 sc, * skip next sc, 7 sc under ch-5, skip 1 sc, 1 sc in each of next 2 sc; rep from *, ending skip 1 sc, 1 sc in each of last 2 sc. Ch 2, turn.

Row 5: Skip first sc, 1 hdc in next sc, * ch 3, skip 3 sc, 1 sc in center st of 7-sc group, ch 3, skip 3 sc, 1 hdc in each of next 2 sc; rep from *, ending 1 hdc in each of last 2 sc. Ch 2, turn.

Repeat from Row 2 for pattern.

No. 2

Chain a multiple of 12 plus 8.

Row 1: Work 3 dc in 4th ch from hook, skip 3 ch, 4 dc in next ch (a double shell), * ch 4, skip 3 ch, 1 sc in next ch, ch 4, skip 3 ch, 4 dc in next ch, skip 3 ch, 4 dc in next ch; rep from * to end. Ch 3, turn.

Row 2: 3 dc in first dc, 4 dc in last dc of other half of double shell, * ch 4, 1 sc in next sc, ch 4, 1 shell in first dc of next shell, 1 shell in last dc of 2nd shell; rep from * to end, working last shell in top of turning ch. Ch 3, turn.

Row 3: Rep Row 2. Ch 6, turn.

Row 4: * 1 sc in sp between 2 shells, ch 4, shell in last dc of 2nd shell, skip sc, shell in first dc of next shell, ch 4; rep from *, ending ch 4, 1 sc between last 2 shells, ch 4, 1 dc in top of turning ch. Ch 6, turn.

Row 5: 1 sc in first sc, * ch 4, shell in first dc of first shell, shell in last dc of 2nd shell, ch 4, 1 sc in next sc; rep from *, ending ch 4, 1 dc in 2nd ch of turning ch. Ch 6, turn.

Row 6: Rep Row 5. Ch 3, turn.

Row 7: 3 dc in first dc, * skip next sc, shell in first dc of next shell, ch 4, 1 sc in sp between next double shell, ch 4, shell in last dc of 2nd shell; rep from *, ending with 2nd shell of last double shell in 2nd ch of turning ch. Ch 3, turn.

Repeat from Row 2 for pattern.

No. 3

Chain a multiple of 4 plus 2.

Foundation Row: Work 1 sc in 2nd ch from hook and in each ch to end. Turn.

Row 1: * Draw up a ½ inch loop, draw yarn thru loop, work 1 sc between the 2 strands of the loop and the single strand of yarn (knot st), rep from * once (double knot st), skip 3 sc, 1 sc in next sc; rep from *, ending double knot st, 1 sc in last sc. Turn.

Row 2: Work double knot st, * 1 sc in center st of first double knot st of last row, work double knot st, skip next sc, 1 sc in center of next double knot; rep from * to end. Turn.

Repeat Row 2 for pattern.

No. 4

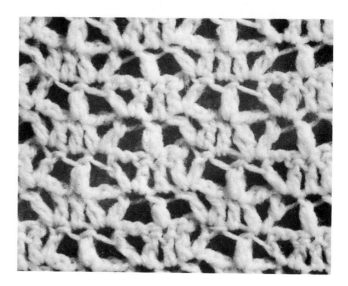

Chain a multiple of 8 plus 1.

Row 1: Yo, draw up loop in 4th ch from hook, yo, draw up loop in same ch, yo and draw thru 4 loops, yo and draw thru 2 loops (cluster), * skip 2 ch, work (1 dc, ch 2, 1 dc) in next ch, 1 dc in next ch, (1 dc, ch 2, 1 dc) in next ch, skip 2 ch, cluster in next ch; rep from * to last 5 ch, skip 2 ch, (1 dc, ch 2, 1 dc) in next ch, 1 dc in each of last 2 ch. Ch 3, turn.

Row 2: Skip first dc, * cluster in next dc, skip next dc and ch-2, (1 dc, ch 2, 1 dc) in next dc, 1 dc in cluster, (1 dc, ch 2, 1 dc) in next dc, skip next ch-2 and dc; rep from *, ending 1 dc in cluster, 1 dc in top of turning ch. Ch 3, turn.

Repeat Row 2 for pattern.

No. 5

Chain an uneven number.

Row 1: 1 sc in 3rd ch from hook, * ch 1, skip 1 ch, 1 sc in next ch; rep from * to end. Ch 2, turn.

Row 2: 1 sc in first ch-1 sp, * ch 1, 1 sc in next sp; rep from *, ending ch 1, 1 sc in top of turning ch. Ch 1, turn.

Row 3: 1 sc in first sc, * draw up a ½ inch loop, draw yarn thru loop, work 1 sc between the 2 strands of loop and single strand of yarn (knot st), work 2nd knot st, 1 sc in next sp; rep from *, ending 2 knot sts, 1 sc in top of turning ch. Ch 4, turn.

Row 4: 1 sc in knot between 2 knot sts, * ch 1, sc in knot between next 2 knot sts; rep from * to end. Ch 2, turn.

Rows 5 and 6: Rep Row 2.
Repeat Rows 3 thru 6 for pattern.

No. 6

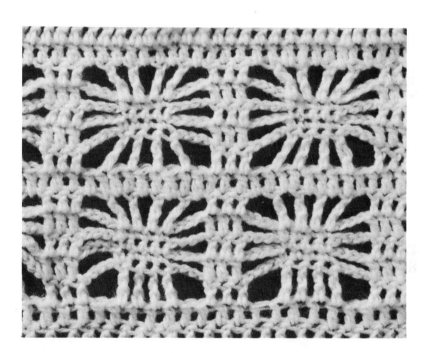

Chain a multiple of 9 plus 2.

Foundation Row: Work 1 dc in 3rd ch from hook and in each ch to end. Ch 4, turn.

Row 1: Skip first dc, tr in next dc, * ch 4, skip 1 dc, 1 dc in each of next 3 dc, ch 4, skip 1 dc, 1 tr in each of next 4 dc; rep from *, ending ch 4, skip next dc, 1 tr in next dc, 1 tr in top of turning ch. Ch 1, turn.

Row 2: 1 sc in each of first 2 tr, * ch 4, 1 dc in each of next 3 dc, ch 4, 1 sc in each of next 4 tr; rep from *, ending ch 4, 1 sc in last tr, 1 sc in top of turning ch. Ch 1, turn.

Row 3: 1 sc in each of first 2 sc, * ch 4, 1 dc in each of next 3 dc, ch 4, 1 sc in each of next 4 sc; rep from *, ending ch 4, 1 sc in each of last 2 sc. Ch 1, turn.

Row 4: Rep Row 3, ch 4, turn.

Row 5: 1 tr in 2nd sc, * ch 1, 1 dc in each of next 3 dc, (ch 1, 1 tr in next sc) 4 times; rep from *, ending (ch 1, 1 tr in next sc) twice. Ch 3, turn.

Row 6: 1 dc in next tr, * 1 dc in next ch-1 sp, 1 dc in each of next 3 dc, (1 dc in next ch-1 sp, 1 dc in next tr) 4 times; rep from *, ending 1 dc in each of next 3 dc, 1 dc in next ch-1 sp, 1 dc in next tr, 1 dc in top of turning ch. Ch 4, turn.

Row 7: 1 tr in 2nd dc, * ch 4, skip next dc, 1 dc in each of next 3 dc, ch 4, (skip next dc, 1 tr in next dc) 4 times; rep from *, ending ch 4, 1 tr in last dc, 1 tr in top of turning ch. Ch 1, turn.

Repeat from Row 2 for pattern.

No. 7

Chain a multiple of 6 plus 2.

Row 1: Ch 9 more, sl st in 10th ch from hook, sl st in next ch, ch 9, sl st in same ch as last sl st, * ch 5, skip 4 ch, sl st in next ch, ch 9, sl st in same ch as last sl st, sl st in next ch, ch 9, sl st in same ch as last sl st; rep from * to end. Ch 5, turn.

Row 2: 1 sc under first ch-9 loop, * ch 4, 1 sc under each of next 2 ch-9 loops; rep from *, ending ch 4, 1 sc under last loop. Ch 9, turn.

Row 3: Sl st in first sc, * ch 5, sl st in next sc, ch 9, sl st in same sc as last sl st, sl st in next sc, ch 9, sl st in same sc as last sl st; rep from *, ending ch 5, sl st in last sc, ch 9, sl st in same sc as last sl st. Ch 5, turn.

Row 4: 1 sc in each of first 2 loops, * ch 4, 1 sc in each of next 2 loops; rep from * to end. Ch 9, turn.

Row 5: Sl st in first sc, sl st in next sc, ch 9, sl st in same sc as last sl st, * ch 5, sl st in next sc, ch 9, sl st in same sc as last sl st, sl st in next sc, ch 9, sl st in same sc as last sl st; rep from * to end. Ch 5, turn.

Repeat from Row 2 for pattern.

No. 8

Chain a multiple
of 14 plus 4.

Row 1: 1 dc in 3rd ch from hook, 1 dc in next ch (3 dc group), * ch 3, skip 3 ch, 1 sc in each of next 5 ch, ch 3, skip 3 ch, 1 dc in each of next 3 ch; rep from * to end. Ch 4, turn.

Row 2: 3 dc under first ch-3, * ch 3, skip 1 sc, 1 sc in each of next 3 sc, ch 3, (3 dc under next ch-3) twice; rep from *, ending ch 3, 3 dc under last ch-3, ch 3, 1 dc in top of turning ch. Ch 3, turn.

Row 3: 1 dc under first ch-3, ch 3, 3 dc under next ch-3, * ch 3, skip 1 sc, 1 dc in next sc, ch 3, 3 dc under next ch-3, ch 3, 1 dc in sp between next 2 groups, ch 3, 3 dc under next ch-3; rep from *, ending ch 3, 1 dc under turning ch, 1 dc in 2nd ch of turning ch. Ch 1, turn.

Row 4: 1 sc in first dc, 1 sc in next sp, * ch 3, (3 dc in next sp) twice, ch 3, 1 sc in next sp, 1 sc in next dc, 1 sc in next sp; rep from *, ending ch 3, 1 sc in last sp, 1 sc in top of turning ch. Ch 1, turn.

Row 5: 1 sc in each of first 2 sc, 1 sc in sp, * ch 3, 3 dc in sp between 2 groups, ch 3, 1 sc in next sp, 1 sc in each of next 3 sc, 1 sc in next sp; rep from *, ending ch 3, 1 sc in last sp, 1 sc in each of last 2 sc. Ch 1, turn.

Row 6: 1 sc in each of first 2 sc, * ch 3, (3 dc in next sp) twice, ch 3, skip 1 sc, 1 sc in each of next 3 sc; rep from *, ending ch 3, 1 sc in each of last 2 sc. Ch 4, turn.

Row 7: 3 dc in first sp, * ch 3, 1 dc in sp between next 2 groups, ch 3, 3 dc in next sp, ch 3, skip 1 sc, 1 dc in next sc, ch 3, 3 dc in next sp; rep from *, ending ch 3, 3 dc in last sp, ch 3, 1 dc in last sc. Ch 2, turn.

Row 8: 2 dc in first sp, * ch 3, 1 sc in next sp, 1 sc in next dc, 1 sc in next sp, ch 3, (3 dc in next sp) twice; rep from *, ending ch 3, 2 dc under turning ch, 1 dc in 2nd ch of turning ch. Ch 2, turn.

Row 9: 1 dc in each of first 2 dc, * ch 3, 1 sc in next sp, 1 sc in each of next 3 sc, 1 sc in next sp, ch 3, 3 dc in sp between next 2 groups; rep from *, ending ch 3, 1 dc in each of last 2 dc, 1 dc in top of turning ch. Ch 4, turn.
Repeat from Row 2 for pattern.

No. 9

Chain a multiple of 8 plus 6.

Foundation Row: Work 1 sc in 2nd ch from hook and in each ch to end. Ch 1, turn.

Row 1: 1 sc in first sc, * ch 5, skip 3 sc, 1 sc in next sc; rep from * to end. Ch 1, turn.

Row 2: 1 sc in first sc, * 5 sc under next ch-5 (arch), 3 sc under next ch-5, ch 5, turn, sl st in 3rd sc of arch, turn; in new ch-5 loop, work 2 sc, ch 2, 2 sc; 2 sc in same ch-5 loop with 3 sc; rep from *, ending 5 sc under last ch-5, 1 sc in last sc, ch 5, turn, sl st in 3rd sc of last arch, turn, 3 sc under new ch-5 just made (½ arch). Ch 1, turn.

Row 3: 1 sc in first sc, ch 5, skip first arch, * 1 sc between skipped arch and next arch (directly over sc 2 rows below), ch 5, sc under ch-2 of next arch, ch 5; rep from *, ending ch 5, 1 sc in last sc. Ch 1, turn.

Row 4: 1 sc in first sc, 3 sc under next ch-5, ch 5, turn, sl st in first sc of this row, * turn; under new ch-5 loop, work 2 sc, ch 2, 2 sc; 2 sc under same ch-5 with 3 sc, 5 sc under next ch-5, 3 sc under next ch-5, ch 5, turn, sl st in 3rd sc of arch; rep from *, ending turn, under new ch-5 loop, work 2 sc, ch 2, 2 sc; 2 sc under same ch-5 with 3 sc, 1 sc in last sc. Ch 1, turn.

Row 5: 1 sc in first sc, * ch 5, 1 sc in first ch-2 sp, ch 5, 1 sc between next 2 arches; rep from *, ending ch 5, 1 sc in last ch-2 sp. Ch 1, turn.
Repeat from Row 2 for pattern.

No. 10

Chain a multiple of 6 plus 4.

Foundation Row: Work 1 sc in 2nd ch from hook and in each ch to end. Ch 3, turn.

Row 1: Skip first sc, in next sc (yo twice, draw up loop, yo and thru 2 loops twice) 3 times, yo and thru 4 loops (cluster), * ch 4, skip 2 sc, 1 sc in next sc, ch 4, skip 2 sc, cluster in next sc; rep from *, ending 1 dc in last sc. Ch 1, turn.

Row 2: 1 sc in st at top of cluster, 1 sc in next st, * ch 4, 1 sc in next sc, ch 4, 1 sc in top of next cluster; rep from *, ending 1 sc in last cluster, 1 sc in top of turning ch. Ch 1, turn.

Row 3: 1 sc in each of first 2 sc, * ch 4, cluster in next sc, ch 4, 1 sc in next sc; rep from *, ending 1 sc in each of last 2 sc. Ch 1, turn.

Row 4: 1 sc in each of first 2 sc, * ch 4, 1 sc in top of cluster, ch 4, 1 sc in next sc; rep from *, ending 1 sc in each of last 2 sc. Ch 3, turn.

Row 5: Skip first sc, cluster in next sc, * ch 4, 1 sc in next sc, ch 4, cluster in next sc: rep from *, ending 1 dc in last sc. Ch 1, turn.
Repeat from Row 2 for pattern.

No. 11

Chain a multiple of 8 plus 4.

Foundation Row: Work 1 sc in 2nd ch from hook and in each ch to end. Ch 1, turn.

Row 1 (right side): 1 sc in first sc, 1 sc in each of next 2 sc, * ch 3, skip 2 sc; in next sc work (1 dc, ch 3, 1 dc, ch 3), skip 2 sc, 1 sc in each of next 3 sc; rep from * to end. Ch 1, turn.

Row 2: 1 sc in first sc, * 7 dc in sp between next 2 dc, ch 3, 1 sc in center st of 3-sc, ch 3; rep from *, ending 1 sc in last sc. Ch 2, turn.

Row 3: 1 dc in first sc, * ch 3, 1 sc in each of next 7 dc; rep from *, ending ch 3, 1 dc in last sc. Ch 2, turn.

Row 4: 1 dc in first dc, * ch 3, skip 2 sc, 1 sc in each of next 3 sc, ch 3, in center st of ch-3 work (1 dc, ch 3, 1 dc); rep from *, ending 1 sc in each of 3 sc, ch 3, 1 dc in top of turning ch. Ch 2, turn.

Row 5: 3 dc under first ch-3, * ch 3, 1 sc in center st of 3-sc, ch 3, 7 dc in sp between 2 dc; rep from *, ending 3 dc under ch-3, 1 dc in top of turning ch. Ch 1, turn.

Row 6: 1 sc in each of first 4 dc, * ch 3, 1 sc in each of next 7 dc; rep from *, ending 1 sc in each of last 3 dc, 1 sc in top of turning ch. Ch 1, turn.

Row 7: 1 sc in first sc, * ch 3, in center st of ch-3 work (1 dc, ch 3, 1 dc), ch 3, skip 2 sc, 1 sc in each of next 3 sc; rep from *, ending ch 3, 1 sc in last sc. Ch 1, turn. Repeat from Row 2 for pattern.

No. 12

Chain a multiple of 8 plus 4.

Foundation Row: Work 1 sc in 2nd ch from hook and in each ch to end. Ch 1, turn.

Row 1: 1 sc in each of first 4 sc, * ch 5, skip 3 sc, 1 sc in each of next 5 sc; rep from *, ending 1 sc in each of last 4 sc. Ch 1, turn.

Row 2: 1 sc in each of first 3 sc, * ch 3, skip next sc, 1 sc under next ch-5, ch 3, skip 1 sc, 1 sc in each of next 3 sc; rep from * to end. Ch 1, turn.

Row 3: 1 sc in each of first 2 sc, * ch 3, 1 sc under next ch-3, 1 sc in next sc, 1 sc under next ch-3, ch 3, skip 1 sc, 1 sc in next sc; rep from *, ending ch 3, 1 sc in each of last 2 sc. Ch 1, turn.

Row 4: 1 sc in first sc, ch 3, * 1 sc under next ch-3, 1 sc in each of next 3 sc, 1 sc under next ch-3, ch 5, skip 1 sc; rep from *, ending last rep ch 3 (instead of ch 5), skip 1 sc, 1 sc in last sc. Ch 1, turn.

Row 5: 1 sc in first sc, 1 sc under next ch-3, ch 3, skip 1 sc, 1 sc in each of next 3 sc, ch 3, skip 1 sc, * 1 sc under next ch-5, ch 3, skip 1 sc, 1 sc in each of next 3 sc, ch 3, skip 1 sc; rep from *, ending ch 3, 1 sc under next ch-3, 1 sc in last sc. Ch 1, turn.

Row 6: 1 sc in each of first 2 sc, * 1 sc under next ch-3, ch 3, skip 1 sc, 1 sc in next sc, ch 3, skip 1 sc, 1 sc under next ch-3, 1 sc in next sc; rep from *, ending 1 sc in each of last 2 sc. Ch 1, turn.

Row 7: 1 sc in each of first 3 sc, * 1 sc under next ch-3, ch 5, skip 1 sc, 1 sc under next ch-3, 1 sc in each of next 3 sc; rep from * to end.
Repeat from Row 2 for pattern.

No. 13

Chain a multiple of 6 plus 2.

Row 1: Work 1 sc in 2nd ch from hook and in each ch to end. Ch 3, turn.

Row 2: 1 dc in first sc, * skip 2 sc, in next sc work (1 dc, ch 1, 1 dc); rep from * to end. Ch 3, turn.

Row 3: 1 dc in first ch-1 sp, * in next ch-1 sp work (3 dc, ch 1, 3 dc) shell, (1 dc, ch 1, 1 dc) in next ch-1 sp; rep from *, ending 1 dc, ch 1, 1 dc under turning ch. Ch 3, turn.

Row 4: 1 dc in first ch-1 sp, * in next ch-1 sp work (1 dc, ch 1, 1 dc); rep from * ending (1 dc, ch 1, 1 dc) under turning ch. Ch 3, turn.
Repeat Rows 3 and 4 for pattern.

No. 14

Chain a multiple of 8 plus 4.

Row 1: 1 sc in 4th ch from hook, ch 3, 1 sc in same ch as before (½ clover), * ch 3, skip 3 ch, 1 dc in next ch, ch 3, skip 3 ch, in next ch work 1 sc (ch 3, 1 sc) 3 times (clover); rep from *, ending ch 3, skip 3 ch, 1 sc (ch 3, 1 sc) twice in last ch (½ clover). Ch 1, turn.

Row 2: 1 sc in first loop of ½ clover, * ch 3, clover in next dc, ch 3, 1 sc in center loop of next clover; rep from *, ending 1 sc in last loop of ½ clover. Ch 3, turn.

Row 3: In first sc work (1 sc, ch 3, 1 sc), * ch 3, 1 sc in center loop of next clover, ch 3, clover in sc over clover; rep from *, ending ½ clover in last sc. Ch 1, turn.

Row 4: 1 sc in first loop of ½ clover, * ch 3, clover in sc over clover, ch 3, 1 sc in center loop of next clover; rep from *, ending 1 sc in last loop of ½ clover. Ch 3, turn. Repeat Rows 3 and 4 for pattern.

No. 15

Chain a multiple of 3 plus 1.

Foundation Row: 1 sc in 2nd ch from hook and in each ch to end. Ch 2, turn.

Row 1: 1 dc in **back** loop of 3rd sc, ch 4, 1 dc in top of last dc, * yo twice, insert hook in **back** loop of next sc and draw up loop (4 loops on hook), yo and thru 2 loops, yo, skip next sc, insert hook in **back** loop of next sc and draw up loop (5 loops on hook), (yo and thru 2 loops) 4 times, ch 1, 1 dc in center of cross; rep from * to end. Ch 1, turn.

Row 2: 1 sc in **front** loop of each dc and in each ch-1, ending 1 sc in last dc, 1 sc in top of ch-4, 1 sc in next ch of ch-4. Ch 2, turn.
Repeat Rows 1 and 2 for pattern.

No. 16

Chain an even number.

Foundation Row: 1 sc in 2nd ch from hook and in each ch to end. Ch 1, turn.

Row 1: 1 sc in first sc, * skip 1 sc, in next sc work (1 dc, ch 2, 1 dc, ch 2, 1 dc) group, skip 1 sc, 1 sc in next sc; rep from * to end. Ch 5, turn.

Row 2: 1 dc in first sc, * 1 sc in center dc of next group, work group in next sc; rep from *, ending with (1 dc, ch 2, 1 dc) in last sc. Ch 1, turn.

Row 3: 1 sc in first dc, * group in next sc, 1 sc in center dc of next group; rep from *, ending 1 sc in 3rd ch of turning ch. Ch 5, turn.
Repeat Rows 2 and 3 for pattern.

No. 17

Chain a multiple of 5 plus 3.

Foundation Row: 1 sc in 2nd ch from hook and in each ch to end. Turn.

Row 1: Ch 7, 1 sc in 2nd sc, ch 3, 1 sl st in same sc, ch 3, * skip 2 sc, 1 sc in next sc, ch 3, 1 sl st in same sc (picot), ch 7, 1 sc in next sc, ch 3, sl st in same sc (the ch-3 at each side of ch-7 forms a picot), ch 3, rep from *, ending skip 2 ch, picot in last sc, ch 3, 1 dc in last sc. Ch 3, turn.

Row 2: 1 sc in first dc, * ch 3, 1 sc under ch-7, ch 3, 1 sc under same ch-7; rep from * to end. Turn.

Row 3: Ch 7, 1 sc under first ch-3 loop, ch 3, sl st under same loop, * ch 3, skip next ch-3, 1 sc under next ch-3 loop, ch 3, sl st under same loop, ch 7, 1 sc under same loop, ch 3, sl st under same loop; rep from *, ending ch 3, 1 sc in last ch-3 loop, ch 3, sl st under same loop, ch 3, 1 dc under same loop. Ch 3, turn.
Repeat Rows 2 and 3 for pattern.

No. 18

Chain a multiple of 4.

Row 1: Yo twice and draw up loop in 4th ch from hook, * yo and thru 2 loops, yo, skip 1 ch, draw up loop in next ch, (yo and thru 2 loops) 4 times, ch 2, 1 dc in joining of the 2 sts, ch 2, skip 1 ch, yo twice and draw up loop in next ch; rep from *, ending ch 1, skip 1 ch, 1 dc in last ch. Ch 3, turn.

Row 2: * Yo twice and draw up loop in first vertical st, yo and thru 2 loops, yo and draw up loop in next vertical st, (yo and thru 2 loops) 4 times, ch 2, 1 dc in joining, ch 2, skip 2 ch; rep from *, ending ch 1, 1 dc in 2nd ch of turning ch. Ch 3, turn.
Repeat Row 2 for pattern.

No. 19

Chain a multiple
of 12 plus 2.

Foundation Row: 1 sc in 2nd ch from hook and in each ch to end. Ch 1, turn.

Row 1: 1 sc in each of first 3 sc, * ch 4, skip 3 sc, 1 tr in next sc, ch 4, skip 3 sc, 1 sc in each of next 5 sc; rep from *, ending ch 4, 1 sc in each of last 3 sc. Ch 2, turn.

Row 2: Skip first sc, 1 dc in each of next 2 sc, * ch 3, 1 sc under ch-4, 1 sc in tr, 1 sc under next ch-4, ch 3, skip 1 sc, 1 dc in each of next 3 sc; rep from *, ending 1 dc in each of last 3 sc. Ch 2, turn.

Row 3: Skip 1 dc, 1 dc in each of next 2 dc, * ch 4, 1 sc in each of next 3 sc, ch 4, 1 dc in each of next 3 dc; rep from *, ending 1 dc in each of last 2 dc, 1 dc in top of turning ch. Ch 1, turn.

Row 4: 1 sc in each of first 3 dc, * ch 3, 1 tr in center sc of 3-sc, ch 3, 1 sc under next ch, 1 sc in each of next 3 dc, 1 sc under next ch; rep from *, ending tr, ch 3, 1 sc in each of last 2 dc, 1 sc in top of turning ch. Ch 1, turn.

Row 5: 1 sc in each sc, in each ch and in each tr across. Ch 1, turn.

Row 6: 1 sc in first and in each sc to end. Ch 7, turn.

Row 7: Skip first 4 sc, * 1 sc in each of next 5 sc (3rd is over tr below), ch 4, skip 3 sc, 1 tr in next sc, ch 4, skip 3 sc; rep from *, ending ch 4, 1 dc in last sc. Ch 1, turn.

Row 8: 1 sc in first dc, 1 sc under next ch, * ch 3, skip 1 sc, 1 dc in each of next 3 sc, ch 3, 1 sc under next ch, 1 sc in tr, 1 sc under next ch; rep from *, ending 1 sc under ch-7, 1 sc in 3rd ch of ch-7. Ch 1, turn.

Row 9: 1 sc in each of first 2 sc, * ch 3, 1 dc in each of next 3 dc, ch 3, 1 sc in each of next 3 sc; rep from *, ending 1 sc in each of last 2 sc. Ch 6, turn.

Row 10: * 1 sc under ch, 1 sc in each dc, 1 sc under ch, ch 3, 1 tr in center sc of 3-sc, ch 3; rep from *, ending ch 3, 1 dc in last sc. Ch 1, turn.

Row 11: Rep Row 5, ending 1 sc in each of 4 ch of turning ch. Ch 1, turn.

Row 12: 1 sc in first and in each sc to end. Ch 1, turn.

Repeat from Row 1 for pattern.

No. 20

Chain a multiple
of 5 plus 4.

Row 1: 1 sc in 2nd ch from hook and in each ch to end. Ch 3, turn.

Row 2: Skip first sc, 1 dc in next sc, * ch 5, skip 4 sc, in next sc work (2 dc, ch 1, 2 dc) shell; rep from *, ending ch 5, 1 dc in each of last 2 sc. Ch 3, turn.

Row 3: Skip first dc, 1 dc in next dc, * ch 5, shell under ch-1 of next shell; rep from *, ending ch 5, 1 dc in last dc, 1 dc in top of turning ch. Ch 3, turn.

Row 4: Skip first dc, 1 dc in next dc, * ch 2, 1 sc in center ch of ch-5 of Row 2 working over the ch-5 of last row, ch 2, shell in center of next shell; rep from *, ending 1 dc in last dc, 1 dc in top of turning ch. Ch 3, turn.

Row 5: Skip first dc, 1 dc in next dc, * ch 5, shell in next shell; rep from *, ending 1 dc in last dc, 1 dc in top of turning ch. Ch 3, turn.

Repeat from Row 3 for pattern.

No. 21

Chain a multiple
of 6 plus 2.

Foundation Row: 1 sc in 2nd ch from hook and in each ch to end. Ch 4, turn.

Row 1: 1 dc in first sc, ch 2, skip 2 sc, 1 sc in next sc (half shell), * ch 2, skip 2 sc, in next sc work (1 dc, ch 1, 1 dc, ch 1, 1 dc) shell, ch 2, skip 2 sc 1 sc in next sc; rep from *, ending ch 2, skip 2 sc, (1 dc, ch 1, 1 dc) in last sc (half shell). Ch 1, turn.

Row 2: 1 sc in first dc, * ch 2, work shell in sc between shells of last row, ch 2, 1 sc in center dc of next shell; rep from *, ending ch 2, 1 sc in 3rd ch of turning ch. Ch 4, turn.

Row 3: 1 dc in first sc, ch 2, 1 sc in center dc of next shell, * ch 2, shell in sc between shells, ch 2, 1 sc in center dc of next shell; rep from *, ending ch 2, (1 dc, ch 1, 1 dc) in last sc. Ch 1, turn.

Repeat Rows 2 and 3 for pattern.

No. 22

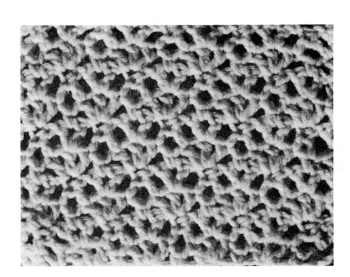

Chain a multiple of 4 plus 1.

Row 1: 1 dc in 5th ch from hook, * ch 1, skip 1 ch, 1 sc in next ch, ch 1, skip 1 ch, in next ch work (1 dc, ch 1, 1 dc, ch 1, 1 dc) group; rep from *, ending (1 dc, ch 1, 1 dc) in last ch. Ch 4, turn.

Row 2: 1 dc in first dc, * ch 1, work a 2-in-1 dc by yo, draw up loop in next dc, yo and thru 2 loops, yo, draw up a loop in first dc of next group, yo and thru 2 loops, yo and thru all 3 loops on hook, ch 1; in center dc of same group work (1 dc, ch 1, 1 dc); rep from *, ending ch 1, (1 dc, ch 1, 1 dc) in 3rd ch of turning ch. Ch 1, turn.

Row 3: 1 sc in first dc, 1 sc in ch-1 sp between first 2 dc; * ch 1, group in the 2-in-1 dc, ch 1, 1 sc in ch-1 sp between next 2 dc; rep from *, ending ch 1, 1 sc under turning ch, 1 sc in 3rd ch of turning ch. Ch 3, turn.

Row 4: Yo, draw up loop in first dc of next group, (yo, thru 2 loops) twice, ch 1, * in center dc of same group work (1 dc, ch 1, 1 dc), ch 1, work 2-in-1 dc in last dc of same group and in first dc of next group, ch 1; rep from *, ending with 2-in-1 dc in last dc and in last sc. Ch 4, turn.

Row 5: 1 dc in first 2-in-1 dc, * ch 1, 1 sc under ch-1 between next 2 dc, ch 1, group in next 2-in-1 dc; rep from *, ending 1 dc under turning ch, ch 1, 1 dc in 3rd ch of turning ch. Ch 3, turn.

Repeat from Row 2 for pattern.

No. 23

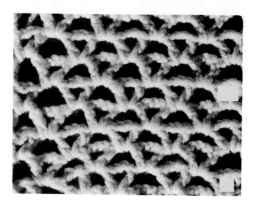

Chain a multiple of 4 plus 2.

Row 1: 1 dc in 6th ch from hook, ch 3, 1 dc in same ch, * ch 1, skip 3 ch, in next ch work (1 dc, ch 3, 1 dc) V st; rep from * to end. Ch 5, turn.

Row 2: 1 dc in first dc, * 1 dc under next ch-1, ch 3, 1 dc under same ch, ch 1; rep from *, ending V st under turning ch. Ch 5, turn.
Repeat Row 2 for pattern.

No. 24

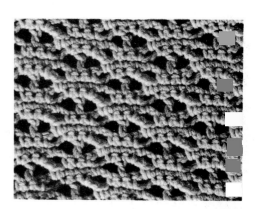

Chain a multiple of 10 plus 2.

Row 1: 1 sc in 2nd ch from hook and in each of next 2 ch; * ch 2, skip 2 ch, 1 dc in next ch, ch 2, skip 2 ch, 1 sc in each of next 5 ch; rep from *, ending ch 2, skip 2 ch, 1 sc in each of last 3 ch. Ch 1, turn.

Row 2: 1 sc in each of first 2 sc, * ch 2, skip next sc, 1 sc under next ch-2, 1 sc in next dc, 1 sc under next ch-2, ch 2, skip 1 sc, 1 sc in each of next 3 sc; rep from *, ending ch 2, skip 1 sc, 1 sc in each of last 2 sc. Ch 5, turn.

Row 3: Skip first 2 sc, * 1 sc under next ch-2, 1 sc in each of next 3 sc, 1 sc under next ch-2, ch 2, skip 1 sc, 1 dc in next sc, ch 2, skip 1 sc; rep from *, ending ch 2, skip 1 sc, 1 dc in last sc. Ch 1, turn.

Row 4: 1 sc in first dc, * 1 sc under next ch-2, ch 2, skip 1 sc, 1 sc in each of next 3 sc, ch 2, skip 1 sc, 1 sc under next ch-2, 1 sc in next dc; rep from *, ending ch 2, skip 1 sc, 1 sc under turning ch, 1 sc in 3rd ch of turning ch. Ch 1, turn.

Row 5: 1 sc in each of first 2 sc, * 1 sc under ch-2, ch 2, skip 1 sc, 1 dc in next sc, ch 2, skip 1 sc, 1 sc under next ch-2, 1 sc in each of next 3 sc; rep from *, ending ch 2, skip 1 sc, 1 sc under next ch-2, 1 sc in each of last 2 sc. Ch 1, turn.
Repeat from Row 2 for pattern.

No. 25

Chain a multiple of 8 plus 4.

Row 1: 1 dc in 4th ch from hook, * draw up loop ½ inch, 1 sc between single strand and loop (knot st), skip 3 ch, 1 sc in next ch, knot st, skip 3 ch, in next ch (yo and draw up loop) 3 times, yo and thru 7 loops, ch 1 (Puff st); rep from * to end. Ch 1, turn.

Row 2: * 1 sc in next Puff st, knot st, Puff st in next sc, knot st; rep from *, ending 1 sc in top of turning ch. Ch 1, turn.

Row 3: Puff st in first sc, * knot st, 1 sc in next Puff st, knot st, Puff st in next sc; rep from * to end. Ch 1, turn.
Repeat Rows 2 and 3 for pattern.

No. 26

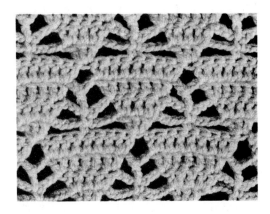

Chain a multiple of 20 plus 6.

Row 1: 1 dc in 5th ch from hook, * ch 4, skip next 4 ch, 1 sc in next ch, ch 4, skip next 4 ch, 3 dc in next ch; rep from *, ending 1 dc in each of last 2 ch. Ch 2, turn.

Row 2: Skip first dc, * 2 dc in next dc, ch 3, 1 sc in next sc, ch 3, 2 dc in next dc, 1 dc in next dc; rep from *, ending 2 dc in last dc, 1 dc in top of turning ch. Ch 2, turn.

Row 3: Skip first dc, 1 dc in next dc, * 2 dc in next dc, ch 2, 1 dc in next sc, ch 2, 2 dc in next dc, 1 dc in each of next 3 dc; rep from *, ending 2 dc in next dc, 1 dc in next dc, 1 dc in top of turning ch. Ch 2, turn.

Row 4: Skip first dc, 1 dc in each of next 2 dc, 2 dc in next dc, * ch 1, 2 dc in next dc, 1 dc in each of next 5 dc, 2 dc in next dc; rep from *, ending 2 dc in next dc, 1 dc in each of next 2 dc, 1 dc in top of turning ch. Ch 1, turn.

Row 5: 1 sc in first dc, * ch 4, 3 dc in next ch-1, ch 4, skip 4 dc, 1 sc in next dc; rep from *, ending skip 4 dc, ch 4, 1 sc in top of turning ch. Ch 1, turn.

Row 6: 1 sc in first sc, * ch 3, 2 dc in next dc, 1 dc in next dc, 2 dc in next dc, ch 3, 1 sc in next sc; rep from *, ending ch 3, 1 sc in last sc. Ch 5, turn.

Row 7: * 2 dc in next dc, 1 dc in each of next 3 dc, 2 dc in next dc, ch 2, 1 dc in next sc, ch 2; rep from *, ending ch 2, 1 dc in last sc. Ch 3, turn.

Row 8: * 2 dc in next dc, 1 dc in each of next 5 dc, 2 dc in next dc, ch 1; rep from *, ending 1 tr in 3rd ch of turning ch. Ch 2, turn.

Row 9: 1 dc in tr, * ch 4, skip 4 dc, 1 sc in next dc, ch 4, 3 dc in next ch-1; rep from *, ending ch 4, 2 dc in top of turning ch. Ch 2, turn.

Repeat from Row 2 for pattern.

No. 27

Chain a multiple of 3 plus 2.

Foundation Row: 1 sc in 2nd ch from hook, * ch 2, skip 2 ch, 1 sc in next ch; rep from * to end. Ch 1, turn.

Row 1: 1 sc in first sc, * 3 sc in next ch-2 sp; rep from *, ending 1 sc in last sc. Ch 4, turn.

Row 2: Skip first sc, * yo and draw up loop in next sc, yo and thru 2 loops, skip 1 sc, yo and draw up loop in next sc, (yo and thru 2 loops) 3 times to complete V st, ch 2; rep from *, ending ch 1, 1 dc in last sc. Ch 1, turn.

Row 3: 1 sc in first sc, * ch 2, 1 sc under next ch-2; rep from *, ending ch 2, 1 sc in 3rd ch of turning ch. Ch 1, turn.

Row 4: 1 sc in first sc, 1 sc under first ch-2, * ch 2, 1 sc under next ch-2; rep from *, ending 1 sc under last ch-2, 1 sc in last sc. Ch 1, turn.

Row 5: 1 sc in each of first 2 sc, * 3 sc in next ch-2 sp; rep from *, ending 1 sc in each of last 2 sc. Ch 5, turn.

Row 6: Skip first 2 sc, * work V st over next 3 sts, ch 2; rep from *, ending ch 2, skip 1 sc, 1 dc in last sc. Ch 1, turn.

Row 7: 1 sc in first dc, 1 sc under first ch-2, * ch 2, 1 sc under next ch-2; rep from *, ending ch 2, 1 sc under turning ch, 1 sc in 3rd ch of turning ch. Ch 1, turn.

Row 8: 1 sc in first sc, * ch 2, 1 sc under next ch-2; rep from *, ending ch 2, skip 1 sc, 1 sc in last sc. Ch 1, turn.

Repeat from Row 1 for pattern.

No. 28

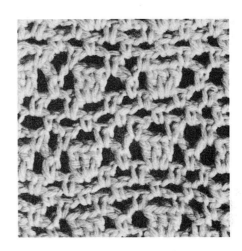

Chain a multiple of 6 plus 5.

Row 1: 1 sc in 2nd ch from hook, * ch 2, skip 2 ch, 1 sc in next ch; rep from * to end. Ch 2, turn.

Row 2 (right side): 2 dc in first ch-2 sp, * ch 2, 1 sc in next sp, ch 2, 3 dc in next sp; rep from *, ending 2 dc in last sp, 1 dc in last sc. Ch 1, turn.

Row 3: 1 sc in first dc, ch 2, 1 sc in first ch-2 sp, * ch 2, 1 sc in next sp; rep from *, ending 1 sc under last ch-2, ch 2, 1 sc in top of turning ch. Ch 1, turn.

Row 4: 1 sc in first sc, ch 2, 1 sc in first ch-2 sp, * ch 2, 3 dc in next sp, ch 2, 1 sc in next sp; rep from *, ending ch 2, skip last ch-2 sp, 1 sc in last sc. Ch 1, turn.

Row 5: 1 sc in first sc, ch 2, 1 sc in first sp, * ch 2, 1 sc in next sp; rep from *, ending ch 2, skip last sp, 1 sc in last sc. Ch 2, turn.

Row 6: 2 dc in first ch-2 sp, * ch 2, 1 sc in next sp, ch 2, 3 dc in next sp; rep from *, ending ch 2, 2 dc in last sp, 1 dc in last sc. Ch 1, turn.

Repeat from Row 3 for pattern.

No. 29

Chain a multiple of 6.

Row 1: 1 sc in 4th ch from hook (counts as picot), ch 1, skip 1, 1 sc in next ch, *
ch 4, 1 sc in 4th ch from hook (picot), ch 1, skip 2 ch, 1 sc in next ch; rep from * to end.
Ch 5, turn.

Row 2: 1 sc in 4th ch from hook, ch 1, 1 sc in center of first picot, * ch 4, 1 sc in
4th ch from hook, ch 1, 1 sc in center of next picot; rep from * to end. Ch 5, turn.
Repeat Row 2 for pattern.

No. 30

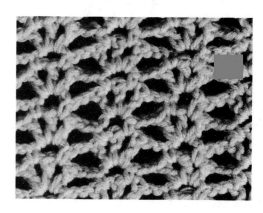

Chain a multiple of 10 plus 4.

Row 1: 1 sc in 2nd ch from hook, * ch 3, skip 1 ch, 1 sc in next ch, ch 2, skip 3
ch, in next ch work (1 dc, ch 1, 1 dc, ch 1, 1 dc) shell, ch 2, skip next 3 ch, 1 sc in next
ch; rep from *, ending ch 3, skip 1 ch, 1 sc in last ch. Ch 2, turn.

Row 2: Shell under next ch-3, ch 2, * 1 sc in sp after next dc, ch 3, 1 sc in sp
after next dc, ch 2, shell under next ch-3, ch 2; rep from *, ending 1 dc in last sc. Ch 1,
turn.

Row 3: 1 sc in first dc, * ch 2, shell under next ch-3, ch 2, 1 sc in sp after next
dc, ch 3, 1 sc in sp after next dc, ch 2, shell under next ch-3, ch 2; rep from *, ending
1 sc in top of turning ch. Ch 2, turn.
Repeat Rows 2 and 3 for pattern.

Shell Patterns

One thing usually leads to another. A stitch in a stitch is fine, but can also be boring. Why not 2 stitches in one? Or 3, or 4 or more? No doubt it was tried first with single crochet and the result was none too pleasing. But with double crochet—an entirely new look. A shell pattern is a group of individual and complete yarn over stitches, all worked in one stitch and so having a common base. The variety of shells that can be made is almost limitless. A shell can consist of all one stitch (as double crochet) or a combination of stitches by height, with the tallest ones in the center; these individual stitches can be fanned out wider, by separating them with one or two chain stitches; or they can be pyramided, first with the individual stitches, the next row with the same stitches divided by a chain 1 and the next row divided by a chain 2. There must be 3 or more stitches in a common base to be considered a shell and the majority of shells are made with an uneven number of stitches, so that there is always a center stitch. The most common shell pattern (and perhaps the oldest), still widely used today, is the shell alternated with a single crochet and staggered every other row.

No. 1

Chain a multiple of 6 plus 3.

Row 1: Work 2 dc in 3rd ch from hook, * skip 2 ch, 1 sc in next ch, skip 2 ch, 5 dc in next ch (shell); rep from *, ending skip 2 ch, 3 dc in last ch. Ch 1, turn.

129

Row 2: 1 sc in first dc, * 5 dc in next sc, 1 sc in center dc of shell; rep from *, ending 1 sc in top of turning ch. Ch 2, turn.

Row 3: 2 dc in first sc, * 1 sc in center dc of shell, shell in next sc; rep from *, ending 3 dc in top of turning ch. Ch 1, turn.

Repeat Rows 2 and 3 for pattern.

No. 2

Chain a multiple of 5 plus 1.

Row 1: In 4th ch from hook work (2 dc, ch 1, 2 dc) shell, * yo, draw up loop in next ch, yo and thru 2 loops, yo, skip 2 ch, draw up loop in next ch, (yo and thru 2 loops) 3 times, shell in next ch; rep from *, ending skip 1 ch, 1 dc in last ch. Ch 3, turn.

Row 2: Shell under ch-1 of first shell, * yo, draw up loop in next dc of same shell, yo and thru 2 loops, yo, skip 3 sts, draw up loop in next dc (2nd dc of shell), (yo and thru 2 loops) 3 times, shell under next ch-1; rep from *, ending shell under ch-1, 1 dc in top of turning ch. Ch 3, turn.

Repeat Row 2 for pattern.

No. 3

Chain a multiple of 7 plus 5.

Row 1: 1 sc in 2nd ch from hook, skip 2 ch, 3 dc in next ch, * ch 3, skip 3 ch, 1 sc in next ch, skip 2 ch, 3 dc in next ch; rep from * to end. Ch 1, turn.

Row 2: 1 sc in first dc, 3 dc in next sc, * ch 3, 1 sc under ch-3, 3 dc in next sc; rep from * to end. Ch 1, turn.

Repeat Row 2 for pattern.

No. 4

Chain a multiple of 13 plus 1.

Foundation Row: 1 dc in 3rd ch from hook and in each ch to end. Ch 2, turn.

Row 1: 1 dc in each of next 2 dc, * ch 3, skip 3 dc, 1 sc in next dc, ch 3, skip 3 dc, 1 dc in each of next 6 dc; rep from *, ending 1 dc in each of last 2 dc, 1 dc in top of turning ch. Ch 2, turn.

Row 2: 1 dc in each of next 2 dc, * ch 1, 1 sc under ch-3, ch 3, 1 sc under next ch-3, ch 1, 1 dc in each of next 6 dc; rep from *, ending 1 dc in each of last 2 dc, 1 dc in top of turning ch. Ch 2, turn.

Row 3: 1 dc in each of next 2 dc, * 7 dc under ch-3, 1 dc in each of next 6 dc; rep from *, ending 1 dc in each of last 2 dc, 1 dc in top of turning ch. Ch 2, turn.

Repeat from Row 1 for pattern.

No. 5

Chain a multiple of 6 plus 2.

Row 1: 1 sc in 2nd ch from hook, 1 sc in next ch ,* ch 3, skip 3 ch, 1 sc in each of next 3 ch; rep from *, ending ch 3, skip 3 ch, 1 sc in each of last 2 ch. Ch 1, turn.

Row 2: 1 sc in first sc, * 5 dc (shell) under ch-3, skip 1 sc, 1 sc in next sc, skip next sc; rep from *, ending skip 1 sc, 1 sc in last sc. Turn.

Row 3: * Ch 3, 1 sc in each of 3 center dc of shell; rep from *, ending ch 2, 1 sc in last sc. Ch 2, turn.

Row 4: 2 dc under ch-2, * skip 1 sc, 1 sc in next sc; skip next sc, shell under ch-3; rep from *, ending 3 dc under turning ch-3. Ch 1, turn.

Row 5: 1 sc in each of first 2 dc, * ch 3, 1 sc in each of 3 center dc of shell; rep from *, ending 1 sc in last dc, 1 sc in top of turning ch. Ch 1, turn.
Repeat from Row 2 for pattern.

No. 6

Chain a multiple of 4 plus 2.

Row 1: 1 sc in 2nd ch from hook, skip 1 ch, in next ch work (2 dc, ch 1, 2 dc) shell, * skip 1 ch, 1 sc in next ch, skip 1 ch, shell in next ch; rep from *, ending skip 1 ch, 1 sc in last ch. Ch 2, turn.

Row 2: 2 dc in first sc, * 1 sc in ch-1 of shell, work shell in back loop of next sc; rep from *, ending 3 dc in last sc. Ch 1, turn.

Row 3: 1 sc in first dc, * work shell in back loop of next sc, 1 sc in ch-1 of next shell; rep from *, ending 1 sc in top of turning ch. Ch 2, turn.
Repeat Rows 2 and 3 for pattern.

No. 7

Chain a multiple of 3 plus 1.

Row 1: 1 sc in 3rd ch from hook, * work 2 dc in same ch (shell), skip 2 ch, 1 sc in next ch; rep from * ending shell in next to last ch, 1 sc in last ch. Ch 3, turn.
Row 2: Skip first sc, 1 sc in next sc (of shell), * 2 dc in same sc, 1 sc in next sc; rep from *, ending shell in last shell, 1 sc in top of turning ch. Ch 3, turn.
Repeat Row 2 for pattern.

No. 8

Chain a multiple of 6 plus 2.

Row 1: 1 sc in 2nd ch from hook, * skip 2 ch, work 7 dc (shell) in next ch, skip 2 ch, 1 sc in next ch; rep from * to end. Ch 2, turn.
Row 2 (right side): * Yo, draw up loop in next dc, yo and thru 2 loops *; rep from * to * in each of next 2 dc, yo and thru all 4 loops on hook, ch 1 for eye of inverted shell, ch 2, 1 sc in next dc; ** ch 2, rep from * to * in each of next 3 dc, the sc and the

next 3 dc, yo and thru all 8 loops, ch 1 for eye, ch 2, 1 sc in next dc **; rep from ** to **, ending with ch 2; rep from * to * in each of last 3 dc and in last sc, yo and thru 5 loops (½ shell), ch 1 for eye, ch 2, turn.

Row 3: 3 dc in eye of inverted shell, * 1 sc in next sc, 7 dc in eye of next shell *; rep from * to *, ending 1 sc in sc, 4 dc in eye of last shell. Ch 1, turn.

Row 4: 1 sc in first dc, rep from ** to ** of Row 2, ending with 1 sc in top of turning ch. Ch 1, turn.

Row 5: Rep from * to * of Row 3, ending with 1 sc in last sc. Ch 2, turn.
Repeat from Row 2 for pattern.

No. 9

Chain a multiple of 6 plus 4.

Row 1: 1 sc in 4th ch from hook, * skip 2 ch, 3 dc (shell) in next ch, skip 2 ch, 1 sc in next ch; rep from *, ending skip 2 ch, 1 sc in last ch. Ch 2, turn.

Row 2: 1 dc in first sc, * 1 sc in center dc of next shell, 3 dc in next sc; rep from *, ending 1 sc in turning ch. Ch 2, turn.
Repeat Row 2 for pattern.

No. 10

Chain a multiple of 6 plus 2.

Row 1: 1 sc in 2nd ch from hook, * skip 2 ch, 3 tr in next ch, ch 1, 3 tr in same ch (shell), skip 2 ch, 1 sc in next ch; rep from * to end. Ch 4, turn.

Row 2: 2 tr in first sc (½ shell), 1 sc under ch-1 of first shell, * shell in next sc, sc under ch-1 of next shell; rep from *, ending 3 tr in last sc (½ shell). Ch 1, turn.

Row 3: Sc in first tr, * shell in next sc, sc under ch-1 of next shell; rep from *, ending 1 sc in top of turning ch. Ch 4, turn.
Repeat Rows 2 and 3 for pattern.

No. 11

Chain a multiple of 8 plus 3.

Row 1: Work 3 dc in 3rd ch from hook, * skip 3 ch, (1 dc, ch 1, 1 dc) in next ch (V st), skip 3 ch, 7 dc (shell) in next ch; rep from *, ending skip 3 ch, 4 dc in last ch. Ch 3, turn.

Row 2: Skip first dc, 1 dc in each of next 2 dc, * V st under ch-1, skip first dc of shell, 1 dc in each of next 5 dc; rep from *, ending skip 1 dc, 1 dc in each of next 2 dc, 1 dc in top of turning ch. Ch 3, turn.

Row 3: 1 dc in next dc, * shell under next ch-1 of V, V in center dc of next shell; rep from *, ending shell under last V, dc in last dc, ch 1, dc in top of turning ch (V). Ch 3, turn.

Row 4: 1 dc under first ch-1, * skip first dc of shell, 1 dc in each of next 5 dc, V in ch-1 of next V; rep from *, ending V under turning ch. Ch 3, turn.

Row 5: 3 dc under ch-1 of V, * V in center dc of shell, shell in ch-1 of next V; rep from *, ending 3 dc under turning ch, 1 dc in 2nd ch of turning ch. Ch 3, turn.
Repeat from Row 2 for pattern.

No. 12

Chain a multiple of 5 plus 1.

Foundation Row: 2 dc in 4th ch from hook, ch 1, 2 dc in next ch, * skip 3 ch, 2 dc in next ch, ch 1, 2 dc in next ch; rep from *, ending 1 dc in last ch. Ch 3, turn.

Row 1: Under first and each ch-1 of last row work (2 dc, ch 1, 2 dc) shell, ending 1 dc in top of turning ch. Ch 3, turn.

Row 2: Shell under first ch-1, ch 2, insert hook in space between first 2 shells 2 rows below and work a tight sc, * ch 2, shell under next ch-1, ch 2, work tight sc between this shell and next shell 2 rows below; rep from *, ending shell under last ch-1, 1 dc in top of turning ch. Ch 3, turn.

Row 3: Same as Row 1.

Repeat these 3 rows for pattern.

No. 13

Chain a multiple of 6 plus 2.

Row 1: 1 sc in 2nd ch from hook, * skip 2 ch, 5 dc in next ch, skip 2 ch, 1 sc in next ch; rep from * to end. Ch 2, turn.

Row 2: 1 dc in first sc, ch 1, 1 sc in center st of 5-dc group, * ch 1, in next sc work (3 dc, ch 1, 3 dc), ch 1, 1 sc in center st of 5-dc group; rep from *, ending ch 1, 2 dc in last sc. Ch 1, turn.

Row 3: 1 sc in first dc, 5 dc in next sc, * 1 sc in next ch-1 between 3-dc groups, 5 dc in next sc; rep from *, ending skip last dc, 1 sc in top of turning ch. Ch 2, turn. Repeat Rows 2 and 3 for pattern.

No. 14

Chain a multiple of 10 plus 7.

Row 1: 1 sc in 3rd ch from hook, * ch 3, skip 3 ch, 1 sc in next ch, ch 2, skip 2 ch, (1 dc, ch 1, 1 dc) in next ch (V st), ch 2, skip 2 ch, 1 sc in next ch; rep from *, ending ch 3, skip 3 ch, 1 dc in last ch. Ch 3, turn.

Row 2: * 5 dc under ch-3 (shell), ch 2, 1 sc under ch-1 of V, ch 2; rep from *, ending shell under last ch-3, 1 dc in last sc. Ch 4, turn.

Row 3: * V in center dc of shell, ch 2, 1 sc under next ch-2, ch 3, 1 sc under next ch-2, ch 2; rep from *, ending V in center of last shell, ch 2, 1 dc in top of turning ch. Ch 4, turn.

Row 4: *1 sc under ch-1 of next V, ch 2, shell under ch-3, ch 2; rep from *, ending 1 sc under V, ch 2, 1 dc in 2nd ch of turning ch. Ch 1, turn.

Row 5: 1 sc under ch-2, * ch 3, 1 sc under next ch-2, ch 2, V in center of next shell, ch 2, 1 sc under next ch-2; rep from *, ending ch 3, 1 sc in 2nd ch of turning ch. Ch 3, turn.
Repeat from Row 2 for pattern.

No. 15

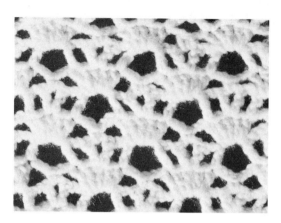

Chain a multiple of 8 plus 2.

Row 1: 1 sc in 2nd ch from hook, * ch 2, skip 3 ch, 5 dc (shell) in next ch, ch 2, skip 3 ch, 1 sc in next ch; rep from * to end. Ch 4, turn.

Row 2: Skip first sc, * 1 dc in first dc of shell, ch 2, skip 1 dc, in next dc work (1 dc, ch 2, dc), ch 2, 1 dc in last dc of shell, ch. 1, skip next sc; rep from *, ending ch 1, 1 dc in last sc. Ch 3, turn.

Row 3: 2 dc in sp under first ch-1, * ch 2, skip 1 sp, 1 sc in center sp over shell, ch 2, skip 1 sp, 5 dc shell in sp under next ch-1; rep from *, ending 2 dc in last sp, 1 dc in 2nd ch turning ch. Ch 4, turn.

Row 4: 1 dc in first dc, ch 2, skip 1 dc, 1 dc in next dc, ch 1; rep from * of Row 2, ending (1 dc, ch 2, 1 dc) in top of turning ch. Ch 1, turn.

Row 5: 1 sc in first sp, ch 2, skip 1 sp, shell in sp under next ch-1; rep from * of Row 3, ending ch 2, 1 sc under turning ch. Ch 4, turn.
Repeat from Row 2 for pattern.

No. 16

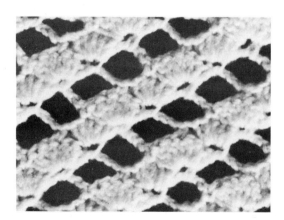

Chain a multiple of 8 plus 6.

Foundation Row: 1 sc in 2nd ch from hook, * ch 5, skip 3 ch, 1 sc in next ch; rep from * to end. Turn.

Row 1: Ch 2, 2 dc in first sc (half shell), 1 sc under first ch-5, * ch 5, 1 sc under next ch-5, 5 dc in next sc (shell), 1 sc under next ch-5; rep from *, ending ch 5, 1 sc in last sc. Ch 2, turn.

Row 2: Half shell in first sc, 1 sc under next ch-5, * ch 5, 1 sc in center dc of shell, shell in next sc, 1 sc under next ch-5; rep from *, ending 1 sc in top of turning ch. Ch 6, turn.

Row 3: 1 sc under first ch-5; * shell in next sc, 1 sc in center of next shell, ch 5, 1 sc under next ch-5; rep from *, ending shell in last sc, 1 sc in top of turning ch. Ch 6, turn.

Row 4: 1 sc in center of next shell, * shell in next sc, 1 sc under next ch-5, ch 5, 1 sc in center of next shell; rep from *, ending 1 sc in center of last shell, shell in next sc, 1 sc in 3rd ch of ch-6. Ch 2, turn.

Row 5: Half shell in first sc, 1 sc in center of next shell, * ch 5, 1 sc under next ch-5, shell in next sc, 1 sc in center of next shell; rep from *, ending ch 5, 1 sc in 3rd ch of ch-6. Ch 2, turn.

Repeat from Row 2 for pattern.

No. 17

Chain a multiple of 25 plus 7.

Foundation Row: Work 1 sc in 2nd ch from hook and in each ch to end. Ch 4, turn.

Row 1: 1 dc in 4th sc, * ch 2, skip 2 sc, 1 dc in next sc; rep from * to end. Ch 1, turn.

Row 2: 1 sc in first dc, 1 sc in next sp, ch 3, 1 sc in next sp, * in next sp work (2 dc, 4 tr, 2 dc) shell, 1 sc in next step sp, (ch 3, 1 sc in next sp) 3 times; rep from *, ending shell, 1 sc in next sp, ch 3, 1 sc under turning ch, 1 sc in 2nd ch of turning ch. Ch 4, turn.

Row 3: 1 sc in first sp, ch 3, *1 sc in first tr of shell, ch 3, skip 2 tr, 1 sc in next tr, (ch 3, 1 sc in next sp) 3 times, ch 3; rep from *, ending 1 sc in last sp, ch 3, 1 sc in last sc. Ch 1, turn.

Row 4: 1 sc in first sc, 1 sc in next sp, ch 3, 1 sc in next sp; rep from * of Row 2. Ch 4, turn.

Repeat Rows 3 and 4 for pattern.

No. 18

Chain a multiple of 8 plus 2.

Row 1: 1 sc 2nd ch from hook, * skip 3 ch, in next ch work (1 dc, ch 1) 4 times and 1 dc (shell), skip next 3 ch, 1 sc in next ch; rep from * to end. Ch 5, turn.

Row 2: * 1 sc in center dc of next shell, ch 3, 1 dc in next sc, ch 3; rep from *, ending 1 dc in last sc. Ch 1, turn.

Row 3: 1 sc in first dc, * shell in next sc, 1 sc in next dc; rep from *, ending 1 sc in 3rd ch of ch-5. Ch 5, turn.

Repeat Rows 2 and 3 for pattern.

No. 19

Chain a multiple of 3.

Row 1: 1 dc in 3rd ch from hook and in each ch to end. Ch 3, turn.

Row 2: Skip first 2 dc, * in next dc work (1 dc, ch 1, 1 dc), skip 2 dc; rep from *, ending skip 1 dc, 1 dc in top of turning ch. Ch 2, turn.

Row 3: * 3 dc under next ch-1; rep from *, ending 3 dc under last ch-1, 1 dc in top of turning ch. Ch 2, turn.

Repeat Rows 2 and 3 for pattern.

No. 20

Chain a multiple of 6 plus 5.

Foundation Row: 1 sc in 2nd ch from hook and in each ch to end. Ch 3, turn.

Row 1: Skip first sc, 3 dc in next sc (shell), * skip 2 sc, shell in next sc; rep from *, ending skip 1 sc, 1 dc in last sc. Ch 3, turn.

Row 2: * 1 dc in 3rd dc of next shell, ch 1, 1 dc in first dc of same shell (cross st); rep from *, ending 1 dc in top of turning ch. Ch 3, turn.

Row 3: Work a shell under each ch-1 of each cross st, ending 1 dc in top of turning ch. Ch 3, turn.

Repeat Rows 2 and 3 for pattern.

No. 21

Chain a multiple of 3.

Row 1: 2 hdc in 3rd ch from hook, * skip 2 ch, 3 hdc in next ch (shell); rep from *, ending skip 2 ch, 1 hdc in last ch. Ch 2, turn.

Row 2: 2 hdc in first hdc, * skip 2 hdc, shell in next hdc; rep from *, ending skip 2 hdc, 1 hdc in top of turning ch. Ch 2, turn.

Repeat Row 2 for pattern.

No. 22

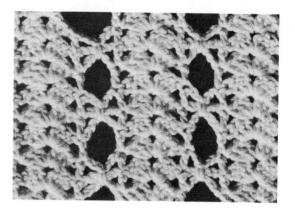

Chain a multiple of 12 plus 10.

Row 1: 1 dc in 3rd ch from hook, * skip next 2 ch, in next ch work (3 dc, ch 2, 3 dc) shell, skip 2 ch, 1 dc in next ch; ch 5, skip 5 ch, 1 dc in next ch; rep from *, ending shell, skip 2 ch, 1 dc in each of last 2 ch. Ch 3, turn.

Row 2: Skip first dc, * 1 dc in next dc, shell under ch-2 of next shell, 1 dc in next single dc, ch 5; rep from *, ending shell over shell, 1 dc in last dc, 1 dc in top of turning ch. Ch 3, turn.

Row 3: Skip first dc, * 1 dc in next dc, shell over shell, 1 dc in next single dc, ch 2, 1 sc under chs of last 2 rows, ch 2; rep from *, ending shell over shell, 1 dc in last dc, 1 dc in top of turning ch. Ch 3, turn.

Row 4: Rep Row 2.

Repeat from Row 2 for pattern.

No. 23

Chain a multiple of 6 plus 4.

Row 1: Skip 4 ch, * 3 dc in next ch, skip next 2 ch, 1 sc in next ch, ch 2, skip 2 ch; rep from *, ending 1 sc in next ch, ch 1, skip 1 ch, 1 dc in last ch. Ch 3, turn.

Row 2: 3 dc in first sc, * 1 sc in 3rd dc of 3-dc group, ch 2, 3 dc in next sc; rep from *, ending 1 sc in last dc of group, ch 1, 1 dc in 2nd ch of turning ch. Ch 3, turn.

Repeat Row 2 for pattern.

No. 24

Chain a multiple of 6 plus 3.

Row 1: 1 dc in 3rd ch from hook, skip 2 ch, * in next ch work (2 dc, ch 2, 2 dc) shell, skip 2 ch, 1 dc in next ch, skip 2 ch; rep from *, ending 2 dc in last ch. Ch 2, turn.

Row 2: 1 dc in first dc, * shell under ch-2 of next shell, 1 dc in next single dc; rep from *, ending shell in last shell, 2 dc in top of turning ch. Ch 2, turn.

Row 3: 1 dc in first dc, 1 dc under ch-2 of next shell, * shell in next single dc, 1 dc under ch-2 of next shell; rep from *, ending 2 dc in top of turning ch. Ch 2, turn.

Row 4: 1 dc in first dc, 1 dc in single dc, * shell under ch-2 of next shell, 1 dc in single dc; rep from *, ending 2 dc in top of turning ch. Ch 2, turn.

Row 5: 1 dc in first dc, shell in single dc, * 1 dc under ch-2 of next shell, shell in next single dc; rep from * ending 2 dc in top of turning ch. Ch 2, turn.
Repeat from Row 2 for pattern.

No. 25

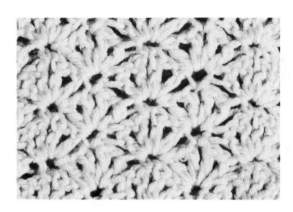

Chain 6 plus 2.

Row 1: 1 sc in 2nd ch from hook, * skip 2 ch, in next ch work (1 dc, ch 1, 1 dc, ch 1, 1 dc, ch 1, 1 dc) shell, skip 2 ch, 1 sc in next ch; rep from * to end. Ch 4, turn.

Row 2: 1 dc in first sc, * 1 sc in center ch-1 sp of next shell, shell in next sc; rep from *, ending (1 dc, ch 1, 1 dc) in last sc. Ch 1, turn.

Row 3: 1 sc in first dc, * shell in next sc, 1 sc in center ch-1 sp of next shell; rep from *, ending 1 sc in 3rd ch of turning ch. Ch 4, turn.
Repeat Rows 2 and 3 for pattern.

No. 26

Chain a multiple of 4 plus 2.

Row 1 (right side): 1 sc in 2nd ch from hook and in each ch to end. Ch 2, turn.

Row 2: Skip first 2 sc, * 3 dc shell in next sc, skip 1 sc, 1 sc in next sc, skip 1 sc; rep from *, ending shell in next sc, skip 1 sc, 1 dc in last sc. Ch 1, turn.

Row 3: 1 sc in first and in each st across, ending 1 sc in top of turning ch. Ch 2, turn.

Repeat Rows 2 and 3 for pattern.

No. 27

Chain a multiple of 10 plus 3.

Foundation Row: 1 dc in 4th ch from hook, * 1 hdc in each of next 2 ch, 1 sc in each of next 3 ch, 1 hdc in each of next 2 ch, 1 dc in each of next 3 ch; rep from *, ending 1 dc in each of last 2 ch. Ch 1, turn.

Row 1: 1 sc in each of first 2 dc, * skip next 3 sts, 7 tr in next st (shell), skip 3 sts, 1 sc in each of next 3 dc; rep from *, ending 1 sc in last dc, 1 sc in top of turning ch. Ch 2, turn.

Row 2: 1 dc in 2nd sc and in each st, ending 1 dc in last sc. Ch 2, turn.

Row 3: 3 tr in first st, * skip next 3 sts, 1 sc in each of next 3 sts, skip next 3 sts, 7 tr in next st; rep from *, ending 3 tr and 1 dc in top of turning ch. Ch 2, turn.

Row 4: 1 dc in first tr and each st, ending 1 dc in top of turning ch.

Repeat from Row 1 for pattern.

No. 28

Chain a multiple of 6 plus 3.

Foundation Row: 1 sc in 2nd ch from hook and in each ch to end. Ch 4, turn.

Row 1: Skip first sc, * skip next 3 sc, 1 tr in each of next 3 sc, 1 tr in each of 3 skipped sc (crossed shell); rep from *, ending 1 tr in last sc. Ch 4, turn.

Row 2: * Skip first 3 tr of next crossed shell, 1 tr in each of next 3 tr, 1 tr in each skipped tr; rep from *, ending 1 tr in top of turning ch. Ch 4, turn.

Repeat Row 2 for pattern.

Filet Crochet

There is a very good reason for the omission of a large number of filet patterns. The easiest way to work any filet pattern is by using a graph and graphs make very poor reading! Filet crochet is a series of boxes worked in double crochet. Filled-in boxes create the design, open boxes or mesh form the background. Or vice versa. If you are interested in filet, from the simple examples shown, here is your opportunity to create your own patterns, working them out first on graph (squared) paper, by filling in the squares to be worked solid. Geometric patterns are a breeze, but many intricate designs can be worked out to be easily followed. Filet had its heyday in the United States during the 1800's but had lost a lot of popularity around the time of World War I, when knitting became the patriotic thing to do. At the peak of its popularity, filet was used mainly for what today we call Home Decor. Fine table linens were trimmed with filet insertions and edgings. Many of us still remember learning filet crochet as a child, making yards and yards of fine insertion with very fine thread and with a No. 14 hook. Monograms were the big thing, but roses ran a close second and a parade of ducks was bound to keep little hands busy. This insertion was used in bed linens. Hems of sheets and pillow slips were torn off, the insertion added and the hems sewn back on. Give a thought to the work involved—no doubt this had a great deal to do with filet's loss of popularity! Many other fascinating filet creations can be found in old crochet books—yokes for camisoles, bread tray covers with the word "bread" carefully worked in on a background of roses, lamp shades that are unbelievable, and no living room of the day was complete without antimacassars adorning the back and arms of the overstuffed furniture. Possibly the most amazing pattern ever printed and shown in filet crochet was a detailed and completely recognizable reproduction of Leonardo Da Vinci's "Last Supper".

This is an example of Filet Crochet worked in 3 different ways, using one basic motif—that of a diamond. Beginning at the lower edge, the first 6 rows are worked with only an open mesh outline of the diamond on a solid background; the middle 6 rows are worked with a solid diamond on an open background; the last 6 rows are worked with an open diamond on a solid background.

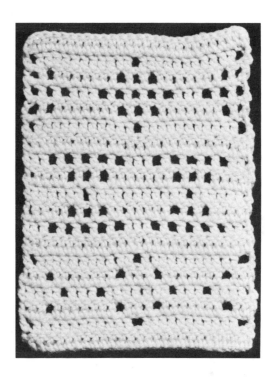

Beginning at lower edge, chain 28.

Row 1: 1 dc in 3rd ch from hook and in each ch to end. Ch 3, turn.

Row 2: Skip first 2 dc, 1 dc in each of next 11 dc, ch 1, skip next dc, 1 dc in each of next 11 dc, ch 1, skip last dc, 1 dc in top of turning ch. Ch 2, turn.

Row 3: Skip first dc, 1 dc in ch-1 and in next dc, ch 1, skip next dc, 1 dc in each of next 7 dc, ch 1, skip next dc, 1 dc in next dc, in ch-1 and in next dc, ch 1, skip next dc, 1 dc in each of next 7 dc, ch 1, skip next dc, 1 dc in next dc, 1 dc in each of next 2 chs of turning ch. Ch 2, turn.

Row 4: Skip first dc, 1 dc in each of next 2 dc, in ch-1 and in next dc, ch 1, skip next dc, 1 dc in each of next 3 dc, ch 1, skip next dc, 1 dc in next dc, in ch-1, in each of next 3 dc, in ch-1 and in next dc, ch 1, skip next dc in each of next 3 dc, ch 1, skip next dc, 1 dc in next dc, in ch-1, in each of last 2 dc, 1 dc in top of turning ch. Ch 2, turn.

Row 5: Work to correspond to Row 3. Ch 3, turn.

Row 6: Work to correspond to Row 2. Ch 3, turn.

This completes the diamond outlined in mesh.

Row 7: Skip first dc, 1 dc in each ch and in each dc across row, ending with 1 dc in 2nd ch of turning ch. Ch 2, turn.

Row 8: Skip first dc, 1 dc in each of next 2 dc, (ch 1, skip next dc, 1 dc in next dc) 5 times, 1 dc in each of next 2 dc, (ch 1, skip 1 dc, 1 dc in next dc) 5 times, 1 dc in last dc, 1 dc in top of turning ch. Ch 2, turn.

Row 9: Skip first dc, 1 dc in each of next 2 dc, in ch-1 and in next dc, (ch 1, 1 dc in next dc) 3 times, 1 dc in next ch-1, in each of next 3 dc, in next ch-1 and in next dc, (ch 1, 1 dc in next dc) 3 times, 1 dc in ch-1 and in each of last 2 dc, 1 dc in top of turning ch. Ch 2, turn.

Row 10: Skip first dc, 1 dc in each of next 4 dc, in next ch-1 and in next dc, ch 1, 1 dc in next dc, in next ch-1, in each of next 7 dc, in next ch-1, in next dc, ch 1, 1 dc in next dc, in ch-1 and in each of last 4 dc, 1 dc in top of turning ch. Ch 2, turn.

Row 11: Work to correspond to Row 9. Ch 2, turn.

Row 12: Work to correspond to Row 8. Ch 2, turn.

This completes the solid diamond on open background.

Row 13: Skip first dc, 1 dc in each ch and in each dc across row, ending with 1 dc in top of turning ch. Ch 3, turn.

Row 14: Skip first 2 dc, 1 dc in each of next 11 dc, ch 1, skip next dc, 1 dc in each of next 11 dc, ch 1, skip last dc, 1 dc in 2nd ch of turning ch. Ch 3, turn.

Row 15: Skip first dc, 1 dc in next dc, ch 1, skip next dc, 1 dc in each of next 7 dc, ch 1, skip next dc, 1 dc in next dc, ch 1, 1 dc in next dc, ch 1, skip 1 dc, 1 dc in each of next 7 dc, ch 1, skip next dc, 1 dc in next dc, ch 1, 1 dc in 2nd ch of turning ch. Ch 3, turn.

Row 16: Skip first dc, 1 dc in next dc, ch 1, 1 dc in next dc, ch 1, skip 1 dc, 1 dc in each of next 3 dc, ch 1, skip next dc, 1 dc in next dc, (ch 1, 1 dc in next dc) 3 times, ch 1, skip next dc, 1 dc in each of next 3 dc, ch 1, skip next dc, 1 dc in next dc, ch 1, 1 dc in next dc, ch 1, 1 dc in 2nd ch of turning ch. Ch 3, turn.

Row 17: Work to correspond to Row 15. Ch 3, turn.

Row 18: Work to correspond to Row 14. Ch 2, turn.

This completes the open diamond on a solid background.

Last Row: Same as Row 13.

No. 1

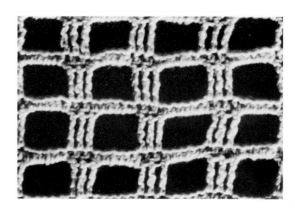

Chain a multiple of 8 plus 4.

Row 1: 1 hdc in 3rd ch from hook and in each ch to end. Ch 5, turn.

Row 2: Skip first hdc, 1 dtr in each of next 2 hdc, * ch 5, skip 5 hdc, 1 dtr in each of next 3 hdc; rep from * to end. Ch 1, turn.

Row 3: 1 hdc in first dtr and in each of next 2 dtr, * 1 hdc in each ch of ch-5, 1 hdc in each of next 3 dtr; rep from *, ending with last hdc in top of turning ch. Ch 5, turn.

Rep Rows 2 and 3 for pattern.

No. 2

Chain a multiple of 8 plus 4.

Row 1: 1 dc in 3rd ch from hook, 1 dc in next ch, * (ch 1, skip 1 ch, 1 dc in next ch) 3 times, 1 dc in each of next 2 ch; rep from * to end. Ch 3, turn.

Row 2: Skip next dc, 1 dc in next dc, * (ch 1, 1 dc in next dc) twice, 1 dc in ch-1, 1 dc in next dc, ch 1, skip next dc, 1 dc in next dc; rep from *, ending ch 1, skip last dc, 1 dc in top of turning ch. Ch 3, turn.

Row 3: 1 dc in next dc, * ch 1, skip next dc, 1 dc in next dc, 1 dc in ch-1, 1 dc in next dc, (ch 1, 1 dc in next dc) twice; rep from *, ending ch 1, 1 dc in 2nd ch of turning ch. Ch 3, turn.

Row 4: 1 dc in next dc, * 1 dc in ch-1, 1 dc in next dc, ch 1, skip next dc, 1 dc in next dc, (ch 1, 1 dc in next dc) twice; rep from *, ending ch 1, 1 dc in 2nd ch of turning ch. Ch 2, turn.

Row 5: 1 dc in first ch-1, 1 dc in next dc, * (ch 1, 1 dc in next dc) twice, ch 1, skip next dc, 1 dc in next dc, 1 dc in ch-1, 1 dc in next dc; rep from *, ending skip next dc, 1 dc in last dc, 1 dc in each of the next 2 ch of turning ch. Ch 3, turn.

Repeat from Row 2 for pattern.

No. 3

Chain a multiple of 4.

Row 1: 1 dc in 4th ch from hook, * ch 2, skip 2 ch, 1 dc in each of next 2 ch; rep from *, ending skip 2 ch, 1 dc in last ch. Ch 1, turn.

Row 2: 1 sc in each of first 2 dc, * 1 sc in each ch of ch-2, 1 sc in each of next 2 dc; rep from * ending 1 sc in last dc, 1 sc in top of turning ch. Ch 2, turn.

Row 3: Skip first sc, 1 dc in next sc * ch 2, skip next 2 sc, 1 dc in each of next 2 sc, rep from * to end. Ch 1, turn.

Repeat Rows 2 and 3 for pattern.

No. 4

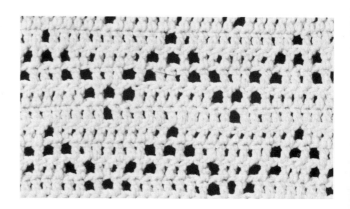

Chain a multiple of 12 plus 1.

Note: When a number is given in sts, count each dc and each ch.

Row 1: 1 dc in 4th ch from hook and in each of next 9 ch, * ch 1, skip next ch, 1 dc in each of next 11 ch; rep from * to end. Ch 4, turn.

Row 2: Skip first 2 dc, 1 dc in each of next 7 dc, * (ch 1, skip 1 st, 1 dc in next st), 3 times, 1 dc in each of next 6 dc; rep from *, ending ch 1, skip last dc, 1 dc in 3rd ch of turning ch. Ch 4, turn.

Row 3: Skip first dc, 1 dc in next dc, ch 1, skip next dc, 1 dc in each of next 3 dc, * ch 1, skip 1 dc, 1 dc in next dc, ch 1, skip 1 st, 1 dc in each of next 3 sts, ch 1, 1 dc in next dc, ch 1, skip next dc, 1 dc in each of next 3 dc; rep from *, ending ch 1, skip next dc, 1 dc in next dc, ch 1, skip next ch, 1 dc in next ch of turning ch. Ch 2, turn.

Row 4: Skip first dc, 1 dc in ch-1, 1 dc in next dc, ch 1, 1 dc in next dc, ch 1, skip next dc, 1 dc in next dc, ch 1, skip 1 st, * 1 dc in each of next 7 sts, ch 1, 1 dc in next dc, ch 1, skip next dc, 1 dc in next dc, ch 1, skip 1 st; rep from *, ending 1 dc in last dc, 1 dc in each of next 2 ch of turning ch. Ch 2, turn.

Row 5: Skip first dc, 1 dc in each of next 4 sts, * ch 1, skip ch-1, 1 dc in each of next 11 sts; rep from *, ending ch 1, 1 dc in each of next 4 sts, 1 dc in top of turning ch. Ch 2, turn.

Row 6: Skip first dc, 1 dc in each of next 10 sts, * ch 1, skip next dc, 1 dc in each of next 11 dc; rep from *, ending last (11th) dc in top of turning ch. Ch 4, turn.

Repeat from Row 2 for pattern.

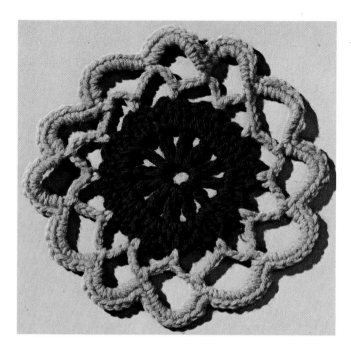

No. 33

No. 34

No. 33

Worked with 2 colors, A and B.

With A, chain 8. Join with sl st to form a ring.

Rnd 1: Ch 5, in ring work (1 dc, ch 2) 11 times. Join with sl st to 3rd ch of ch-5.

Rnd 2: Ch 1, 1 sc in joining, * ch 1, 3 dc in next ch-2 sp, ch 1, 1 sc in next dc; rep from * around, ending with ch 1. Join with sl st to first sc. Fasten off.

Rnd 3: Attach B to center dc on one petal, (ch 7, 1 sc in center dc of next petal) 11 times, ch 3, join with 1 dc in first sc (so yarn will be at center of this loop).

Rnd 4: (Ch 8, 1 sc in next loop) 12 times.

Rnd 5: Work 11 sc in each loop around. Join and fasten off.

No. 34

Worked with 2 colors, A and B.

With A, chain a multiple of 4 plus 2.

Row 1: 1 sc in 2nd ch from hook and in each ch to end. Ch 1, turn.

Row 2: 1 sc in each of first 3 sc, * ch 1, skip next sc (to be worked later), 1 sc in each of next 3 sc; rep from *, ending ch 1, skip 1 sc, 1 sc in last sc. Pull B thru loop, drop and tighten A. Ch 1, turn.

Row 3: 1 sc in first sc, 1 sc in next ch, 1 sc in next sc, yo and draw up long loop in skipped sc of row below, (yo and thru 2 loops) twice for a diagonal dc, skip next sc, 1 sc in next sc, * 1 sc in next ch, 1 sc in next sc, diagonal dc in next skipped sc below, skip next sc, 1 sc in next sc; rep from * to end. Ch 1, turn.

Row 4: 1 sc in first sc, 1 sc in diagonal dc, 1 sc in next sc, diagonal dc in first skipped sc of last row, skip next sc, 1 sc in next sc, * sc in diagonal dc, 1 sc in next sc, diagonal dc in next skipped sc below, skip next sc, 1 sc in next sc; rep from * to end. Draw A thru loop, drop and tighten B. Ch 1, turn.

Repeat Row 4 for pattern, alternating 2 rows A and 2 rows B.

No. 35

Worked with 3 colors, A, B, and C.

With A, chain an even number.

Row 1: 1 sc in 2nd ch from hook and in each ch to end. Ch 1, turn.

Row 2: 1 sc in first sc and in each sc to end. Drop A, join B. Ch 1, turn.

Row 3: 1 sc in first sc, * 1 dc thru next sc 2 rows below, skip sc behind dc, 1 sc in next sc; rep from * to end. Ch 1, turn.

Row 4: 1 sc in first sc and in each st to end. Drop B, join C. Ch 1, turn.

Row 5: 1 dc in first sc 2 rows below, * skip sc behind dc, 1 sc in next sc, 1 dc in next sc 2 rows below; rep from * to end. Ch 1, turn.

Row 6: Rep Row 4. Draw A thru loop, drop C. Ch 1, turn.

Repeat from Row 3 for pattern, changing colors every 2 rows.

No. 36

Worked with 2 colors, A and B.

With A, chain an uneven number.

Work a row of basic afghan st. Draw B thru loop, drop A.

Row 1—First Half: Skip first bar, * work a P st in next bar, with yarn at back, draw up loop in next bar; rep from *, ending draw up loop in last bar.

Row 1—Second Half: Work off loops in basic afghan st. Draw A thru loop, drop B.

Repeat Row 1, alternating colors every row.

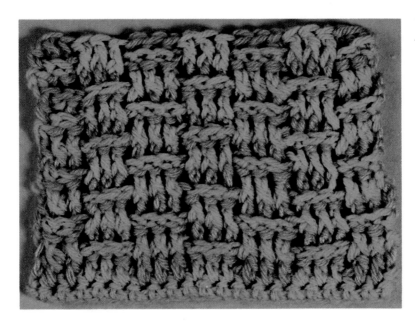

No. 35

No. 36

No. 37

No. 38

No. 37

Worked with 2 colors, A and B.

With A, chain an uneven number.

    Row 1—First Half: Basic afghan st.

    Row 1—Second Half: Join B and work off loops in basic afghan st.

    Row 2—First Half: With B, skip first bar, * work a P st in next bar, draw up loop in next bar; rep from * to end.

    Row 2—Second Half: With A, work off loops in basic afghan st.

Repeat Row 2 for pattern, alternating colors as before.

No. 38

Worked with 2 colors, A over B.

With A, chain a multiple of 3 plus 2.

    Foundation Row: 1 sc in 2nd ch from hook and in each ch to end. Ch 1, turn.

Note: All rows are worked with A over B, holding B at top of row. Be certain B is not drawn too tightly.

    Row 1: 1 sc in first sc, * ch 2, skip 2 sc, 1 sc in next sc; rep from * to end. Ch 1, turn.

    Row 2: 1 sc in first sc, * 1 sc under next ch-2, ch 2; rep from *, ending 1 sc under last ch-2, 1 sc in last sc. Ch 1, turn.

    Row 3: 1 sc in first sc, * ch 2, 1 sc under next ch-2; rep from *, ending 1 sc in last ch-2, skip next sc, 1 sc in last sc. Ch 1, turn.

Repeat Rows 2 and 3 for pattern.

No. 39

Worked with 3 colors, A, B, and C.
With A, chain 7.

 Rnd 1: (1 tr, ch 2) 5 times in 7th ch from hook. Join with sl st in 4th ch of ch-7. (6 tr, counting turning ch). Ch 1, turn.

 Rnd 2: 1 sc in joining, * 3 sc in next sp, 1 sc in next tr; rep from * around. Join with sl st in back loop of first sc. Draw B thru loop, break A.

 Rnd 3: Ch 8, drop B from hook; join C in next sc, ch 8, * drop C loop, pick up B loop in back of C, 1 tr in next sc, ch 5, drop B; pick up C loop in back of B, 1 tr in next sc, ch 5; rep from * around, ending with first B ch in front, first C ch in back, join last C ch-5 to 3rd ch of first C ch-8 and fasten off C; keeping first B ch at back, join last B ch-5 in 3rd ch of first B ch-8. Fasten off.

No. 40

Worked in 3 colors, A, B, and C.
With A, chain a multiple of 6 plus 2.

 Foundation Row: 1 sc in 2nd ch from hook and in each ch to end. Ch 1, turn.

 Rows 1, 2 and 3: 1 sc in first sc and in each sc to end. Ch 1, turn at end of Rows 1 and 2. At end of Row 3, draw B thru loop, break A.

 Row 4: 1 sc in first sc, * 1 sc at base of next sc, 1 sc at base of next sc 2 rows below, 1 sc at base of next sc 3 rows below, 1 sc at base of next sc 2 rows below, 1 sc at base of next sc, 1 sc in next sc; rep from *, ending 1 sc in last sc. Ch 1, turn.

 Rows 5, 6 and 7: 1 sc in first sc and in each sc to end. Ch 1, turn at end of Rows 5 and 6. At end of Row 7, draw C thru loop, break B. With C, rep Rows 4 thru 7. Draw A thru loop. Break C.

Repeat from Row 4 for pattern, changing colors as established.

No. 39

No. 40

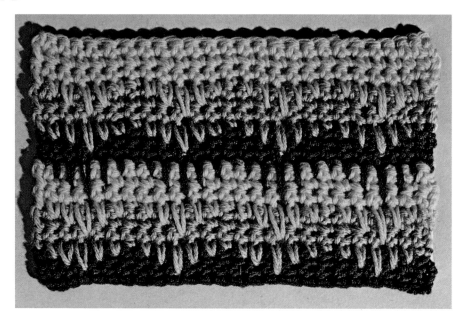

No. 41

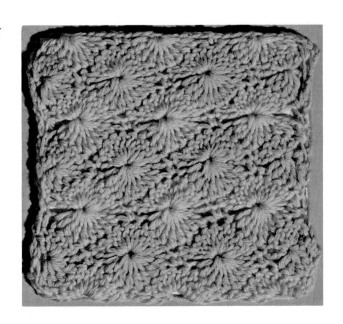

No. 42

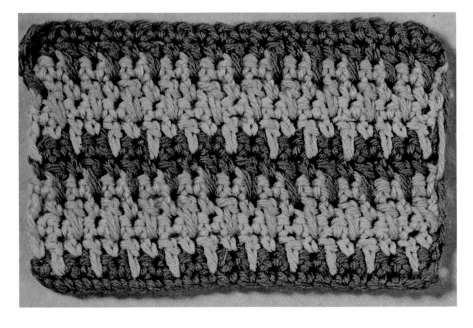

No. 41

Worked in 2 colors, A and B.

With A, chain a multiple of 8 plus 2.

Row 1: 1 sc in 2nd ch from hook, * skip 3 ch, 9 dc in next ch, skip 3 ch, 1 sc in next ch; rep from * to end. Draw B thru loop, ch 3, turn.

Row 2: 1 sc in first sc, ch 3, (yo, draw up a loop in next dc, yo and thru 2 loops) 4 times, yo and thru 5 loops on hook, ch 1 to form eye (½ shell), * ch 3, 1 sc in next dc, ch 3, (yo, draw up loop in next st, yo and thru 2 loops) 9 times, yo and thru 10 loops on hook, ch 1 (shell); rep from *, ending (yo, draw up loop in next st, yo and thru 2 loops) 4 times, yo and thru 5 loops, ch 1 for eye, ch 3, 1 sc in last sc. Ch 3, turn.

Row 3: 1 sc in first sc, 4 dc in first eye, * 1 sc in next sc, 9 dc in next eye; rep from *, ending 4 dc in last eye, 1 sc in last sc. Draw A thru loop, ch 3, turn.

Row 4: 1 sc in first dc, * ch 3, (yo, draw up loop in next st, yo and thru 2 loops) 9 times, ch 1 (eye), ch 3, 1 sc in next dc; rep from *, ending 1 sc in last sc, Ch 3, turn.

Row 5: 1 sc in first sc, * 9 dc in next eye, 1 sc in next sc; rep from *, ending 1 sc in last sc. Draw B thru loop, ch 3, turn.

Repeat from Row 2 for pattern.

No. 42

Worked with 2 colors, A and B.

With A, chain a multiple of 6 plus 4.

Foundation Row: 1 sc in 2nd ch from hook and in each ch to end. Always change color by drawing new color thru last 2 loops of last dc of previous color. Carry color not in use loosely at wrong side of work.

Row 1 (right side): Draw B thru, ch 3, skip first sc, 1 dc in each of next 2 sc, * draw A thru and work 1 dc in each of next 3 sc draw B thru and work 1 dc in each of next 3 sc; rep from *, ending 3 B. Draw A thru, ch 3, turn.

Row 2: With A, dc from back around post of each of next 2 dc, * with B dc from front around post of each of next 3 dc, with A dc from back around post of each of next 3 dc; rep from * ending with A. Draw B thru, ch 3, turn.

Row 3: Reversing colors, work same as Row 2, ending 3 B. Draw A thru, ch 3, turn.

Repeat Rows 2 and 3, reversing colors every row.

No. 43

Worked with 2 colors, A and B.

With A, chain a multiple of 6 plus 4.

Note: Always change colors by working off the last 2 loops of last dc with new color. Carry color not in use across back, working over it.

Row 1: 1 dc in 3rd ch from hook, 1 dc in next ch, drawing B thru last 2 loops, * with B work 1 dc in each of next 3 ch, with A work 1 dc in each of next 3 ch; rep from *, ending 3 A and drawing B thru last 2 loops. Ch 2, turn.

Row 2: Skip first dc, 1 dc in each of next 2 dc, * with A work 1 dc in each of next 3 dc, with B work 1 dc in each of next 3 dc; rep from *, ending with B and working last dc in top of turning ch. Ch 2, turn.

Repeat Row 2 for pattern, alternating colors.

No. 44

Worked with 3 colors, A, B, and C.

With A, chain a multiple of 4.

Row 1: 1 sc in 2nd ch from hook and in each of next 2 ch, * 1 tr in next ch, 1 sc in each of next 3 ch; rep from * to end. Ch 1, turn.

Row 2: 1 sc in first sc and in each sc and in each tr to end. Draw B thru last 2 loops. Ch 1, turn.

Row 3: 1 sc in first sc, 1 tr in next sc, * 1 sc in next sc, 1 dc from front around post of tr 2 rows below, 1 sc in next sc, 1 tr in next sc; rep from *, ending 1 sc in last sc. Ch 1, turn.

Row 4: 1 sc in first sc and in each st to end. Draw C thru last 2 loops. Ch 1, turn.

Row 5: 1 sc in first sc, 1 dc from front around post of B tr below, * 1 sc in next sc, 1 tr in next sc, 1 sc in next sc, 1 dc from front around post of B tr below; rep from *, ending 1 sc in last sc. Ch 1, turn.

Row 6: 1 sc in first sc and in each st to end. Draw A thru last 2 loops, ch 1, turn.

Repeat from Row 3 for pattern, changing colors every 2 rows.

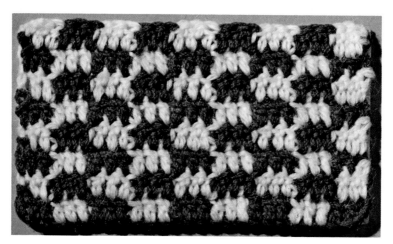

No. 43

No. 44

No. 45

No. 46

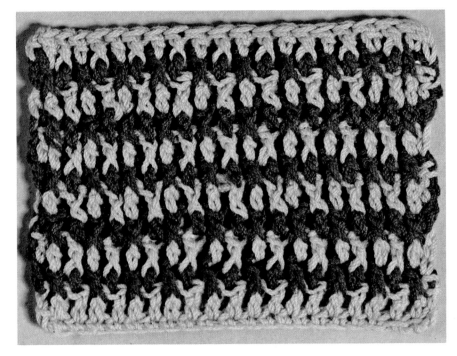

No. 45

Worked with 2 colors, A and B.
With A, chain a multiple of 8 plus 2.

Row 1: 1 sc in 2nd ch from hook, * 1 hdc in next ch, 1 dc in each of next 2 ch, 1 tr in next ch, 1 dc in each of next 2 ch, 1 hdc in next ch, 1 sc in next ch; rep from * to end. Ch 1, turn.

Row 2: 1 sc in first and each st to end, drawing B thru 2 loops of last sc. Ch 4. turn.

Row 3: With B, skip first sc, * 1 dc in each of next 2 sc, 1 hdc in next sc, 1 sc in next sc, 1 hdc in next sc, 1 dc in each of next 2 sc, 1 tr in next sc; rep from *, ending 1 tr in last sc. Ch 1, turn.

Row 4: 1 sc in first and each st to end, working last sc in top of turning ch and drawing A thru last 2 loops. Ch 1, turn.

Row 5: 1 sc in first sc, * 1 hdc in next sc, 1 dc in each of next 2 sc, 1 tr in next sc, 1 dc in each of next 2 sc, 1 hdc in next sc; 1 sc in next sc; rep from * to end. Ch 1, turn.

Repeat from Row 2 for pattern.

No. 46

Worked with 2 colors, A and B.
With A, chain an even number.

Foundation Row: 1 dc in 5th ch from hook, * ch 1, 1 dc in next ch; rep from * to end. Drop A, join B.

Row 1: With B, ch 3, skip first dc, 1 dc in next dc, * 1 dc from front around post of next dc, 1 dc in next dc; rep from *, ending 1 dc in last dc, skip next ch of turning ch, 1 dc in next ch. Drop B. Do not turn.

Row 2: Draw A thru top of ch at opposite side, ch 3, skip first dc, * 1 dc from front around post of next dc, 1 dc in next dc; rep from * to end. Draw B thru loop, turn.

Row 3: With B, ch 3, skip first dc, 1 dc in next dc, * 1 dc from back around post of next dc, 1 dc in next dc; rep from *, ending 1 dc in last dc, 1 dc in top of turning ch. Drop B.

Row 4: Draw A thru top of ch at opposite side, ch 3, skip first dc, * 1 dc from back around post of next dc, 1 dc in next dc; rep from * to end. Draw B thru loop, drop A.

Repeat from Row 1 for pattern.

No. 47

Worked with 2 colors, A and B.

With A, chain a multiple of 6 plus 4.

    Row 1: 2 dc in 4th ch from hook, * skip 2 ch, 1 sc in next ch, skip 2 ch, 5 dc in next ch; rep from *, ending 3 dc in last ch. Ch 1, turn.

    Row 2: 1 sc in first dc, * 5 dc in next sc, 1 sc in center dc of next shell; rep from *, ending 1 sc in top of turning ch. Draw B thru loop, drop A, ch 3, turn.

    Row 3: 2 dc in first sc, * 1 sc in center dc of next shell, 5 dc in next sc; rep from *, ending 3 dc in last sc. Ch 1, turn.

    Row 4: Rep Row 2. Draw A thru loop, drop B, ch 3.

Repeat Rows 3 and 4 for pattern, alternating colors every 2 rows.

No. 48

Worked with 2 colors, A and B.

Work over colors when not in use.

With A, chain a multiple of 8 plus 3.

    Foundation Row: 1 sc in 2nd ch from hook and in each ch to end, drawing B thru last 2 loops of last st. Ch 2, turn. Always change colors in this way.

Following rows are all worked 1 dc in each st, always working last dc in top of turning ch.

    Row 1: Skip first dc, 1 B, * 2 A, 2 B; rep from * to end, drawing A thru last 2 loops of last dc. Ch 2, turn.

    Row 2: Skip first dc, 1 A, * 6 B, 2 A; rep from * to end. Ch 2, turn.

    Row 3: Skip first dc, 1 A, * 2 B, 2 A; rep from * to end. Ch 2, turn.

    Row 4: Same as Row 2, drawing B thru last 2 loops of last dc. Ch 2, turn.

    Row 5: Skip first dc, 1 B, * 2 A, 2 B; rep from * to end. Ch 2, turn.

    Row 6: Skip first dc, 3 B, * 2 A, 6 B; rep from *, ending 4 B. Draw A thru last 2 loops of last dc. Ch 2, turn.

    Row 7: Skip first dc, 1 A, * 2 B, 2 A; rep from * to end, drawing B thru last 2 loops of last dc. Ch 2, turn.

    Row 8: Same as Row 6. Do not change colors at end of row. Ch 2, turn.

Repeat from Row 1 for pattern.

No. 47

No. 48

No. 5

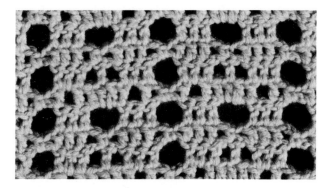

Chain a multiple of 12 plus 9.

Row 1: 1 dc in 4th ch from hook, * ch 1, skip next ch, 1 sc in next ch, ch 1, skip next ch, 1 dc in next ch, ch 1, skip 1 ch, 5 dc in next ch, ch 1, skip 1 ch, 1 dc in next ch; rep from *, ending 1 dc in each of last 2 ch. Ch 2, turn.

Row 2: Skip first dc, 1 dc in next dc, * ch 3, 1 dc in next dc, 1 dc under next ch-1, 1 dc in next dc, (ch 1, skip next dc, 1 dc in next dc) twice, 1 dc under next ch-1, 1 dc in next dc; rep from *, ending ch 3, 1 dc in last dc, 1 dc in top of turning ch. Ch 2, turn.

Row 3: Skip first dc, 1 dc in next dc, * ch 1, 1 sc under ch-3, ch 1, 1 dc in each of next 3 dc, ch 1, 1 sc in next dc, ch 1, 1 dc in each of next 3 dc; rep from *, ending ch 1, 1 dc in last dc, 1 dc in top of turning ch. Ch 2, turn.

Row 4: Skip first dc, dc in next dc, * ch 3, 1 dc in each of next 3 dc; rep from *, ending ch 3, 1 dc in last dc, 1 dc in top of turning ch. Ch 2, turn.

Row 5: Skip first dc, 1 dc in next dc, * ch 1, 1 sc under next ch-3, ch 1, 1 dc in next dc, ch 1, skip next dc, 1 dc in next dc, 3 dc under next ch-3, 1 dc in next dc, ch 1, skip next dc, 1 dc in next dc; rep from *, ending ch 1, 1 dc in last dc, 1 dc in top of turning ch. Ch 2, turn.

Repeat from Row 2 for pattern.

No. 6

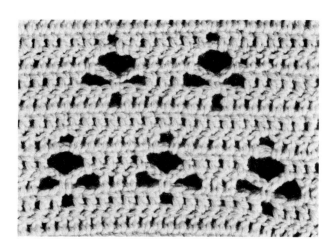

Chain a multiple of 8 plus 5.

Row 1: 1 dc in 4th ch from hook and in each ch to end. Ch 2, turn.

Row 2: 1 dc in 2nd dc and in each dc to end, working last dc in top of turning ch. Ch 2, turn.

Row 3: Skip first dc, 1 dc in each of next 4 dc, * ch 1, skip next dc, 1 dc in each of next 7 dc; rep from *, ending 1 dc in each of last 4 dc, 1 dc in top of turning ch. Ch 2, turn.

Row 4: Skip first dc, 1 dc in each of next 2 dc, * ch 3, skip 2 dc, 1 sc under ch-1, ch 3, skip 2 dc, 1 dc in each of next 3 dc; rep from *, ending 1 dc in each of last 2 dc, 1 dc in top of turning ch. Ch 2, turn.

Row 5: Skip first dc, 1 dc in each of next 2 dc, * 1 dc under next ch-3, ch 3, 1 dc under next ch-3, 1 dc in each of next 3 dc; rep from *, ending 1 dc in each of last 2 dc, 1 dc in top of turning ch. Ch 2, turn.

Row 6: Skip first dc, 1 dc in each of next 3 dc, * 1 dc under next ch-3, ch 1, 1 dc under same ch-3, 1 dc in each of next 5 dc; rep from *, ending 1 dc in each of last 3 dc, 1 dc in top of turning ch. Ch 2, turn.

Row 7: Skip first dc, 1 dc in each dc and under each ch-1 across row, ending 1 dc in top of turning ch. Ch 2, turn.

Row 8: Skip first dc, 1 dc in each of next 8 dc, * ch 1, skip next dc, 1 dc in each of next 7 dc; rep from *, ending ch 1, skip 1 dc, 1 dc in each of last 8 dc, 1 dc in top of turning ch. Ch 2, turn.

Row 9: Skip first dc, 1 dc in each of next 6 dc, * ch 3, skip 2 dc, 1 sc under next ch-1, ch 3, skip 2 dc, 1 dc in each of next 3 dc; rep from *, ending 1 dc in each of last 6 dc, 1 dc in top of turning ch. Ch 2, turn.

Row 10: Skip first dc, 1 dc in each of next 6 dc, * 1 dc under ch-3, ch 3, 1 dc under next ch-3, 1 dc in each of next 3 dc; rep from *, ending 1 dc in each of last 6 dc, 1 dc in top of turning ch. Ch 2, turn.

Row 11: Skip first dc, 1 dc in each of next 7 dc, * 1 dc under ch-3, ch 3, 1 dc under same ch-3, 1 dc in each of next 5 dc; rep from *, ending 1 dc in each of last 7 dc, 1 dc in top of turning ch. Ch 2, turn.

Row 12: Skip first dc, 1 dc in each dc and under each ch-1 across row, ending 1 dc in top of turning ch. Ch 2, turn.

Repeat from Row 3 for pattern.

Motifs

Motifs are as popular today, if not more so, as they were centuries ago. Every motif is a small masterpiece in itself. It's easy to understand the fundamentals of patterns worked in rows, but the variety of shapes and patterns and designs found in motifs is hard to assimilate. Motif is our modern descriptive word, but these small and very individual designs were long referred to as medallions and used as insertions and trims. You can give free rein to your imagination and find a lot of questions but very few answers. Was the first motif designed and drawn by an artist? Or was it laboriously worked out by a simple soul who loved doing handwork and had the artistic ability to create these small designs? Or do you see the fine hand of the mathematician plotting the outline to geometric precision? Let's hope it was the simple soul with great imagination and patience, carrying on a craft handed down from generation to generation, for there is more human interest in that picture. Although it seems there must be a touch of either artist or mathematician or both—it seems too credulous to think that either of the two could transform their work from paper to crochet. Our crocheter may have gotten ideas from the work of the other two, but let's give the credit where it must be due. With the creation of the design settled, up pops a new question. Who in the world came up with the idea of putting motifs together—to create the lovely table linens, bedspreads and afghans as we make them today? Who knows—it might even have been your great, great, great, great grandmother!

No. 1

Chain 5, join with sl st to form a ring.

Rnd 1: Ch 4, * 1 dc in ring, ch 1; rep from * 6 times more, sl st in 3rd ch of ch-4. Do not turn.

Rnd 2: Ch 3, 1 sc in next dc, ch 3, * 1 sc in next dc, ch 3; rep from * 5 times more, sl st in same place as first ch of first ch-3. (8 ch-3 loops).

Rnd 3: Ch 1, 1 sc under first ch-3 loop, ch 6, * 1 sc under next ch-3 loop, ch 6; rep from * 6 times more, sl st in first sc. (8 ch-6 loops).

Rnd 4: Sl st in each of first 3 ch of ch-6, 1 sc under same ch-6 loop, ch 6, * 1 sc under next ch-6, ch-6; rep from * 6 times more, sl st in first sc. Ch 1.

Rnd 5: 1 sc in same place with joining, under first ch-6 work (2 dc, ch 4, 2 dc), 1 sc in first sc, * under next ch-6 work (2 dc, ch 4, 2 dc), 1 sc in next sc; rep from * around. End with sl st in first sc. 8 groups of (2 dc, ch 4, 2 dc).

Rnd 6: Sl st in each of first 2 dc, 1 sc under first ch-4, ch 8, * 1 sc under next ch-4, ch 8; rep from * around. End sl st in first sc.

Rnd 7: Under first ch-8 work (1 sc, 1 hdc, 2 dc, 1 tr, 2 dc, 1 hdc, 1 sc), shell, sl st in next sc, * work shell under next ch-8, sl st in next sc; rep from * around. End sl st in first sc of Rnd 6.

Rnd 8: Work 1 sl st in each of first sc, hdc, 2 dc and tr, 1 sc in same tr, ch 11, * 1 sc in next tr, ch 11; rep from * around. End sl st in first sc.

Rnd 9: Under first ch-11 work (2 sc, 2 hdc, 2 dc, 4 tr, 2 dc, 2 hdc, 2 sc), shell, sl st in first sc, * work shell under next ch-11, sl st in next sc; rep from * around. End sl st in first sc. Fasten off.

No. 2

Ch 4, join with sl st to form a ring.

Rnd 1: * 1 sc in ring, ch 3; rep from * 5 times more. Join with sl st to first sc. (6 ch-3 loops).

Rnd 2: * 1 sc under next ch-3, under same ch-3 work (ch 1, 1 dc) twice, ch 1, 1 sc under same ch-3; rep from * 5 times more. Join with sl st to first sc. (6 petals). Turn work so wrong side faces you.

Rnd 3: From wrong side work 1 sc around bar of first sc of Rnd 1, * ch 5, 1 sc around bar of next sc of Rnd 1; rep from * 4 times more, ch 5. Join with a sl st to first sc. (6 ch-5 loops). Turn work back to right side.

Rnd 4: From right side, * 1 sc under next ch-5, (ch 1, 1 dc under same ch-5) 3 times, ch 1, 1 sc under same ch-5; rep from * 5 times more. Join with sl st to first sc. Turn.

Rnd 5: Rep Rnd 3, working around base of sc on Rnd 3.

Rnd 6: 1 sc under first ch-5, ch 5, * 1 sc under next ch-5, ch 5; rep from * 4 times more. Join with sl st to first sc. Turn.

Rnd 7: 1 sl st in each of first 2 ch of next ch-5, 1 sc under same ch-5, * ch 1, in next sc work (1 long dc, drawing loop up to ¾ inch, ch 1) 4 times, ch 1, 1 sc under next ch-5; rep from * 4 times more, ch 1, in last sc work (1 long dc, ch 1) 4 times. Join with sl st to first sc and fasten off.

No. 3

Chain 8, join with sl st to form a ring.

Rnd 1: Ch 4, work (1 dc, ch 1) in ring 11 times. Join with sl st to 3rd ch of ch-4. (12 dc counting ch-4).

Rnd 2: 1 sc in first ch-1 sp, ch 4, * skip 2 dc, 1 sc in next ch-1 sp, ch 4; rep from * 4 times. Join with sl st to first sc. (6 ch-4 loops).

Rnd 3: 1 sc in same sc with joining, * ch 1, under next ch-4 work (1 long dc drawing loop up to ¾ inch, ch 1) 4 times, 1 sc in next sc; rep from * 4 times, under next ch-4 work (1 long dc, ch 1) 4 times. Join with sl st to first sc.

Rnd 4: Ch 5, 1 tr in same place with joining, ch 1, * skip 2 long dc, 1 sc in next ch-1 sp, ch 1, in next sc work (1 tr, ch 1) 4 times; rep from * around, ending (1 tr, ch 1) twice in same place as joining. Join with sl st to 4th ch of ch-5. Fasten off.

No. 4

Chain 6, join with sl st to form a ring.

Note: On Rnds 1 and 2, draw dc loops up to ¾ inch.

Rnd 1: Ch 4, work in ring 1 dc, * ch 2, 1 dc, ch 1, 1 dc; rep from * 4 times more, ch 2, join with sl st to 3rd ch of ch-4.

Rnd 2: * 1 sc in next sp, in next sp work (1 dc, ch 1) twice, then 1 dc in same sp; rep from * 5 times more. Join with sl st to first sc.

Rnd 3: Ch 4, * 1 sc in next ch-1 sp, ch 1, 1 sc in next ch-1 sp, ch 1, in next sc work (1 long dc, drawing loops to 1-inch, ch 1, 1 long dc, ch 5, 1 long dc, ch 1, 1 long dc) for a corner group, (ch 1, 1 sc in next ch-1 sp) twice, ch 1, 1 dc in next sc, ch 1; rep from * twice more. End with sl st in 3rd ch of ch-4 instead of working last dc. Fasten off.

No. 5

Ch 6, join with sl st to form a ring.

Rnd 1: Ch 3, in ring work 2 dc, ch 7, (3 dc, ch 7) 4 times. Join with sl st to top of ch-3.

Rnd 2: Sl st in each of next 2 dc and under next ch-7, ch 3, under same ch-7 work

2 dc, 3 tr, 5 dtr, 3 tr and 3 dc; under each remaining ch-7 work 3 dc, 3 tr, 5 dtr, 3 tr, 3 dc. Join as before.

Rnd 3: Ch 1, thru back loops only work 1 sc in each st around. Join with sl st to first sc. Fasten off.

No. 6

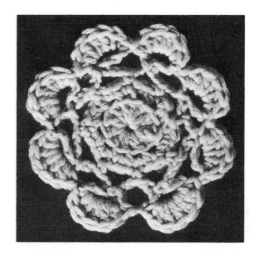

Chain 4, work 11 dc in first ch. (Ch 4 counts as 1 dc). Join with sl st to 3rd ch of ch-4. 12 dc.

Rnd 1: Ch 1, 1 sc in same sl st, thru back loops only work 2 sc in each dc around. Join with sl st. 24 sc.

Rnd 2: * Ch 10, sl st into 8th ch from hook (forming an 8-ch loop), ch 2, skip 2 sc, 1 sc in next sc; rep from * 7 times, ending with sl st (instead of sc) in first ch of first ch-10.

Rnd 3: Sl st in each of first 2 ch, under first ch-8 loop work (1 sc, 5 dc, 1 sc), * under next ch-8 work (1 sc, 5 dc, 1 sc); rep from * around, joining with sl st to first sc. Fasten off.

No. 7

Chain 22.

Row 1: 1 dc in 7th ch from hook, * ch 2, skip 2 ch, 1 dc in next ch; rep from * to end. (6 spaces). Turn.

Row 2: Ch 5, * 1 dc in next dc, ch 2; rep from *, ending skip 2 ch of turning ch, 1 dc in next ch of turning ch. Turn.

Rows 3, 4, 5 and 6: Rep Row 2. Do not turn at end of Row 6.

Rnd 1: Ch 2, 2 sc in first sp, * 3 sc in each of next 3 sps, ch 12, turn, skip 6 sc and sl st in top of dc below, ch 1, turn; under the ch-12 work (3 sc, ch 3) 5 times, then 3 sc under same ch, 3 sc in next sp, in next sp work (3 sc, ch 1, 3 sc) for corner; rep from * ending last corner 3 sc under ch, ch 1, join with sl st to top of ch-2.

Rnd 2: * Ch 8, sl st in 2nd ch-3, ch 9, skip next ch-3, sl st in next ch-3, ch 8, skip next ch-3, sl st in ch-1 sp of corner; rep from *, ending sl st in corner.

Rnd 3: * 10 sc under next ch-8, 11 sc under corner ch-9, 10 sc under next ch-8; rep from *, join with sl st. Ch 1.

Rnd 4: 1 sc in each of next 15 sc, * 3 sc in next sc (corner), 1 sc in each of next 30 sc; rep from *, ending last rep 1 sc in each of last 15 sc. Join with sl st and fasten off.

No. 8

Chain 10, join with sl st to form a ring.

Rnd 1: Ch 1, work 16 sc in ring. Join with sl st to first sc. Fasten off.

Rnd 2: Ch 9, sl st in any sc on ring. Hold chain to left, ch 1 to right of ch, across ch work 1 sc, 1 hdc, 5 dc, 1 hdc, ending 1 sc in last ch. * Ch 17, turn, skip 1 sc on ring, sl st in next sc, ch 1, turn; across half of ch work 1 sc, 1 hdc, 5 dc, 1 hdc, 1 sc; rep from * 6 times. Ch 8, turn, join to end of first petal.

Rnd 3: Ch 1, turn and in each sp around work (2 sc, 2 hdc, 7 dc, 2 hdc, 2 sc). Join and fasten off.

No. 9

Chain 9, join with sl st to form a ring.

Rnd 1: Ch 1, 16 sc in ring, join with sl st to first sc.

Rnd 2: Ch 5, 2 tr in same st with sl st, 3 tr in next sc, (ch 7, skip 2 sc, 3 tr in each of next 2 sc) 3 times, ch 7, join with sl st to top of first ch-5.

Rnd 3: Ch 1, 1 sc in same place, * 1 dc in next tr, 2 dc in next tr, ch 4, sl st thru side-top of last dc (picot), 2 dc in next tr, 1 dc in next tr, 1 sc in end tr, 7 sc under next ch-7, 1 sc in next tr; rep from * around, ending 7 sc under ch-7. Join to first sc and fasten off.

No. 10

Ch 2, work 6 sc in 2nd ch from hook, join with sl st to first sc.

Rnd 1: Ch 10, 1 dc in next sc, (ch 7, 1 dc in next sc) 4 times, ch 7, join with sl st in 3rd ch of ch-10. Ch 3.

Rnd 2: 5 dc in back loop of joining, 1 sc under next ch-7, (6 dc in back loop of next dc, 1 sc under next loop) 5 times, join with sl st in top of ch-3.

Rnd 3: ** Ch 16, * skip 1 ch, 1 sc in next ch, 1 hdc in next ch, 1 dc in next ch; holding back the last loop of each dc work 1 dc in each of next 2 ch, yo and thru all 3 loops (cluster), 1 dc in next ch, 1 hdc in next ch, sl st in next ch, * (ch 9, rep from * to *) twice; sl st in next ch of ch-16, 1 sc in next ch, 1 hdc in next ch, cluster over next 2 dc, 1 tr in next ch, 2 tr in last ch of ch-16; skip 4 dc, sl st in each of next dc, sc, dc; rep from ** around. Join and fasten off.

Rnd 4: Join yarn to first petal of any group, * ch 10, in next petal work (1 dc, ch 5, 1 dc), ch 10, 1 sc in next petal, ch 3, 1 sc in first petal of next group; rep from * around. Join with sl st in each of first 2 ch of next loop.

Rnd 5: Ch 5, skip 2 ch, 1 dc in next ch, (ch 2, skip 2 ch, 1 dc in next ch) 3 times, * ch 5, 1 dc in same st with last dc, (ch 2, skip 2, 1 dc in next ch) 4 times, ch 2, 1 dc in center ch of next ch-3, ch 2, 1 dc in 2nd ch of next ch-10, (ch 2, skip 2 ch, 1 dc in next ch) 4 times; rep from * around. Join with sl st to 3rd ch of ch-5.

Rnd 6: Ch 1, 1 sc in same st, (2 sc in next sp, 1 sc in next dc) 4 times, 5 sc under next ch-5, 1 sc in next dc (2 sc in next sp, 1 sc in next dc) 10 times; rep from * around, join with sl st to first sc. Fasten off.

No. 11

Chain 2, work 6 sc in 2nd ch from hook, join with sl st in back loop of first sc.

Rnd 1: Ch 1, 2 sc in same sc, (2 sc in back loop of next sc) 5 times, join with sl st to back loop of first sc.

Rnd 2: Ch 3, 4 dc in same sc, remove hook, insert it in top of ch-3, catch free loop and draw thru (popcorn), (ch 3, work a 5 dc popcorn in back loop of next sc) 11 times, ch 3, join with sl st in back of first popcorn.

Rnd 3: Ch 1, 1 sc in same st, * (3 sc in next sp, 1 sc in next popcorn); rep from * around. (48 sc). Join with sl st to first sc, sl st in next sc.

Rnd. 4: * Ch 4, 1 tr in same st, (1 tr in next sc, 2 tr in next sc) 3 times, ch 4, turn; holding back the last loop of each tr, work 1 tr in each of first 2 tr, yo and thru 3 loops on hook (cluster), (tr cluster over next 2 tr) 4 times, ch 3, turn; yo, draw up loop in next cluster, yo and thru 2 loops) 5 times; yo and thru 6 loops, ch 3, sl st at base of turning ch, ch 4, sl st at base of turning ch below, ch 4, sl st in last worked sc, sl st in each of next 2 sc on center; rep from * around. Fasten off.

No. 12

Chain 2, work 8 sc in 2nd ch from hook.

Rnd 1: Thru back loops only work sl st in first sc, ch 1, 1 sc in same sc, (ch 5, 1 sc in next sc) 7 times, ch 2, join with dc in first sc.

Rnd 2: (Ch 4, 1 sc in next loop) 8 times.

Rnd 3: * 3 sc under next ch 4 loop, ch 12; turn, sl st in 12th ch from hook to form a ring, ch 1, turn; under ring work (1 sc, 1 hdc, 7 dc, ch 4, sl st in last dc for picot, 7 dc, 1 hdc, 1 sc), sl st at base of ring, 3 sc under same ch-4; rep from * 7 times. Join with sl st to first sc and fasten off.

Rnd 4: Join yarn to 3rd dc to left of any picot, ch 6, * 1 tr in 3rd dc to right of picot on next ring, ch 3, 1 tr in next dc, ch 9, 1 tr in 2nd dc to left of same picot, ch 3, ** 1 tr in next dc, ch 1; rep from * 6 times, then rep from * to ** once. Join with sl st to 5th ch of first ch-6.

Rnd 5: Sl st in next ch-1 sp, ch 3, 1 dc in next ch-3 sp, * ch 2, 1 dc in first ch of next ch-9 loop (ch 2, skip 1 ch, 1 dc in next ch) twice (to center ch), ch 5, 1 dc in same ch, (ch 2, skip 1 ch, 1 dc in next ch) twice, ch 2, 1 dc in next ch-3 sp, ** 1 dc under ch-1, 1 dc in next ch-3 sp; rep from * 6 times, then from * to ** once. Join with sl st to top of first ch-3.

Rnd 6: Ch 1, 1 sc in same st, 1 sc in next dc, * (2 sc in next ch-2 sp, 1 sc in next dc) 3 times, 2 sc under corner ch, 3 sc in 3rd ch of same ch, 2 sc under same ch, (1 sc in next dc, 2 sc in next sp) 3 times, ** 1 sc in center dc of 3-dc group; rep from * around, ending at **, join with sl st to first sc. Fasten off.

No. 13

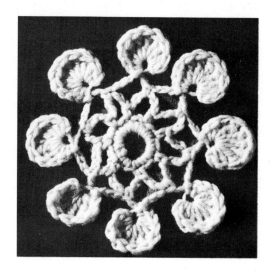

Chain 10, join with sl st to form a ring.

Rnd 1: Ch 1, 16 sc in ring. Join with sl st to first sc.

Rnd 2: (Ch 6, skip 1 sc, 1 sc in next sc) 7 times, ch 3, join with dc in first sc.

Rnd 3: * Ch 5, in 2nd ch from hook work (1 hdc, 1 dc, 5 tr, 1 dc, 1 hdc, ch 1, sl st), ch 3, 1 sc in next loop; rep from * 7 times, ch 3, join with sl st at base of ch-5. Fasten off.

No. 14

Chain 10, join with sl st to form a ring.

Rnd 1: Ch 4, 6 tr in ring, * ch 4, 7 tr in ring; rep from * twice, ch 4, join with sl st in top of first ch-4, Ch 1.

Rnd 2: 1 sc in each tr, 3 sc in each corner. Join with sl st to first sc.

Rnd 3: Ch 5, (skip 1 sc, 1 dc in next sc, ch 2) 4 times, * 1 dc in same sc, (corner), (ch 2, skip 1 sc, 1 dc in next sc) 5 times, ch 2; rep from * around, ending ch 2, 1 dc in same sc, ch 2, join with sl st to 3rd ch of ch-5.

Rnd 4: Sl st in first ch, 1 sc under same ch,* ch 5, 1 sc under next ch-2; rep from * and join with sl st to first sc.

Rnd 5: Sl st in each of first 3 chs of first ch-5, * ch 5, 1 sc in center ch of next ch-5; rep from * around and join with sl st to first sc. Fasten off.

No. 15

Chain 8, join with sl st to form a ring.

Rnd 1: Ch 7, (1 tr in ring, ch 3) 14 times. Join with sl st to 4th ch of ch-7.

Rnd 2: Ch 1, 1 sc in same place, * (ch 1, 3 dc in next sp, ch 1, 1 sc in next tr); rep from * around, ending 3 dc in last sp, ch 1. Join with sl st to back loop of first sc.

Rnd 3: Ch 8, * 1 dc in back loop of the next sc between 3-dc groups, ch 5; rep from * around. Join with sl st to 3rd ch of ch-8.

Rnd 4: Ch 1, 1 sc in same place, * ch 1, in next sp work (1 dc, 5 tr, 1 dc) shell, ch 1, 1 sc in next dc; rep from * around, ending shell, ch 1. Join with sl st to first sc. Fasten off.

Rnd 5: Join yarn to back loop of center tr of any shell, ch 3, 3 dc in same place, * ch 4, 4 dc in back loop of center tr of next shell; rep from * around, ch 4, join with sl st to top of first ch-4.

Rnd 6: Ch 3, 1 dc in same place, (2 dc in next dc) 3 times, * ch 2, 2 dc in each of 4 dc in next group; rep from * around, ch 2, join with sl st to top of ch-3.

Rnd 7: Ch 3, 1 dc in next dc, * 1 tr in next dc, 3 tr in next dc, 2 tr in next dc, 1 tr in next dc, 1 dc in each of next 2 dc, ** 1 dc in each of first 2 dc of next group; rep from * around, ending at **. Join with sl st to top of ch-3.

Rnd 8: Ch 4, 1 dc in 2nd tr of this group, * ch 3, skip 1 tr, in next (center) tr work (1 tr, ch 5, 1 tr), ch 3, skip 1 tr, 1 dc in next tr, ch 4, 1 sc between groups, ** ch 4, 1 dc in 2nd tr of next group; rep from * around, ending at **. Join with sl st and fasten off.

No. 16

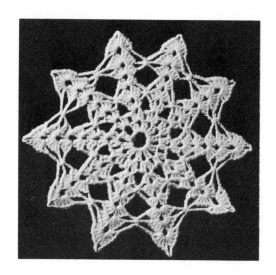

Chain 15, join with sl st to form a ring.

Rnd 1: Ch 3, 1 dc in ring, (ch 2, 2 dc in ring) 9 times, ch 2, join with sl st to top of ch-3.

Rnd 2: Sl st in next dc, sl st in next sp, ch 3, in same sp work (1 dc, ch 2, 2 dc), * ch 2, in next sp work (2 dc, ch 2, 2 dc) shell; rep from * around, ending ch 2, sl st to top of ch 3.

Rnd 3: Sl st in next dc, sl st in next sp, ch 3, in same sp work (1 dc, ch 2, 2 dc), * ch 4, skip next sp, work (2 dc, ch 2, 2 dc) shell under ch-2 of next shell; rep from * around, ending ch 4, sl st in top of ch-3.

Rnd 4: Sl st to next sp, ch 3, in same sp work (2 dc, ch 2, 3 dc), * ch 3, under ch-2 of next shell work (3 dc, ch 2, 3 dc) shell; rep from * around, ch 3 and join with sl st to top of ch-3.

Rnd 5: * Work shell over shell as in Rnd 4, ch 3, 1 sc in next sp 2 rnds below, working over the 2 ch, ch 3; rep from * around and join.

Rnd 6: * Shell over shell, having 4 dc, ch 2, 4 dc for shell, ch 5; rep from * around and join.

Rnd 7: * Work shell over shell, having 5 dc, ch 3, 5 dc for shell, ch 5; rep from * around and join.

Rnd 8: Sl st to center of shell, ch 4, in same sp work (4 dc, ch 3, 4 dc, ch 1, 1 dc), * ch 4, 1 sc in next sp 2 rnds below, working over the 2 ch, ch 4, under ch-3 of next shell work (1 dc, ch 1, 4 dc, ch 3, 4 dc, ch 1, 1 dc); rep from * around, ch 4 and join with sl st to 3rd ch of ch-4 and fasten off.

No. 17

Chain 5, join with sl st to form a ring.

Rnd 1 * Ch 6, 1 sc in ring; rep from * 4 times. Mark end of rnds.

Rnd 2: * Ch 6, skip 3 ch of next ch-6, 1 sc in each of last 3 ch; rep from * 4 times.

Rnd 3: Ch 6, * skip 3 ch, 1 sc in each of next 3 ch, 1 sc in each of 2 sc, ch 6 (skipping last sc); rep from * 4 times.

Rep Rnd 3, always working 3 sc in last 3 ch of each ch-6, 1 sc in each sc, omitting last sc, until there are 13 sc in each section. There are 5 sections.

Next Rnd: * Ch 5, 1 sc in 3rd ch of next ch-6, ch 5, skip 1 sc, 1 sc in each of next 11 sc; rep from * 4 times.

Next Rnd: * Ch 5, 1 sc in 3rd ch of each ch-5, ch 5, skip 1 sc, sc in each of next 9 sc; rep from * 4 times.

Rep last rnd with 1 less sc at each side of group each rnd and 1 more ch-5 loop between sc groups, until there are 3 sc and 6 loops in each section. End with 3 sc.

Last Rnd: * (Ch 3, 1 sc in 3rd ch of next ch-5) 6 times, ch 3, 1 dc in center sc of group; rep from * around. Join and fasten off.

No. 18

Ch 10, join with sl st to form a ring.

Rnd 1: Ch 3, 23 dc in ring, join with sl st to top of ch-3.

Rnd 2: Ch 10, work cross st as follows: yo twice, insert hook in 8th ch from hook, draw up loop (4 loops on hook), yo, skip 1 dc, draw up loop in next dc (6 loops on hook), (yo and thru 2 loops) 5 times; *ch 3, yo 4 times draw up loop in next dc, (yo and thru 2 loops) twice, yo, skip 1 dc, draw up loop in next dc, (yo and thru 2 loops) 5 times, ch 3, 1 dc in center of cross; rep from * 6 times, ch 3. Join with sl st in 7th ch of ch 10.

Rnd 3: Work 5 sc in each sp of previous rnd.

Rnds 4, 5 and 6: 1 sc in each sc.

Rnd 7: Ch 3, skip first sc, 1 dc in each sc around. Join with sl st to top of ch-3.

Rnd 8: Ch 10 and work cross sts as in Rnd 2, skipping 2 dc in working each cross st and working ch 3 between cross sts. 20 cross sts.

Rnd 9: Sl st to center of cross st, ch 5, 1 dc in same sp, * ch 3, 1 sc in next loop, ch 3, 1 dc in top loop of cross, ch 3, 1 dc in same loop; rep from * around.

Rnd 10: Sl st to center of first loop, ch 6, 1 dc in same loop, * ch 4, 1 sc in next sc, ch 4, 1 dc in next loop, ch 3, 1 dc in same loop; rep from * around. Join and fasten off.

No. 19

Chain 8, join with sl st to form a ring.

Rnd 1: Ch 7, (1 tr in ring, ch 3) 7 times. Join with sl st to 4th ch of ch-7.

Rnd 2: Sl st in first sp, ch 4, holding back on hook the last loop of each tr, work 5 tr in same sp, yo and thru all loops on hook (cluster), * ch 10, work a 6 tr cluster in next sp; rep from * around, ending ch 10, join with sl st to top of first cluster.

Rnd 3: 15 sc in next loop, * 5 sc in next loop, ch 10, turn; skip 4 sc of previous loop, sl st in next sc, turn; 13 sc in loop just formed, 10 sc in uncompleted loop; rep from * around, ending with sl st in each of first 5 sc of first loop. Ch 10, turn; skip 4 sc of previous loop, sl st in next sc, turn; 13 sc in loop, sl st at base of ch 10.

Rnd 4: Ch 3, * (skip 2 sc, 1 dc in next sc) twice, (ch 2, skip 2 sc, 1 dc in next sc) twice, ch 3, 1 dc in same sc as last dc, (ch 2, skip 2 sc, 1 dc in next sc) twice; rep from * around. Join and fasten off.

No. 20

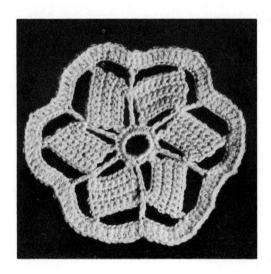

Chain 10, join with sl st to form a ring.

Rnd 1: 24 sc in ring. Join with sl st to first sc.

Rnd 2: Ch 12, ** skip next sc, 1 sc in next sc, ch 1, turn; 1 sc in each of next 8 ch, ch 1, turn; * 1 sc in each sc across, ch 1, turn; rep from * until there are 6 rows of sc; skip next sc of ring, 1 tr in next sc, ch 8; rep from ** around, ending with 6th row of sc, sl st to 4th ch of ch-12.

Rnd 3: Ch 12, * 1 sc in free tip of next sc-section, ch 8, 1 tr in next tr, ch 8; rep from * around, ending ch 8, sl st in 4th ch of ch-12.

Rnd 4: Ch 3, * 1 dc in each ch of next 8-ch, 1 dc in each sc, 1 dc in each ch of next ch-8, 1 dc in each tr; rep from * around. Join with sl st in top of ch-3. Fasten off.

No. 21

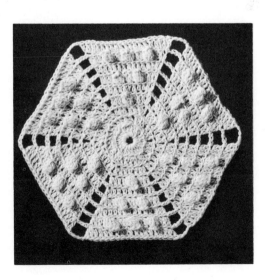

Ch 6, join with sl st to form a ring.

Rnd 1: Ch 3, 19 dc in ring. Join with sl st in top of ch-3. (Counting ch-3 as first dc, there are 20 dc in ring).

Note: In the following rnds, work thru back loop only of each dc.

Rnd 2: Ch 3, 1 dc in same st as joining, 1 dc in next dc, * 2 dc in next dc, 1 dc in next dc; rep from * around. Join with sl st in top of ch-3. (30 dc in rnd).

Rnd 3: Ch 3, 1 dc in joining st, * 1 dc in each of next 3 dc, 2 dc in next dc, ch 1, 2 dc in next dc; rep from * around, ending with 1 dc in each of next 3 dc, 2 dc in last dc, ch 1. Join with sl st in top of ch-3. (6 groups of 7-dc with ch-1 between groups).

Rnd 4: Ch 3, 1 dc in joining st, 1 dc in each of next 2 dc, 5 dc in next dc, drop loop from hook, insert hook in top of first dc of 5-dc group, catch dropped loop and draw thru and tighten (popcorn), 1 dc in each of next 2 dc, 2 dc in next dc, * ch 2, 2 dc in first dc of next group, 1 dc in each of next 2 dc, popcorn in next dc, 1 dc in each of next 2 dc, 2 dc in next dc (last dc of group); rep from * around, ending with ch-2, sl st in top of ch 3.

Rnd 5: Ch 3, 1 dc in joining st, * 1 dc in each of next 3 dc, 1 dc in popcorn, 1 dc in each of next 3 dc, 2 dc in next dc, ch 2, 2 dc in first dc of next group; rep from * around, ending ch 2, sl st in top of ch-3.

Rnd 6: Ch 3, 1 dc in joining st, 1 dc in each of next 2 dc, popcorn in next dc, 1 dc in each of next 3 dc, popcorn in next dc, 1 dc in each of next 2 dc, 2 dc in last dc of group, ch 3, 2 dc in first dc of next group; continue around in this manner, ending ch-3, sl st in top of ch-3.

Rnd 7: Ch 3, 1 dc in joining st, 1 dc in each of next 11 dc, 2 dc in last dc of group, * ch 3, 2 dc in first dc of next group, 1 dc in each of next 11 dc, 2 dc in last dc of group; rep from * around, ending ch 3, sl st in top of ch-3.

Rnd 8: Ch 3, 1 dc in joining st, * 1 dc in each of next 2 dc, popcorn in next dc, (1 dc in each of next 3 dc, popcorn in next dc) twice, 1 dc in each of next 2 dc, 2 dc in last dc of group, ch 4, 2 dc in first dc of next group; rep from * around, ending ch 4, sl st in top of ch-3.

Rnd 9: Ch 3, 1 dc in joining st, * 1 dc in each of next 15 sts, 2 dc in last dc of group, ch 4, 2 dc in first dc of next group, rep from * around, ending ch-4, sl st in top of ch-3. Fasten off.

No. 22

Chain 8, join with sl st to form a ring.

First Motif: Ch 3, 1 dc in ring, * ch 3, sl st in top of last dc (picot), 2 dc in ring; rep from * until 12th picot is completed, join with sl st in top of ch-3. Fasten off.

2nd Motif: Ch 8, join with sl st to form a ring. Ch 3, 1 dc in ring, ch 2, drop loop from hook, insert hook in any picot of first motif and in dropped loop, draw loop thru, ch 1, complete picot on 2nd motif, 2 dc in ring of 2nd motif, join with picot to next free picot on first motif, continue as in first motif until 12th picot is completed (including the 2 joined picots), join and fasten off.

Note: Count picots clockwise to determine joining.

Rep 2nd motif, joining first 2 picots to 7th and 8th picot of previous motif. There will be 4 free picots on each side of joinings. Continue in this manner for desired width.

Row 2—First Motif: Follow directions for 2nd motif of Row 1, but join the first 2 picots of this motif to the 4th and 5th picots of first motif in Row 1.

2nd Motif: Work as before, joining first 2 picots to 10th and 11th picots of next motif in Row 1 and the 4th and 5th picots to 4th and 5th picots of first motif of Row 2. Continue in this manner. 1 picot of each motif remains free between joinings.

No. 23

Chain 6.

Row 1: 1 sc in 2nd ch from hook and in each of next 4 ch. Ch 1, turn.

Row 2: * 1 sc in first and in each sc. (5 sc.) Ch 1, turn.

Rep from * 3 times more. Turn.

Rnd 1: 2 sc in first sc, 1 sc in each of next 3 sc, 3 sc in last sc (corner), 3 sc along side of square, 3 sc in corner (beg ch), 1 sc in each of next 3 sts of beg ch, 3 sc in corner (last st of beg ch), 3 sc along side, ending with 1 sc in first sc (corner). Join with sl st to first sc.

Rnd 2: Ch 14, 1 dc in center sc of next corner, (ch 11, 1 dc in center sc of next corner) twice, ch 11, sl st in 3rd ch of ch-14.

Rnd 3: Ch 1, 1 sc in same st with joining, * 15 sc under next loop, 1 sc in next dc; rep from * around. Join with sl st to first sc.

Rnd 4: Ch 5, holding back on hook the last loop of each dtr, work 2 dtr in same st with joining, yo and thru all loops (cluster), (ch 7, skip 3 sc, 3 dtr cluster in next sc) 15 times, ch 7, sl st in top of first cluster.

Rnd 5: Sl st under next ch 7, ch 3, 3 dc under same ch, * 5 dc in center ch of same ch-7, 2 dc under same ch, (holding back on hook the last loop, work 2 dc under same ch, 2 dc under next ch-7, yo and thru all loops), 2 dc under same ch; rep from * around, ending with a 2-dc cluster, sl st in first dc. Fasten off.

No. 24

Chain 8. Join with sl st to form a ring.

Rnd 1: 16 sc in ring. Join with sl st to first sc.

Rnd 2: Ch 8, 1 dc in 6th ch from hook, * skip next sc, 1 dc in next sc, ch 5, 1 dc in top of last dc made; rep from * around. Join with sl st to 3rd ch of ch-8.

Rnd 3: Ch 9, 1 dc in 6th ch from hook, * 1 dc in next loop, ch 5, 1 dc in top of last dc made, 1 tr in next dc, ch 5, 1 dc in top of last tr; rep from * around. Join with sl st to 4th ch of ch-9. Fasten off.

No. 25

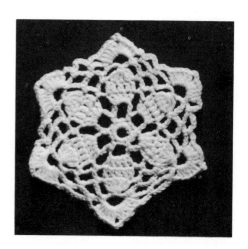

Chain 6. Join with sl st to form a ring.

Rnd 1: Ch 1, work 12 sc in ring. Join with sl st to first sc.

Rnd 2: * Ch 7, skip 1 sc, 1 sc in next sc; rep from * until there are 5 ch-7 loops, ch 3, 1 dc in same place as joining. (Yarn is now at center of loop).

Rnd 3: Ch 3, 4 dc under loop just completed, * ch 3, 5 dc under next loop; rep from * around, ending ch 3, sl st in top of first ch-3.

Rnd 4: Ch 3, 1 dc in each of next 4 dc, * ch 3, 1 sc under next ch-3, ch 3, 1 dc in each of next 5 dc; rep from * around, ending ch 3, 1 sc under last ch-3, ch 3, sl st in top of first ch-3.

Rnd 5: Ch 3, yo and draw up loop in next dc, yo and thru 2 loops (incomplete dc) work an incomplete dc in each of next 3 dc, yo and thru all loops on hook (cluster), * ch 5, 1 sc under next ch-3, ch 5, 1 sc under next ch-3, ch 5, work cluster over next 5 dc; rep from * around, ending ch 5, 1 sc under next ch-3, ch 5, 1 sc under next ch-3, ch 2, 1 dc in top of first cluster.

Rnd 6: * Ch 5, 1 sc under next ch-5; rep from * around, ending ch 2, 1 dc in top of dc of last joining.

Rnd 7: * Ch 3, under next ch-5 work (5 dc, ch 3, 5 dc) for corner, ch 3, 1 sc under next ch-5, ch 5, 1 sc under next ch-5; rep from * around, ending ch 5, sl st in top of dc of last joining. Fasten off.

No. 26

Chain 8. Join with sl st to form a ring.

Rnd 1: 16 sc in ring. Join with sl st to first sc.

Rnd 2: Ch 12, * skip next sc, 1 tr in next sc, ch 8; rep from * around. Join with sl st to 4th ch of ch-12.

Rnd 3: * In next sp work (1 sc, 1 hdc, 1 dc, 3 tr) ch 5, sl st in top of last tr made, in same sp work (3 tr, 1 dc, 1 hdc, 1 sc); rep from * around. Join with sl st to first sc. Fasten off.

No. 27

Chain 10. Join with sl st to form a ring.

Rnd 1: Ch 4, 31 tr in ring. Join with sl st in top of ch-4.

Rnd 2: Ch 3, in same place with sl st work (1 dc, ch 3, 2 dc) starting shell, * ch 7, skip 3 tr, in next tr work (2 dc, ch 3, 2 dc) shell; rep from * around, ending ch 7, join with sl st in top of ch-3, sl st to center ch-3 of starting shell.

Rnd 3: Ch 3, complete starting shell under same ch-3 (shell over shell), * ch 7, under center ch of next shell work (2 dc, ch 3, 2 dc) shell over shell; rep from * around, ending ch 7, join with sl st in top of ch-3, sl st to center ch of starting shell.

Rnd 4: * Shell over shell, ch 4, work 1 sc over both ch-7 loops of Rnds 2 and 3, ch 4; rep from * around. Join and sl st to center ch of shell.

Rnd 5: * Shell over shell, ch 16, sl st in 13th ch from hook to form a ring, ch 3 and drop loop from hook, turn work around, insert hook thru top of last dc made and pull dropped loop thru; work 6 dc in ring, turn; work 1 sc in sc over two ch-7 loops, turn; work 8 more dc in ring, turn (lower half of circle completed); rep from * around. Join and sl st to center ch of shell.

Rnd 6: * Shell over shell, ch 1, sl st loosely in same place where dropped loop was picked up, work 16 dc in ring for upper half of circle, sl st in last dc of lower half to join circle, ch 1; rep from * around. Join and sl st to center of shell. Fasten off.

No. 28

Chain 5. Join with sl st to form a ring.

Rnd 1: Ch 3, 2 dc in ring, (ch 5, 3 dc in ring) 5 times, ch 5. Join with sl st to top of ch-3.

Rnd 2: Ch 4, holding back on hook the last loop of each tr, work 1 tr in each of next 2 dc, yo and thru all loops (cluster), * ch 4, under next ch-5 work (1 sc, ch 3, 1 sc), ch 4, work cluster over next 3 dc; rep from * around. Join with sl st to top of ch-4. Fasten off.

No. 29

Chain 12. Join with sl st to form a ring.

Rnd 1: Ch 4, 31 tr in ring. Join with sl st in top of ch-4.

Rnd 2: Ch 4, holding back on loop the last loop of each tr work 2 tr in same place with sl st, yo and thru all loops (cluster), * ch 5, 3-tr cluster in same st as last cluster, ch 5, skip 3 tr, 1 sc in next tr, ch 5, skip 3 tr, 3-tr cluster in next tr; rep from * around, ending ch 5, sl st in top of first cluster.

Rnd 3: Ch 4, 2-tr cluster in same place with sl st, * ch 4, in next sp work (3-tr cluster, ch 5, 3-tr cluster), ch 4, cluster in tip of next cluster, ch 5, holding back on hook the last loop of each dc work 1 dc in each of next 2 sps, yo and thru all loops, ch 5, cluster in tip of next cluster; rep from * around. Join with sl st to top of ch-4. Ch 4.

Rnd 4: 2-tr cluster in same place as sl st, * ch 5, cluster in tip of next cluster, ch 5, in next sp work (cluster, ch 5, cluster), (ch 5, cluster in tip of next cluster) twice; (ch 5, 1 sc in next sp) twice; ch 5, cluster in tip of next cluster; rep from * around. Join with sl st to tip of first cluster.

Rnd 5: Ch 4, 2-tr cluster in same place as sl st, * (ch 5, cluster in tip of next cluster) twice; ch 5, in next sp work (cluster, ch 5, cluster); ch 5, (cluster in tip of next cluster, ch 5) twice; (cluster in tip of next cluster) twice; rep from * around. Join with sl st to top of ch-4. Fasten off.

No. 30

Chain 4. Join with sl st to form a ring.

First Motif—Rnd 1: Ch 1, 8 sc in ring. Join with sl st to first sc.

Rnd 2: Ch 2, 1 dc in same place as sl st, * ch 3, 1 sc in next sc, ch 3, holding back on hook the last loop of each dc work 2 dc in next sc, (yo and thru 2 loops) twice (cluster); rep from * twice, ch 3, 1 sc in next sc, ch 3, join with sl st in top of ch 2.

Rnd 3: Ch 6, in same place as sl st work (1 dc, ch 3) twice and 1 dc, * in top of next cluster work (1 dc, ch 3) 3 times and 1 dc; rep from * 2 more times. Join with sl st in 3rd ch of ch-6. Fasten off.

Second Motif: Work same as first motif until 2nd rnd is completed.

Rnd 3: Ch 6, 1 dc in same place as sl st, ch 1, sl st in center loop of a corner on last motif, ch 1, in same place as last dc work (1 dc, ch 3, 1 dc), in top of next cluster work (1 dc, ch 3, 1 dc), ch 1, sl st in center loop of next corner on last motif, ch 1, in same place as last dc work (1 dc, ch 3, 1 dc). Complete same as first motif.

Continue in this manner for desired width and length. Where 4 corners meet, join 2nd and 3rd corners in the 2 loops of the first joining sl st.

No. 31

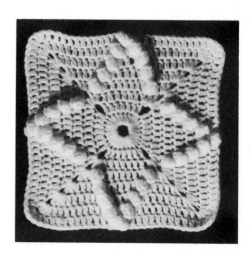

Chain 6. Join with sl st to form a ring.

Rnd 1: Ch 2, 27 dc in ring. Join with sl st to top of ch-2.

Rnd 2: Ch 2, skip first dc, 1 dc in each of next 6 dc, * ch 2, 1 dc in each of next 7 dc; rep from * around, ending ch 2, sl st in top of first ch-2.

Rnd 3: Ch 2, skip first dc, 1 dc in each of next 6 dc, under next ch-2 work (2 dc, ch 2, 2 dc), * 1 dc in each of next 7 dc, under next ch-2 work (2 dc, ch 2, 2 dc); rep from * around. Join with sl st to top of ch-2.

Rnd 4: Ch 2, skip first dc, 1 dc in each of next 6 dc, * 5 dc in next dc, drop loop from hook, insert hook in first of the 5-dc and dropped loop, draw loop thru (popcorn), 1 dc in next dc, under next ch-2 work (2 dc, ch 2, 2 dc), 1 dc in next dc, popcorn in next dc, 1 dc in each of next 7 dc; rep from * around, ending with popcorn. Join.

Rnd 5: Sl st in next dc, ch 2, 1 dc in each of next 4 dc, * popcorn in next dc, 1 dc in tip of next popcorn, 1 dc in each of next 3 dc, under next ch-2 work (2 dc, ch 2, 2 dc), 1 dc in each of next 3 dc, 1 dc in tip of next popcorn, popcorn in next dc, 1 dc in each of next 5 dc; rep from * around, ending with popcorn. Join.

Rnd 6: Sl st in next dc, ch 2, 1 dc in each of next 2 dc, * popcorn in next dc, 1 dc in tip of next popcorn, 1 dc in each of next 6 dc, under next ch-2 work (2 dc, ch 2, 2 dc), 1 dc in each of next 6 dc, 1 dc in tip of next popcorn, popcorn in next dc, 1 dc in each of next 3 dc; rep from * around, ending with popcorn. Join.

Rnd 7: Ch 2, work 5 dc popcorn in same place as joining, 1 dc in next dc, * popcorn in next dc, 1 dc in tip of next popcorn, 1 dc in each of next 9 dc, 3 dc under next ch-2, 1 dc in each of next 9 dc, 1 dc in tip of next popcorn, popcorn in next dc, 1 dc in next dc; rep from * around, ending 1 dc in tip of next popcorn. Join with sl st to first popcorn.

Rnd 8: Sl st in next dc, ch 2, popcorn in same dc, * dc in tip of next popcorn, 1 dc in each of next 11 dc, 3 dc in next dc, 1 dc in each of next 11 dc, 1 dc in tip of next popcorn, popcorn in next dc; rep from * around. Join and fasten off.

No. 32

Chain 5. Join with sl st to form a ring.

Rnd 1: Ch 6, (1 dc in ring, ch 3) 7 times. Join with sl st to 3rd ch of ch-6. (8 loops)

Rnd 2: Ch 3, (4 dc in next ch-3 loop, 1 dc in next dc) 7 times, 4 dc in next ch-3 loop. Join with sl st in top of ch-3.

Rnd 3: (Ch 6, 1 sc in 2nd ch from hook, 1 hdc in next ch, 1 dc in next ch, 1 tr in next ch, 1 dtr in next ch, skip 4 dc, 1 sc in next dc) 8 times, ending last rep with 1 sc in top of ch-3. Fasten off.

No. 33

Chain 8. Join with sl st to form a ring.

Rnd 1: Ch. 7, sl st in 5th ch from hook (picot), * 4 dc in ring, ch 5, sl st in top of last dc made (picot); rep from * 6 times more, ending 3 dc in ring, join with sl st to 2nd ch of ch-7.

Rnd 2: Sl st in 2 chs of picot, sl st under picot, ch 3, in same picot work (1 dc, ch 2, 2 dc), * ch 4, under next picot work (2 dc, ch 2, 2 dc) shell; rep from * around, ending ch 4, join with sl st to top of ch-3.

Rnd 3: Sl st in next dc and under next ch-2, ch 3, under same ch work (1 dc, ch 2, 2 dc), * ch 6, shell under ch-2 of next shell; rep from * around, ending ch 6, join with sl st to top of ch-3.

Rnd 4: Sl st in next dc and under next ch-2, ch 3, under same ch (1 dc, ch 2, 2 dc), * ch 8, shell under ch-2 of next shell; rep from * around, ending ch 8, join with sl st to top of ch-3.

Rnd 5: * Sl st in next dc and under next ch-2, ch 3, 3 dc under same ch, * 1 sc in each ch of ch-8, 4 dc under next ch-2; rep from *, ending 1 sc under each ch of ch-8, join with sl st to top of ch 3. Fasten off.

No. 34

Chain 10. Join with sl st to form a ring.

Rnd 1: Ch 2, 4 dc in ring, (ch 9, 5 dc in ring) 3 times, ch 9. Join with sl st to top of ch-2.

Rnd 2: Ch 2, 1 dc in each of next 2 dc, * ch 2, 1 dc in same dc with last dc, 1 dc in each of next 2 dc, ch 2; under next ch-9 work (3 dc, ch 5, 3 dc) for corner; ch 2, 1 dc in each of next 3 dc; rep from * around, ending ch 2, sl st in top of first ch-2.

Rnd 3: Ch 2, (yo, draw up loop in next dc, yo and thru 2 loops) 5 times, yo and thru 6 loops, * ch 5, skip 1 dc, 1 dc in next dc, ch 3; under next ch-5 work (2 dc, ch 2, 2 dc) ch 3, skip 1 dc, 1 dc in next dc, ch 5, (yo, draw up loop in next dc, yo and thru 2 loops) 6 times, yo and thru 7 loops; rep from * around, ending ch 5, skip 1 dc, 1 dc in next dc, ch 3; under next ch-5 work (2 dc, ch 2, 2 dc), ch 3, skip 1 dc, 1 dc in next dc, ch 5, join with sl st to top of first cluster. Fasten off.

Rnd 4: 1 sc in each ch and in **back** loop of each dc, working 2 dc under ch-2 at each corner. Join and fasten off.

No. 35

Chain 8. Join with sl st to form a ring.

Rnd 1: 1 hdc in ring, * ch 8, 3 hdc in ring; rep from * 6 times more, ch 8, 2 hdc in ring, join with sl st to top of first hdc.

Rnd 2: Sl st to center of first ch-8, 1 hdc under ch, * ch 5, 1 hdc under same ch, ch 5, 1 hdc under next ch-8; rep from *, ending ch 5, join with sl st to first hdc.

Rnd 3: Sl st under first ch-5, under same ch work (1 hdc, ch 5, 1 hdc), * under next ch-5 work (1 hdc, 4 dc, 1 hdc) shell, under next ch-5 work (1 hdc, ch 5, 1 hdc); rep from * around, ending with sl st under first ch of last rnd.

Rnd 4: * Under ch work (1 hdc, ch 5, 1 hdc), ch 5, 1 hdc in center of next shell, ch 5; rep from * around, join with sl st under first ch-5 of last rnd.

Rnd 5: * Under ch work (1 hdc, ch 5, 1 hdc), work a shell under each of next 2 ch; rep from * around, ending join with sl st to first hdc.

Rnd 6: Sl st under first ch-5, * under same ch work (1 hdc, ch 5, 1 hdc), ch 5, 1 hdc between next 2 shells, ch 5; rep from * around, join with sl st to first hdc.

Rnd 7: Sl st under ch-5, * under ch work (1 hdc, ch 5, 1 hdc), under each of next 2 ch work (1 hdc, 5 dc, 1 hdc) shell; rep from * around. Join and fasten off.

No. 36

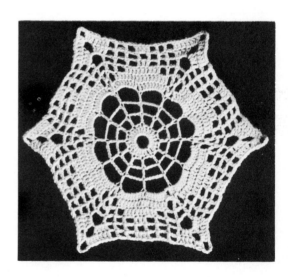

Chain 10. Join with sl st to form a ring.

Rnd 1: Ch 2, 23 dc in ring. Sl st in top of ch-2.

Rnd 2: Ch 6, * skip 1 dc, 1 dc in next dc, ch 3; rep from * around. Sl st in 3rd ch of ch-6.

Rnd 3: Ch 8, * 1 dc in next dc, ch 5; rep from * around. Sl st in 3rd ch of ch-8.

Rnd 4: Ch 10, * 1 dc in next dc, ch 7; rep from * around. Sl st to 3rd ch of ch-10.

Rnd 5: Ch 6, 1 dc in same place as sl st, * 8 dc in sp, 1 dc in next dc, 8 dc in next sp, in next dc work (1 dc, ch 3, 1 dc); rep from * around. Sl st to 3rd ch of ch-6.

Rnd 6: Sl st in sp, ch 6, 1 dc in same sp, * ch 2, skip first dc of 17-dc, 1 dc in each of next 15 dc, ch 2, in next sp work (1 dc, ch 3, 1 dc); rep from * around. Join.

Rnd 7: Ch 7, * 1 dc in next dc, ch 2, 1 dc in next dc, ch 2, skip 2 dc, 1 dc in each of next 9 dc, ch 2, skip 2 dc, 1 dc in next dc, ch 2, 1 dc in next dc, ch 2; rep from * around. Join.

Rnd 8: Ch 8, * 1 dc in next dc, (ch 2, 1 dc in next dc) twice, ch 2, skip next 2 dc, 1 dc in each of next 3 dc, ch 2, skip 2 dc, 1 dc in next dc, (ch 2, 1 dc in next dc) twice, ch 5; rep from * around. Join.

Rnd 9: Ch 3, * in next sp work (3 dc, ch 5, 3 dc), 1 dc in next dc, (ch 2, 1 dc in next dc) 3 times, ch 2, skip 1 dc, 1 dc in next dc, (ch 2, 1 dc in next dc) 3 times; rep from * around. Join.

Rnd 10: Ch 3, * 1 dc in each of next 3 dc, in next sp work (3 dc, ch 5, 3 dc), 1 dc in each of next 4 dc, (ch 2, 1 dc in next dc) 3 times, 2 dc in next sp, 1 dc in next dc, (ch 2, 1 dc in next dc) 3 times; rep from * around. Join and fasten off.

No 37

Chain 6. Join with sl st to form a ring.

Rnd 1: Ch 2, 15 dc in ring, join with sl st in top of ch-2.

Rnd 2: Ch 7, * skip 1 dc, 1 dc in next dc, ch 4; rep from * around. Join with sl st to 2nd ch of ch-7. (8 sps).

Rnd 3: Sl st under ch, ch 2, 7 dc under same ch, * 8 dc under next ch; rep from * around. Join with sl st to top of ch 2.

Rnd 4 (worked thru back loops): Ch 2, 1 dc in each of next 7 dc, * ch 1, 1 dc in each of next 8 dc; rep from * around, ending ch 1, sl st in top of ch-2.

Rnd 5 (worked thru back loops): Ch 2, 1 dc in each of next 7 dc, * ch 4, 1 sc in 4th ch from hook (picot), ch 1, 1 dc in each of next 8 dc; rep from * around. Join with sl st to top of ch-2.

Rnd 6 (worked thru back loops): Ch 2, 1 dc in each of next 7 dc, * ch 1, picot, ch 2, 1 dc in each of next 8 dc; rep from * around, ending picot, ch 2, join with sl st to top of ch 2. Fasten off.

No. 38

Chain 4.

Rnd 1: 1 dc in 4th ch from hook, ch 3, sl st in same ch, * ch 4, 1 dc in 4th ch from hook, ch 3, sl st in same ch; rep from * until there are 8 petals. Join with sl st in starting st, then sl st to top of first dc of first petal.

Rnd 2: * Ch 12, 1 dc in 9th ch from hook, ch 3, 1 sc in top of next petal; rep from * around, ending ch 3, sl st in first 4 sts of ch-12.

Rnd 3: Ch 3 (count as 1 dc), * in next ch-8 loop work (1 hdc, 7 sc, 1 hdc), 1 dc in next dc, 1 dc in 4th ch on next loop; rep from * around. Join with sl st in top of ch-3 and in next 5 sts.

Rnd 4: * Ch 3, skip next sc, 1 sc in next sc, ch 3, 1 sc in angle between next 2 dc's, ch 3, skip hdc and 1 sc, 1 sc in next sc, ch 3, skip 1 sc, in next (center) sc work (1 sc, ch 4, 1 sc); rep from * around, ending 1 sc in last sc to be worked, ch 2 (instead of ch-4), 1 hdc in same sc.

Rnd 5: * (Ch 3, 1 sc in next loop) twice, 1 sc in next loop, (ch 3, 1 sc in next loop) twice, ch 4, 1 sc in same loop; rep from * around, ending same as Rnd 5. Fasten off.

No. 39

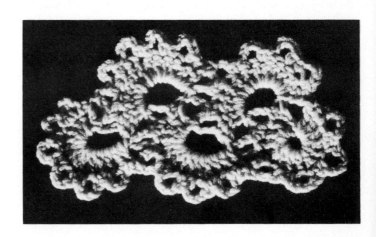

Chain 6. Join with sl st to form a ring.

First Motif: Ch 3 (count as 1 dc), 13 more dc in ring. Ch 1, turn, work 1 sc in first dc, 1 sc in next dc, (ch 4, 1 sc in each of the next 2 dc) 6 times. (Last dc will always be worked in top of turning ch.) Ch 6, turn.

Second Motif: Sl st in first free ch-4 loop, ch 3, turn; 13 dc under ch-6, sl st to first sc of first motif, ch 1, turn; 1 sc in first dc, 1 sc in next dc, (ch 4, 1 sc in each of next 2 dc) 6 times, sl st in next free ch-4 loop of adjoining motif, ch 6, turn.

Third Motif: Sl st in first free ch-4 loop of adjoining motif, ch 3, turn; 13 dc under ch-6, sl st in next free ch-4 loop of adjoining motif, ch 1, turn; 1 sc in first dc from hook, 1 sc in next dc, (ch 4, 1 sc in each of next 2 dc) 6 times, sl st in next free ch-4 loop of adjoining motif, ch 6, turn.

Repeat 3rd motif for pat, leaving 3 ch-4 loops free at each side of strip. When desired length, on last motif, omit last ch 6. Fasten off.

No. 40

Chain 6. Join with sl st to form a ring.

Rnd 1: Ch 5, * 1 dc in ring, ch 2; rep from * until 7 sps. Join last ch 2 to 3rd ch of ch-5. (8 sps).

Rnd 2: Ch 1, * 5 sc in next sp, insert hook in same sp from front to back and bring out in next sp, yo and draw up loop, yo and thru both loops (raised sc-Rsc); rep from * around, ending with Rsc, sl st in first sc.

Rnd 3: Ch 1, * 1 sc in each of next 4 sc, insert hook in next st and bring out in next st and complete Rsc; rep from * around. Join.

Rnd 4: Ch 1, 1 sc in same place as joining, 1 sc in each of next 3 sc, * Rsc over Rsc, 2 sc in next sc, 1 sc in each of next 2 sc; rep from * around. Join.

Rnd 5: Ch 2 (count as 1 dc), * 1 sc in each of next 2 sc, 1 dc in next sc, ch 5, skip Rsc, 1 dc in next sc; rep from * around, ending ch 5, sl st in top of ch-2.

Rnd 6: Ch 3, * holding back on hook the last loop of each dc work 1 dc in each of next 2 sc, yo, insert hook from front between 2nd sc below and next dc and bring out in next sp, yo and draw up loop, yo and thru 2 loops, yo and thru remaining loops (cluster), ch 5, 1 sc in sp, ch 5, yo, insert hook in next sp and out between dc and sc, yo and draw up loop, yo and thru 2 loops on hook; rep from * around, ending ch 5, sl st in tip of first cluster.

Rnd 7: Ch 8, * 1 sc in next loop, 1 sc in next sc, 1 sc in next loop, ch 5, 1 dc in tip of next cluster, ch 5; rep from * around, ending ch 5, sl st in 3rd ch of ch-8.

Rnd 8: Ch 10, * 1 sc in center sc of next 3-sc group, ch 7, 1 dc in next dc, ch 7; rep from * around, ending ch 7, sl st in 3rd ch of ch-10.

Rnd 9: Ch 1, 1 sc in same place as sl st, * 10 sc in next loop, 1 sc in next sc, 10 sc in next loop, 1 sc in next dc; rep from * around. Join with sl st in first sc.

Rnd 10: Ch 6, 1 dc in same place as sl st, * (ch 2, skip 2 sc, 1 dc in next sc) 3 times, (skip 1 sc, 1 dc in next sc) twice, (ch 2, skip 2 sc, 1 dc in next sc) 3 times, ch 3, 1 dc in same place as last dc; rep from * around. Join last ch-2 with sl st to 3rd ch of ch-6. Fasten off.

Insertions and Edgings

The sampling here is not a large one, but does give you some idea of the sheer ingenuity used in creating them. Patterns for insertions and edgings have withstood the ups and downs of interest in crochet much better than the majority of crochet patterns. They appear in the oldest instruction books as well as current ones and hundreds of interesting examples are available. Only two other forms of crochet have held their own as well during the ages—motifs and afghan stitch. Try some of these patterns and you will realize you must bid a fond goodbye to our early ancestor. Civilization must have been well on its way when these patterns were created. They turn and twist, they go up and down, they go back and forth, and you will be convinced that what you are doing will result in nothing more than wasted time and effort and a tangle of something or other. If any crochet pattern has rhyme and reason, these are the ones. When all the manuevering is over it isn't a tangle at all—it's a well planned design, leaving you wondering how the original designer ever did it in the first place.

INSERTIONS

No. 1

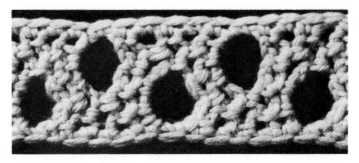

Chain 16.

Row 1: 1 sc in 7th ch from hook, (ch 2, skip 2 ch, 1 sc in next ch) 3 times. Ch 4, turn.

Row 2: 1 sc under first ch-2, (ch 2, 1 sc under next ch-2) twice, ch 2, skip next 2 ch of turning ch, 1 sc in next ch. Ch 1, turn.

Row 3: 1 sc in first sc, ch 7, skip next 2 ch-2, 1 sc under next ch-2, ch 2, skip next 2 ch of turning ch, 1 sc in next ch. Ch 4, turn.

Row 4: 1 sc under first ch-2, under ch-7 work (ch 2, 1 sc) twice, ch 2, 1 sc in last sc. Ch 4, turn.

Repeat from Row 2 for pattern, ending with Row 4. Ch 1, turn. Work 1 row sc around 4 sides, spacing sts to keep edge flat and working 3 sc at each corner. Join with sl st and fasten off.

No. 2

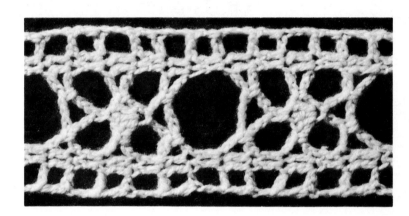

Chain 24.

Row 1: Skip 8 ch from hook, 1 dc in each of next 2 ch, ch 2, skip 2 ch, 1 sc in next ch, ch 5, skip 3 ch, 1 sc in next ch, ch 2, skip 2 ch, 1 dc in each of next 2 ch, ch 2, skip 2 ch, 1 dc in last ch. Ch 5, turn.

Row 2: Skip first dc, 1 dc in each of next 2 dc, ch 5, 1 sc under ch-5, ch 5, 1 dc in each of next 2 dc, ch 2, skip 2 ch, 1 dc in next ch of turning ch. Ch 5, turn.

Row 3: Skip first dc, 1 dc in each of next 2 dc, ch 2, 1 sc under next ch-5, 3 dc in next sc, 1 sc under next ch-5, ch 2, 1 dc in each of next 2 dc, ch 2, 1 dc in 3rd ch of turning ch. Ch 5, turn.

Row 4: Skip first dc, 1 dc in each of next 2 dc, ch 5, 1 sc in center dc of 3-dc group, ch 5, skip last dc of group, 1 dc in each of next 2 dc, ch 2, 1 dc in 3rd ch of turning ch. Ch 5, turn.

Row 5: Skip first dc, 1 dc in each of next 2 dc, ch 2, 1 sc under next ch-5, ch 4, 1 sc under next ch-5, ch 2, 1 dc in each of next 2 dc, ch 2, 1 dc in 3rd ch of turning ch. Ch 5, turn.

Row 6: Skip first dc, 1 dc in each of next 2 dc, ch 9, 1 dc in each of last 2 dc, ch 2, 1 dc in 3rd ch of turning ch. Ch 5, turn.

Row 7: Skip first dc, 1 dc in each of next 2 dc, ch 2, 1 sc under ch-9, ch 5, 1 sc under ch-9, ch 2, 1 dc in each of last 2 dc, ch 2, 1 dc in 3rd ch of turning ch. Ch 5, turn.
Repeat from Row 2 for pattern.

No. 3

Chain 11.

Row 1: 1 sc in 8th ch from hook, ch 4, skip 2 ch, 1 sc in last ch. Ch 13, turn.
Row 2: 1 sc under the ch-4, ch 4, 1 sc under turning ch-7. Ch 13, turn.
Row 3: 1 sc under ch-4, ch 4, 1 sc under ch-13. Ch 6, turn.
Row 4: 1 sc under ch-4, ch 4, 1 sc under ch-13. Ch 6, turn.
Row 5: 1 sc under ch-4, ch 4, 1 sc under ch-6. Ch 13, turn.
Row 6: 1 sc under ch-4, ch 4, 1 sc under ch-6. Ch 13, turn.
Repeat from Row 3 for pattern, ending with Row 3 and 1 sc under ch-13. Do not turn.
Rnd 7: 1 sc under same ch-13, * ch 6, 2 sc under next ch-13; rep from * around, working 3 sc under each of 2 small loops at short ends and ending ch 6, join with sl st to first sc. Fasten off.

No. 4

Chain 10.

Row 1: 1 sc in 2nd ch from hook and in each of next 2 ch, ch 7, 1 tr in last ch. Ch 1, turn.
Row 2: 1 sc in tr, 1 sc in each of next 2 ch, ch 6, 1 sc in each of last 2 sc. Ch 13, turn.
Row 3: Skip ch, 1 sc in each of last 3 sc. Ch 1, turn.

Row 4: 1 sc in each of first 2 sc, ch 6, skip next sc and next 5 ch, 1 sc in each of next 3 ch. Ch 1, turn.

Row 5: 1 sc in each of first 3 sc, ch 7, 1 tr in last sc. Ch 1, turn.

Repeat from Row 2 for pattern.

Work 1 row sc across each long side, spacing sts to keep edge flat.

No. 5

Chain a multiple of 6 plus 4.

Row 1: 1 dc in 3rd ch from hook and in each ch to end. Ch 2, turn.

Row 2: Skip first dc, 1 dc in each dc across, ending 1 dc in top of turning ch. Ch 2, turn.

Row 3: 1 dc in next dc, * ch 6, skip 5 dc, in next dc work (2 dc, ch 1, 2 dc) group; rep from *, ending skip last 5 dc, 1 dc in last dc, 1 dc in top of turning ch. Ch 2, turn.

Row 4: Skip first dc, 1 dc in next dc, * ch 4, group in ch-1 sp at center of next group; rep from *, ending ch 4, 1 dc in last dc, 1 dc in top of turning ch. Ch 2, turn.

Row 5: Same as Row 4.

Row 6: Skip first dc, 1 dc in next dc, * ch 3, work 1 dc inserting hook under the 3 chains below, ch 3, group in center of next group; rep from *, ending dc under chains, ch 3, 1 dc in last dc, 1 dc in top of turning ch. Ch 1, turn.

Row 7: 1 sc in each of first 2 dc, * ch 5, 1 sc in ch-1 of next group; rep from *, ending ch 5, 1 sc in last dc, 1 sc top of turning ch. Ch 2, turn.

Row 8: 1 dc in each sc and in each ch. Ch 2, turn.

Row 9: Skip first dc, 1 dc in each dc to end, 1 dc in top of turning ch. Fasten off.

No. 6

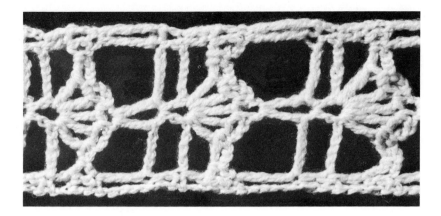

Chain 20.

Row 1: 1 dc in 5th ch from hook, ch 3, skip 6 ch, in next ch work (1 dc, ch 1) 4 times and 1 dc (shell), ch 3, skip 6 ch, 1 dc in each of last 2 ch. Ch 2, turn.

Row 2: Skip first dc, 1 dc in next dc, ch 1, 1 sc under next ch-3, (ch 3, 1 sc under next ch-1) 4 times, ch 3, 1 sc under next ch-3, ch 1, 1 dc in last dc, 1 dc in top of turning ch. Ch 6, turn.

Row 3: Skip first dc, 1 tr tr in next dc (wrap yarn 4 times, draw up loop in st, yo and thru 2 loops 5 times), ch 5, in center ch-3 of group below work (1 tr, ch 2, 1 tr), ch 5, 1 tr tr in last dc, 1 tr tr in top of turning ch. Ch 2, turn.

Row 4: Skip first tr tr, 1 dc in next tr tr, ch 5, under ch-2 work (1 dc, ch 2, 1 dc), ch 5, 1 dc in last tr tr, 1 dc in top of turning ch. Ch 2, turn.

Row 5: Skip first dc, 1 dc in next dc, ch 3, shell under ch-3, ch 3, 1 dc in last dc, 1 dc in top of turning ch. Ch 2, turn.
Repeat from Row 2 for pattern.

No. 7

Chain 22.

Row 1: 1 dtr in 7th ch from hook, ch 4, skip 5 ch, 2 dtr in next ch, 1 dtr in next ch, 2 dtr in next ch, ch 4, turn; skip first dtr, 1 sc in next dtr, (ch 3, 1 sc in next dtr) 3 times, ch 5, turn; (1 sc under next ch 3, ch 4) 4 times, sl st in top of last dtr, ch 4, skip 5 ch, 1 dtr in each of last 2 ch. Ch 8, turn.

Row 2: Skip first dtr, 1 tr tr in next dtr, ch 4, skip first loop, 1 dc in next loop, ch 5, skip next loop, 1 dc in next loop, ch 4, 1 tr tr in last dtr, 1 tr tr in top of turning ch. Ch 5, turn.

Row 3: Skip first tr tr, 1 dtr in next tr tr, ch 4, 5 dtr under ch-5, ch 4, turn; skip first dtr, 1 sc in next dtr, (ch 3, 1 sc in next dtr) 3 times, ch 5, turn; (1 sc under next ch-3 loop, ch 4) 4 times, sl st in top of last dtr, ch 4, 1 dtr in last tr tr, 1 dtr in top of turning ch. Ch 8, turn.

Repeat Rows 2 and 3 for pattern.

No. 8

Chain a multiple of 4 plus 3.

Row 1: 1 sc in 2nd ch from hook and in each ch to end. Ch 1, turn.

Rows 2, 3 and 4: 1 sc in first sc and in each sc to end. Ch 1, turn. At end of Row 4, ch 5, turn.

Row 5: 1 dc in first sc, * skip 2 sc, in next st (1 dc, ch 2, 1 dc) V st; rep from *, ending with V st in last sc. Ch 4, turn.

Row 6: 1 dc under first ch-2, * V st under next ch-2; rep from *, ending 1 V st under turning ch. Ch 4, turn.

Rows 7 and 8: Rep Row 6, ending ch 1, turn at end of Row 8.

Row 9: 1 sc in first dc, 1 sc under first ch-2, 1 sc in next dc, * 2 sc under next ch-2; rep from * to last V, 1 sc in last dc, 1 sc under turning ch, 1 sc in 3rd ch of turning ch. Ch 1, turn.

Repeat Rows 2, 3 and 4. Fasten off.

No. 9

Chain 9.

Work 6 rows in basic afghan st.

Row 1—First Half: Skip first bar, draw up loop in next 4 bars, yo and draw up loop in 3rd bar 3 rows below (to right of last picked-up loop on hook), * yo and thru 1 loop, yo and thru 2 loops, yo and thru 1 loop (6 loops on hook) *; yo and draw up loop in 4th bar 4 rows below (to left of long st just worked) and rep from * to * (7 loops on hook); yo twice and draw up loop in 5th bar (center) 5 rows below, yo and thru 1 loop, (yo and thru 2 loops) twice, yo and thru 1 loop (8 loops on hook); yo and draw up loop in 6th bar 4 rows below (left of center long st) and rep from * to * (9 loops on hook); yo and draw up loop in 7th bar 3 rows below and rep from * to * (10 loops on hook); yo and thru 6 loops on hook; draw up loop in each of last 4 bars of Row 6 (9 loops on hook).

Row 1—Second Half: Work off loops in basic afghan st.

Rows 2 thru 5: Basic afghan st.

Repeat from Row 1 for pattern.

No. 10

Chain 12 loosely.

Row 1: 1 dc in 4th ch from hook and in each ch to end. Ch 1, turn.

Row 2: 1 sc in each of first 3 dc, ch 4 loosely, skip next 4 dc, 1 sc in each of last 2 dc, 1 sc in top of turning ch. Ch 1, turn.

Row 3: 1 sc in first sc, 13 dc under ch-4, 1 sc in last sc. Ch 2, turn.

Row 4: Skip first sc and 2 dc, 1 dc in next dc, (ch 2 loosely, skip 1 dc, 1 dc in next dc) 4 times, ch 2, 1 sc in last sc. Ch 1, turn.

Row 5: 1 sc under first ch-2, * skip next dc, 2 sc under next ch-2; rep from *, ending 1 sc under last ch-2. (10 sc). Ch 1, turn.

Row 6: 1 sc in each of first 3 sc, ch 4 loosely, skip next 4 sc, 1 sc in each of last 3 sc. Ch 1, turn.
Repeat from Row 3 for pattern.

No. 11

Chain 4. Join with sl st
to form a ring.

Row 1: Ch 3, 3 dc in ring, ch 2, 4 dc in ring. Ch 3, turn.
Row 2: 3 dc under ch-2, ch 2, 3 dc under same ch-2, 1 dc in top of turning ch. Ch 3, turn.
Repeat Row 2 for pattern.

No. 12

Chain 17 (narrow end).

Row 1: 1 dc in 4th ch from hook, 1 dc in each of next 3 ch, ch 3, skip 2 ch, 1 sc in next ch, ch 3, skip 2 ch, 1 dc in each of next 5 ch. Ch 2, turn.
Row 2: Skip first dc, 1 dc in each of next 4 dc, ch 5, 1 dc in each of last 4 dc, 1 dc in top of turning ch. Ch 6, turn.
Row 3: 1 sc in center dc of 5-dc, ch 3, 5 dc under ch-5, ch 3, 1 sc in center dc of 5-dc, ch 3, 1 dc in top of turning ch. Ch 8, turn.
Row 4: 1 dc in each of next 5 dc, ch 5, 1 dc in 3rd ch of turning ch. Ch 3, turn.
Row 5: 4 dc under first ch-5, ch 3, 1 sc in center dc of 5-dc, ch 3, 4 dc under ch-8, 1 dc in 3rd ch of ch-8 turning ch. Ch 3, turn.
Repeat from Row 2 for pattern to desired length. Do NOT turn at end of last row.

Heading: Ch 5, 1 dc in end of next row, * ch 2, 1 dc in end of next row; rep from *, ending with last dc in beg ch; sl st across short end to opposite corner; ch 5, 1 dc in end of next row; rep from *, ending last dc in last row. Fasten off.

No. 13

Chain 6 (narrow end).

Row 1: In 6th ch from hook work (1 dc, ch 2, 1 dc). Ch 5, turn.

Row 2: Under ch-2 work (1 dc, ch 2, 1 dc) group. Ch 5, turn.
Rep Row 2 to desired length. (There must be multiple of 4 groups plus 3). Ch 2, do NOT turn.

Row 1: * In next ch-5 loop work (4 dc, ch 3, 4 dc); rep from *, ending 4 dc in last ch-5 on this side. Ch 1, turn.

Row 2: 1 sc in first dc, * ch 5, 1 sc in next ch-3 sp; rep from *, ending 1 sc in last sp, ch 3, 1 dc in last dc. Fasten off.
With right side facing, join yarn in first ch-5 loop on opposite edge and work to correspond. Fasten off.

No. 14

Chain 10 (narrow end).

Row 1: 7 dc in first ch. Ch 5, turn.

Row 2: Skip 2 dc, 1 dc in next dc, (ch 2, skip 1 dc, 1 dc in next dc) twice, ch 4, 7 dc under loop. Ch 5, turn.
Repeat Row 2 for desired length, ending last row with 7 dc under loop. Do not turn.

Heading: Ch 7, 1 sc under ch-5 at end of next pattern, * ch 7, 1 sc under next ch-5; rep from * to end. Break. Join yarn and work heading along opposite side. Break and fasten off.

EDGINGS

No. 1

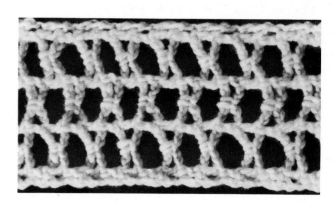

Chain 21 (narrow end).

Row 1: 1 dc in 4th ch from hook, * ch 2, skip next 2 ch, 1 sc in next ch, ch 2, skip next 2 ch, 1 dc in next ch, ch 5, skip next 3 ch, 1 dc in next ch; rep from *, ending 1 dc in each of last 2 ch. Ch 3, turn.

Row 2: Skip first dc, * 1 dc in next dc, ch 5, dc in next dc, ch 2, 1 sc under ch-5, ch 2; rep from *, ending ch 5, 1 dc in last dc, 1 dc in top of turning ch. Ch 3, turn.

Row 3: Skip first dc, * 1 dc in next dc, ch 2, 1 sc under ch-5, ch 2, 1 dc in next dc, ch 5; rep from *, ending 1 dc in top of turning ch. Ch 3, turn.

Repeat Rows 2 and 3 for pattern.

No. 2

Chain a multiple of 6 plus 2.

Foundation Row: 1 sc in 2nd ch from hook and in each ch to end. Ch 2, turn.

Row 1: 2 dc in first sc, * skip next 5 sc, in next sc work (3 dc, ch 2, 3 dc) shell; rep from *, ending skip 5 sc, 3 dc in last sc. Ch 2, turn.

Row 2: 2 dc in first dc, * ch 1, work shell under ch-2 of next shell; rep from *, ending ch 1, 3 dc in top of turning ch. Turn.

Row 3: Ch 4, sl st in 4th ch from hook, 1 sc in first dc, * 3 dc under ch-1 between shells, in ch-2 of next shell work (1 sc, ch 4, sl st in 4th ch from hook, 1 sc) picot group;

rep from *, ending 3 dc under ch-1, 1 sc in top of turning ch, ch 4, sl st in 4th ch from hook, sl st in last sc worked. Turn.

Row 4: Ch 5, skip picot, * in center dc of 3-dc group work (2 dc, ch 4, sl st in 4th ch from hook, 2 dc), ch 2; rep *, ending with picot shell, ch 5, sl st in last st. Fasten off.

No. 3

Chain a multiple of 8 plus 6.

Row 1: 1 dc in 3rd ch from hook and in each ch to end. Ch 1, turn.

Row 2: In first dc work (1 sc, ch 3, 3 dc), * skip next 3 dc, 3 dc in next dc, skip next 3 dc, in next dc work (1 sc, ch 3, 3 dc), rep from *, ending skip 3 dc, 1 dc in top of turning ch. Ch 3, turn.

Row 3: Under first ch-3 work (1 sc, 1 dc, ch 3, 1 dc, 1 sc) shell, * shell in center dc of next 3-dc, shell under next ch-3; rep from *, ending (1 sc, 1 dc, ch 3, 1 dc) under last ch-3, 1 sc in last sc. Ch 1, turn.

Row 4: Sl st under first ch-3, ch 5, 1 dc under same ch-3, * under next ch-3 work (1 dc, ch 3, 1 dc); rep from * ending last pat under turning ch. Ch 1, turn.

Row 5: Under first ch-3 work (1 sc, ch 3, 1 sc), * in sp between next 2 dc work (1 sc, ch 3, 1 sc); under next ch-3 work (1 sc, ch 3, 1 sc); rep from * to end. Fasten off.

No. 4

Chain a multiple of 8 plus 2.

Row 1: 1 sc in 2nd ch from hook and in each ch to end. Ch 1, turn.

Row 2: Working thru front loops only, 1 sc in each of first 4 sc, * in next sc work (1 sc, ch 7, 1 sc), 1 sc in each of next 7 sc; rep from * to last 5 sc, in next sc work (1 sc, ch 8, 1 sc), 1 sc in each of last 4 sc. Ch 3, turn.

Row 3: Working thru back loops only, skip first sc, 1 sc in next sc, * skip next 3 sc, 9 sc under ch-7, skip next 3 sc, 1 sc in next sc, 1 dc in next sc, 1 sc in next sc; rep from *, ending skip next 3 sc, 9 sc under next ch-7, skip next 3 sc, 1 sc in next sc, 1 dc in last sc. Ch 1, turn.

Row 4: 1 sc in first sc, * ch 4, in center sc of next 9-sc work (1 sc, ch 5, 1 sc), ch 4, 1 sc in next dc; rep from *, working last sc in top of turning ch instead of a dc. Ch 1, turn.

Row 5: 1 sc in first sc, * 3 sc under next ch-4, 5 sc under next ch-5, 3 sc under next ch-4, 1 sc in next sc; rep from * to end. Fasten off.

No. 5

Chain a multiple of 4.

Row 1: 1 dc in 4th ch from hook, * ch 2, skip next 2 ch, 1 dc in each of next 2 ch; rep from * to end. Ch 4, turn.

Row 2: * 3 dc in next sp (group), ch 1; rep from *, ending with 1 dc in top of turning ch. Ch 1, turn.

Row 3: 1 sc in first dc, * ch 1, 3 sc in center dc of next group; rep from *, ending ch 1, 1 sc in 2nd ch of turning ch. Ch 3, turn.

Row 4: 1 sc in first sc, * in center sc of next group work (1 sc, 1 dc, ch 4, sl st in 4th ch from hook, 1 dc, 1 sc); rep from *, ending with 1 sc and 1 dc in last sc. Fasten off.

No. 6

Chain a multiple of 8 plus 3.

Row 1: 1 dc in 4th ch from hook and in each ch to end. Ch 5, turn.

Row 2: 1 dc in first dc, * skip next 3 dc, in next dc work (2 dc, ch 3, 2 dc), skip next 3 dc, in next dc work (1 dc, ch 3, 1 dc); rep from *, ending skip last 3 dc, in top of turning ch work (1 dc, ch 2, 1 dc). Ch 1, turn.

Row 3: 1 sc under next ch-2, * ch 7, 1 sc under next ch-3; rep from *, ending ch 7, 1 sc under turning ch. Ch 1, turn.

Row 4: Under each ch-7 work (1 sc, ch 3) 3 times and 1 sc. Fasten off.

No. 7

Chain a multiple of 8 plus 4.

Row 1: 1 dc in 6th ch from hook, * ch 1, skip next ch, 1 dc in next ch; rep from * to end. Ch 1, turn.

Row 2: 1 sc in first dc, * ch 5, skip next dc, 1 sc in next dc; rep from *, ending ch 5, skip last dc and first ch, 1 sc in next ch of turning ch. Ch 1, turn.

Row 3: Work 7 sc under each loop. Ch 5, turn.

Row 4: * 1 sc in center sc of first 7-sc, * ch 3, 1 sc in center sc of next 7-sc; rep from *, ending ch 2, 1 dc in last sc. Ch 3, turn.

Row 5: 1 dc in center ch of first ch-3, ch 1, * 1 dc in next sc, ch 1, 1 dc in center ch of next ch-3, ch 1; rep from *, ending 1 dc in next sc, ch 1, 1 dc in 3rd ch of turning ch. Ch 1, turn.

Row 6: In each sp work (1 sc, ch 3, 1 sc). Fasten off.

No. 8

Chain a multiple of 9 plus 8.

Row 1: 1 dc in 4th ch from hook and in each of next 4 ch, * ch 3, skip next 3 ch, 1 dc in each of next 6 ch; rep from *, to end. Turn.

Row 2: Ch 4 (count as first tr), holding back on hook the last loop of each tr, 1 tr in each of next 2 dc, yo and thru all loops on hook (3-tr cluster), ch 5, 3 tr-cluster over next 3 dc, * ch 5, 1 sc under ch-3, (ch 5, 3-tr cluster over next 3 dc) twice; rep from *, ending with 3-tr cluster over last 2 dc and top of turning ch. Ch 1, turn.

Row 3: Sl st in top of first cluster and sl st under first loop, in same loop work (ch 4, 11 tr), * ch 3, skip next 2 loops, 12 tr in next loop; rep from * to end. Fasten off.

No. 9

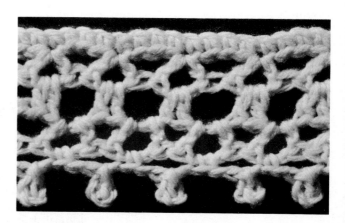

Chain a multiple of 4 plus 2.

Row 1: 1 sc in 2nd ch from hook and in each ch to end. Ch 5, turn.

Row 2: 1 dc in first sc, * skip 3 sc, in next sc work (1 dc, ch 2, 1 dc); rep from * to end. Ch 3, turn.

Row 3: 1 dc under first ch, * ch 2, 2 dc under next ch; rep from *, ending 1 dc under turning ch, 1 dc in 3rd ch of turning ch. Ch 5, turn.

Row 4: Under first ch work (1 dc, ch 2, 1 dc), * under next ch work (1 dc, ch 2, 1 dc); rep from *, ending ch-2, 1 dc in 2nd ch of turning ch. Turn.

Row 5: Sl st under first ch, * ch 6, sl st in 5th ch from hook (picot), ch 1, 1 sc under next ch; rep from *, ending picot, ch 1, sl st to 2nd ch of turning ch. Fasten off.

No. 10

Chain 20 (narrow end).

Row 1: 1 dc in 6th ch from hook, * (ch 1, skip next ch, 1 dc in next ch) 7 times. Ch 7, turn.

Row 2: 1 dc in first dc, (ch 1, 1 dc in next dc) twice, ch 7, skip next 3 dc, (1 dc in next dc, ch 1) twice, skip next ch, 1 dc in next ch. Ch 4, turn.

Row 3: Skip first dc, 1 dc in next dc, ch 1, 1 dc in next dc, (ch 1, skip next ch, 1 dc in next ch) 3 times, (ch 1, 1 dc in next dc) 3 times. Ch 7, turn.
Repeat Rows 2 and 3 for pattern.

No. 11

Chain a multiple of 4 plus 10 to turn.

Row 1: 1 dc in 10th ch from hook, * ch 3, skip next 3 ch, 1 dc in next ch; rep from * to end. Ch 1, turn.

Row 2: 1 sc in first dc, ch 2, in next dc work (3 tr, ch 3, 3 tr) shell, ch 2, 1 sc in next dc, ch 2; rep from *, ending shell in last dc, ch 2, skip next 3 ch of turning ch, 1 sc in next ch. Ch 1, turn.

Row 3: 1 sc in first sc, * ch 4, 1 sc under center ch-3 of shell, ch 4, 1 sc in next sc; rep from * to end. Ch 6, turn.

Row 4: Skip first sc, 1 sc in next sc, * ch 3, 1 dc in next sc, ch 3, 1 sc in next sc; rep from *, ending ch 3, 1 dc in last sc. Fasten off.

Row 5: Join to 3rd ch of ch-6 at beg of last row, 1 sc in same place with joining * ch 2, shell in next sc, ch 2, 1 sc in next dc; rep from * to end. Fasten off.

No. 12

Chain 25 (narrow end).

Row 1: 1 dc in 4th ch from hook, 1 dc in each of next 4 ch, ch 3, skip 2 ch, 1 sc in next ch, ch 3, skip 2 ch, 1 dc in each of next 6 ch, ch 3, skip 2 ch, 1 sc in next ch, ch 3, skip 2 ch, in last ch work (1 dc, ch 5, 1 sl st). Turn.

Row 2: Under ch-5 work (1 sc, 2 hdc, 5 dc), 1 dc in first dc, ch 5, 1 dc in next dc, ch 5, skip next 4 dc, 1 dc in next dc, ch 5, 1 dc in next dc, ch 5, skip next 4 dc, 1 dc in top of turning ch. Ch 2, turn.

Row 3: 4 dc under first ch-5, 1 dc in next dc, ch 3, 1 sc under ch-5, ch 3, 1 dc in next dc, 4 dc under next ch-5, 1 dc in next dc, ch 3, 1 sc under next ch-5, ch 3, 1 dc in next dc, ch 5, sl st in same place as last dc. Turn.
Repeat Rows 2 and 3 for pattern.

No. 13

Chain a multiple of 16 plus 7.

Row 1: 1 dc in 7th ch from hook, * ch 1, skip 1 ch, 1 dc in next ch; rep from * to end. (Number of sps must be a multiple of 8 plus 1). Ch 4, turn.

Row 2: (1 dc in next sp, 1 dc in next dc) twice, * ch 5, skip 2 sps, 1 tr in next sp, ch 5, skip 2 dc, 1 dc in next dc, (1 dc in next sp, 1 dc in next dc) 3 times; rep from *, ending 1 dc in last sp, 1 dc in 3rd ch of turning ch. Ch 3, turn.

Row 3: Skip first dc, 1 dc in each of next 3 dc, * ch 7, 1 sc in next tr, ch 7, skip 1 dc, 1 dc in each of next 5 dc; rep from *, ending 1 dc in each of last 3 dc, 1 dc in top of turning ch. Ch 3, turn.

Row 4: Skip first dc, 1 dc in each of next 2 dc, * ch 7, in next sc work (1 sc, ch 5, 1 sc), ch 7, skip 1 dc, 1 dc in each of next 3 dc; rep from *, ending 1 dc in each of last 2 dc, 1 dc in top of turning ch. Turn.

Row 5: Sl st in next dc, ch 7, holding back last loop of each dtr on hook work 2 dtr in ch-5 loop, yo and thru all loops (cluster), (ch 3, cluster in same loop) 4 times; * ch 3, skip 1 dc, 1 dc in next dc, ch 3, in next ch-5 loop work 5 clusters with ch 3 between; rep from *, ending ch 3, 1 dc in last dc. Turn.

Row 6: Sl st in first sp, 1 sc in same sp, * (ch 5, 1 sc in next sp) 5 times, 1 sc in next sp; rep from *, ending 1 sc in last sp, sl st in last sc. Fasten off.

No. 14

Chain 13 (narrow edge).

Row 1: 1 dc in 6th ch from hook, ch 1, skip 2 ch, 2 dc in next ch, ch 2, 2 dc in next ch (shell), ch 1, skip 2 ch, 1 dc in last ch. Ch 5, turn.

Rows 2 and 3: 1 dc in ch-1 sp, ch 1, in next ch-2 sp work (2 dc, ch 2, 2 dc) shell over shell, ch 1, 1 dc in next ch-1 sp. Ch 5, turn.

Row 4: 1 dc in first ch-1 sp, ch 1, shell over shell, ch 1, 1 dc in next sp, ch 3, do not turn; holding back the last loop of each tr on hook work 3 tr in next ch-5 loop on this edge, yo and thru all loops (3-tr cluster); (ch 3, 3 tr cluster in same loop) 3 times; ch 3, 1 sc in next ch-5 loop on this edge, ch 1, turn.

Row 5: (In next sp work 1 sc, 1 hdc, 1 dc, 1 hdc, 1 sc) 5 times, ch 3, 1 dc in next sp, ch 1, shell over shell, ch 1, 1 dc under turning ch. Ch 5, turn.

Rows 6 thru 9: Rep Rows 2 and 3 twice.

Repeat from Row 4 for pattern until desired length. Fasten off.

No. 15

Chain 6 (narrow end).

Row 1: 1 dc in 6th ch from hook, ch 3, turn.

Row 2: 3 dc in sp, ch 2, 1 tr in same sp. Ch 5, turn.

Row 3: 3 dc in sp, 1 dc in next dc, ch 2, skip 2 dc, 1 dc in top of turning ch. Ch 5, turn.

Row 4: 1 dc in next dc, ch 2, skip 2 dc, 1 dc in next dc, 3 dc in sp, ch 2, 1 tr in same sp. Ch 5, turn.

Row 5: 3 dc in sp, 1 dc in next dc, ch 2, skip 2 dc, 1 dc in next dc, ch 2, 1 dc in next dc, 2 dc under turning ch, 1 dc in 3rd ch of turning ch. Ch 3, turn.

Row 6: 1 dc in each of next 3 dc, 2 dc in sp, 1 dc in next dc, ch 2, 1 dc in next dc, ch 2, skip 2 dc, 1 dc in next dc, 3 dc under turning ch, ch 2, 1 tr under turning ch. Ch 5, turn.

Row 7: 3 dc in sp, 1 dc in next dc, ch 2, skip 2 dc, 1 dc in next dc, ch 2, 1 dc in next dc, 2 dc in sp, 1 dc in next dc. Ch 3, turn.

Row 8: 1 dc in each of next 3 dc, 2 dc in sp, 1 dc in next dc, ch 2, 1 dc in next dc, ch 2, skip 2 dc, 1 dc in next dc, 3 dc in sp, ch 2, 1 tr in same sp. Ch 5, turn.

Row 9: 3 dc in sp, 1 dc in next dc, ch 2, skip 2 dc, 1 dc in next dc, ch 2, 1 dc in next dc, 2 dc in next sp, 1 dc in next dc. Ch 3, turn.

Repeat Rows 8 and 9 to desired length. Fasten off.

Work along scalloped edge as follows: With wrong side facing, join yarn under turning ch of 6-dc group.

Row 1: 1 sc in same sp with joining, ch 5, holding back the last loop of each tr on hook work 2 tr in last dc of same group, yo and thru all loops (cluster), * ch 5, 1 sc under next turning ch (of next group), ch 5, cluster in last dc of same group; rep from *, ending to correspond to beg. Turn.

Row 2: 5 sc under ch-5 loop, * ch 5, 5 sc under each of next 2 ch-5 loops; rep from *, ending 5 sc under last ch-5 loop. Fasten off.

No. 16

Chain a multiple of 16 plus 6.

Row 1: 1 dc in 6th ch from hook, * skip 3 ch, in next ch work (1 dc, ch 3, 1 dc); rep from * to end. (There must be a multiple of 4 plus 1 ch-3 sps). Turn.

Row 2: Sl st in first sp, ch 4, in same sp work (3 tr, ch 3, 4 tr), * 1 dc in next sp, in next sp work (4 tr, ch 3, 4 tr) shell; rep from *, ending last tr of shell under turning ch. Turn.

Row 3: Sl st across to next sp, ch 4 (to count as tr), holding back last loop of each tr on hook work 2 tr in same sp, yo and thru all loops (3-tr cluster), (ch 5, 3 tr cluster in same loop) twice; * in next sp work (3 dc, ch 3, 3 dc), in next sp work three 3-tr clusters with ch 5 between; rep from * to end. Turn.

Row 4: Sl st in sp, ch 5, in same sp work (tr, ch 1) 3 times; * in top of next cluster work (1 tr, ch 3, 1 tr), in next sp work (ch 1, 1 tr) 4 times; in next ch-3 sp work (2 sc, ch 3, 2 sc); in next sp work (1 tr, ch 1) 4 times; rep from *, ending with last tr in top of last cluster. Fasten off.

No. 17

Chain a multiple of 12 plus 2.

Row 1: 1 sc in 2nd ch from hook, * ch 5, skip 3 ch, 1 sc in next ch; rep from * to end. (Number of loops must be a multiple of 3). Ch 1, turn.

Row 2: * (5 sc in next loop) twice, 3 sc in next loop, turn; (ch 5, 1 sc in center sc of next loop) twice, turn; 5 sc in next loop, 3 sc in next loop, turn; ch 5, 1 sc in center sc of last loop, turn; 5 sc in next loop, (2 sc in next loop) twice (completing 5 sc in each loop); rep from * to end. Fasten off.

Row 3: With right side facing, join yarn to center sc of loop at tip of first point, * ch 4, (skip 1 sc, 1 tr in next sc) twice; 1 tr in corresponding sc on next point, (skip 1 sc, 1 tr in next sc) twice, turn; 1 tr at top of ch-4, ch 6, 1 tr in loop formed by last tr, (ch 2, 1 tr in same place) 6 times, 1 dc at base of ch-4, turn; sl st in next tr, 1 sc in sp, (ch 3, 1 sc in next sp) 6 times, ch 3, 1 sc in center sc of next loop (where tr was worked); rep from * to end. Fasten off.

No. 18

Chain 10
(narrow end

Row 1: 1 dc in 4th ch from hook, ch 2, skip 2 ch, 2 dc in next ch, ch 2, 2 dc in next ch, ch 1, skip 1 ch, 1 dc in last ch. Ch 5, turn.

Row 2: Under first ch-2 work (2 dc, ch 2, 2 dc) shell, ch 2, 1 dc in last dc, 1 dc in top of turning ch. Ch 3, turn.

Row 3: 1 dc in next dc, ch 2, shell over shell, ch 1, 1 dc in ch-5 loop, ch 8, 1 sc in same loop. Turn.

Row 4: Work 12 sc in ch-8 loop, ch 5, shell over shell, ch 2, 1 dc in last dc, 1 dc in top of turning ch. Turn.

Row 5: Sl st in next dc, (sl st in 2 ch and in 2 dc) twice, sl st in each of next 3 ch; ch 5, 1 sc in each of next 3 sc, (ch 5, 1 sc in each of next 3 sc) 3 times, ch 5, 1 sc in ch-8 loop. Ch 1, turn.

Row 6: In each ch-5 loop work (1 sc, ch 2, 1 dc, ch 2, 1 tr, ch 3, 1 tr, ch 2, 1 dc, ch 2, 1 sc), ch 5, shell over shell, ch 2, 1 dc in each of last 2 sl sts. Ch 3, turn.

Row 7: 1 dc in next dc, ch 2, shell over shell, ch 1, 1 dc in ch-5 loop. Ch 5, turn.

Row 8: Rep Row 2.

Row 9: Rep Row 7.

Rows 10 thru 13: Rep Rows 2 thru 5.

Row 14: In first ch-5 loop work (1 sc, ch 2, 1 dc, ch 2, 1 tr, ch 1, sl st in corresponding ch-3 between tr's of last scallop, ch 1, 1 tr, ch 2, 1 dc, ch 2, 1 sc); work as for Row 6 over remaining ch-5 loops; ch 5, shell over shell, ch 2, 1 dc in each of last 2 sl sts. Ch 3, turn.

Rows 15, 16 and 17: Rep Rows 7, 2 and 7.
Repeat Rows 10 thru 17 to desired length. Fasten off.

No. 19

Chain a multiple of 15 plus 5.

Row 1: 1 sc in 2nd ch from hook and in each ch to end. Ch 1, turn.

Row 2: 1 sc in first sc, * ch 4, skip 2 sc, 1 sc in next sc; rep from * to end. (There must be a multiple of 5 plus 1 ch-4 loops). Turn.

Row 3: Sl st in first loop, ch 4, in same loop work (3 tr, ch 3, 4 tr), * ch 4, skip 1 loop, 1 sc in next loop, ch 4, 1 sc in next loop, ch 4, skip 1 loop, in next loop work (4 tr, ch 3, 4 tr); rep from * to end. Ch 5, turn.

Row 4: In first ch-3 sp work (1 sc, ch 3) 3 times and 1 sc; * ch 5, 1 sc in next loop, ch 4, skip next loop, 1 sc in next loop, ch 5, under next ch-3 work (1 sc, ch 3) 3 times and 1 sc; rep from *, ending ch 5, sl st in top of turning ch. Fasten off.

No. 20

Chain a multiple of 20 plus 2.

Row 1: 1 sc in 2nd ch from hook, 1 sc in each of next 3 ch, * ch 5, skip 4 ch, 1 dc in each of next 5 ch, ch 5, skip 4 ch, 1 sc in each of next 7 ch; rep from *, ending with 1 sc in each of last 4 sc. Ch 1, turn.

Row 2: 1 sc in each of first 3 sc, * ch 5, 1 dc in last ch of ch-4, 1 dc in each of next 2 dc, ch 3, skip 1 dc, 1 dc in each of next 2 dc, 1 dc in next ch, ch 5, skip 1 sc, 1 sc in each of next 5 sc; rep from *, ending 1 sc in each of last 3 sc. Ch 1, turn.

Row 3: 1 sc in each of first 2 sc, * ch 5, skip 3 ch, 1 dc in each of next 2 ch, 1 dc in next dc, ch 5, 1 sc in next sp, ch 5, skip 2 dc, 1 dc in next dc, 1 dc in each of next 2 ch, ch 5, skip 1 sc, 1 sc in each of next 3 sc; rep from *, ending with 1 sc in each of last 2 sc. Ch 1, turn.

Row 4: 1 sc in first sc, * ch 5, skip 3 ch, 1 dc in each of next 2 ch, 1 dc in next dc, ch 5, 1 sc in next loop, ch 7, 1 sc in next loop, ch 5, skip 2 dc, 1 dc in next dc, 1 dc in each of next 2 ch, ch 5, skip 1 sc, 1 sc in next sc; rep from *, ending 1 sc in last sc. Turn.

Row 5: Sl st in first sc and in each of next 4 ch; ch 3, 1 dc in next ch, 1 dc in next dc, ch 5; holding back on hook the last loop of each tr work 3 tr under ch-7, yo and thru all loops (cluster); * (ch 5, 1 dc in 5th ch from hook, cluster under same ch-7) 4 times; ch 5, skip 2 dc, 1 dc in next dc, 1 dc in each of next 2 ch, skip next sc and next 3 ch, 1 dc in each of next 2 ch, 1 dc in next dc, ch 5, cluster in next ch-7; rep from *, ending with 3 dc to correspond to beg. Fasten off.

No. 21

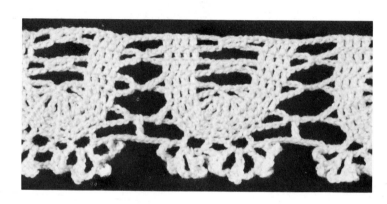

Chain 11 (narrow end).

Row 1: 1 dc in 8th ch from hook and in each of next 3 ch. Ch 7, turn.

Rows 2 thru 7: 1 dc in each of next 4 dc, ch 7, turn.

Row 8: 1 dc in each of next 4 dc, ch 3, 1 sc in next loop on this edge, 1 dc in next loop, ch 3, turn.

Row 9: 1 dc in each of next 4 dc, ch 7, turn.

Row 10: 1 dc in each of next 4 dc, ch 2, 1 sc in sc on opposite loop, ch 2, turn.

Row 11: 1 dc in each of next 4 dc, ch 7, turn.

Row 12: 1 dc in each of next 4 dc, ch 2, 1 dc in dc on opposite loop, ch 2, turn.

Row 13: 1 dc in each of next 4 dc, ch 7, turn.

Row 14: 1 dc in each of next 4 dc, ch 2, 2 tr in corresponding loop on opposite side, ch 3, turn.

Rows 15 and 16: Rep Rows 13 and 14.

Row 17: 1 dc in each of next 4 dc, ch 16, turn.

Row 18: 1 dc in 8th ch from hook and in each of next 3 ch, ch 3, 1 sc in free loop on opposite side, ch 3, turn.

Row 19: 1 dc in each of next 4 ch, ch 7, turn.

Row 20: 1 dc in each of next 4 dc, ch 3, 1 dc in next free loop on opposite side, ch 3, turn.

Row 21: 1 dc in each of next 4 dc, ch 7, turn.

Row 22: 1 dc in each of next 4 dc, ch 3, 1 tr in next free loop on opposite side, ch 3, turn.

Repeat the last 17 rows (Row 6 thru Row 22) for pattern.

No. 22

Chain 6 (narrow end)

Row 1: In 6th ch from hook work 1 dc, ch 2, 1 dc. Ch 5, turn.

Row 2: Under ch-2 work 1 dc, ch 2, 1 dc (group). Ch 5, turn.

Rep Rows 1 and 2 for desired length. (There must be a multiple of 4 plus 3 groups). Ch 2, do not turn. Work across long side.

Row 1: * In next ch-5 loop work (4 dc, ch 3, 4 dc); rep from * to end. Ch 3, turn.

Row 2: * In next ch-3 sp work (1 tr, ch 5) 3 times and 1 tr; 1 sc in next ch-3 sp; rep from *, ending skip 3 dc, sl st in next dc. Ch 1, turn.

Row 3: * In next loop work (3 sc, ch 3, 3 sc); in center loop work (2 sc, ch 3) 3 times and 2 sc; in next loop work (3 sc, ch 3, 3 sc), 1 sc in next sc; rep from *, ending with 1 sc in top of turning ch. Fasten off.

No. 23

Chain a multiple of 12 plus 9.

Row 1: 1 sc in 2nd ch from hook, ch 3, 1 sc in next ch, * ch 7, skip 4 ch, 1 sc in next ch, ch 3, 1 sc in next ch; rep from * to end (uneven number of ch 7 loops). Ch 10, turn.

Row 2: * In next loop work (1 sc, ch 3, 1 sc), ch 7; rep from *, ending ch 5, 1 dtr in last sc. Ch 1, turn.

Row 3: In first loop work (1 sc, ch 3, 1 sc), * ch 7, in next loop work (1 sc, ch 3, 1 sc); rep from * to end. Ch 10, turn.

Rows 4, 5 and 6: Rep Rows 2, 3 and 2. Ch 8, turn.

Row 7: 1 sc in 3rd ch from hook (picot), in first loop work (1 dtr, ch 3, 1 sc in 3rd ch from hook) 5 times and 1 dtr, * in next loop work (1 sc, ch 3, 1 sc), in next loop work (1 dtr and picot) 6 times and 1 dtr; rep from * to end. Fasten off.

No. 24

Chain 8 (narrow end).

Row 1: 1 dc in 4th ch from hook, 1 dc in each of next 2 ch, ch 2, in last ch work (1 dc, ch 2) 3 times, 1 dc. Ch 1, turn.

Row 2: Under first ch-2 work (1 sc, 2 dc, 1 sc), under next ch-2 work (1 sc, 3 dc, ch 2, 3 dc, 1 sc) shell, under next ch-2 work (1 sc, 2 dc, 1 sc), ch 2, 1 dc in each of last 3 dc, 1 dc in top of turning ch. Ch 2, turn.

Row 3: Skip first dc, 1 dc in each of next 3 dc, ch 2, under ch-2 of shell work (1 dc, ch 1) 3 times, 1 dc. Ch 1, turn.
Repeat Rows 2 and 3 to desired length.

No. 25

Chain 9 (narrow end).

Row 1: 2 dc in 4th ch from hook, ch 2, skip next ch, 3 dc in next ch, skip 2 ch, 1 dc in last ch. Ch 3, turn.

Row 2: Under ch-2 work (3 dc, ch 2, 3 dc) shell. Ch 3, turn.

Row 3: Shell under ch-2 of shell, 1 dc under ch-3 at end of row. Ch 3, turn.

Row 4: Shell in shell, turn work, ch 5 and remove hook, insert hook under ch-3 at right, draw dropped loop thru; ch 5, drop loop then draw thru point of next shell at right, ch 1 to fasten.

Row 5: Work 8 sc in loop just made; 3 sc in next loop, ch 6, draw loop thru 4th sc of first loop, ch 1, 8 sc in loop just made, 5 sc in 2nd loop (to complete 8 sc in this loop), shell in shell, 1 dc under ch-3 at end of row. Ch 3, turn.

Repeat from Row 2 for pattern.

No. 26

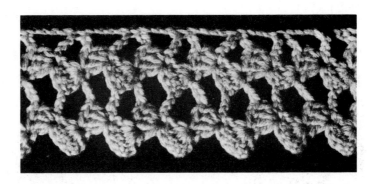

Chain 12 (narrow end).

Row 1: Skip 3 ch, 4 dc in 4th ch from hook, ch 3, skip 3 ch, 4 dc in next ch, ch 3, skip 3 ch, 1 dc in last ch. Ch 6, turn.

Row 2: 4 dc in first dc of first group, ch 3, 4 dc in first dc of next group, ch 3, turn.

Row 3: 4 dc in first dc of first group, ch 3, 4 dc in first dc of next group, ch 3, 1 dc in 3rd ch of turning ch-6. Ch 6, turn.

Repeat from Row 2 for desired length.

No. 27

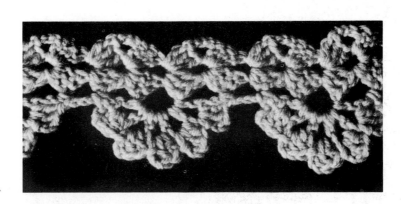

Chain 5 (narrow end).

Row 1: In first ch work (3 dc, ch 3, 3 dc) shell. Ch 3, turn.
Row 2: Shell under ch-3 of shell, ch 3, turn.
Row 3: Shell under ch-3 of shell, ch 5, turn.
Row 4: Shell in shell, ch 3, turn.

Row 5: Shell in shell, ch 2, in next ch-5 loop work (1 dc, ch 2) 5 times and 1 dc, 1 sc in ch-3 loop, turn, ch 3, 2 dc in first ch-2 loop, * sl st in next loop, ch 3, 2 dc in same loop; rep from * 3 times, 1 sc in next loop, ch 3, shell in shell, ch 3, turn.

Row 6: Shell in shell, ch 5, turn.

Row 7: Shell in shell, ch 3, turn.

Repeat from Row 5 for desired length.

Trims

These are only a smattering of survivals that reappear every so often. Yet there was a time in fashion when a crocheted trim was extremely popular. Included here to show you that working with very few stitches can produce a very interesting effect. When you see the commercial trims and braids now on the market and if your imagination is still working, you can well believe that once again the crocheted trim arrived long before the machines took over. Ball fringe, for example, was undoubtedly first a crochet band trimmed with pompons and can faintly be recognized in very, very old fashion pictures.

No. 1

Chain 5.

1 sc in 5th ch from hook, * ch 2, turn, 1 sc in sc; rep from * to desired length. Fasten off.

209

No. 2

Chain 4.

Row 1: In 4th ch from hook work (yo, draw up loop, yo and thru 2 loops) 4 times, yo and thru 5 loops. Ch 4.
Repeat Row 1 to desired length. Fasten off.

No. 3

Chain 4.

Row 1: 1 hdc in 2nd ch from hook, skip next ch, 1 sc in last ch. Ch 1, turn.
Row 2: 1 hdc in sc, 1 sc in hdc. Ch 1, turn.
Repeat Row 2 to desired length. Fasten off.

No. 4

Chain desired length.

Row 1: 1 sc in 2nd ch from hook and in each ch to end. Ch 1, do NOT turn.
Row 2: 1 sc in last sc of Row 1, * 1 sc in next sc to right; rep from * to end.
Fasten off.

No. 5

Chain a multiple
of 10 plus 2.

Foundation Row: 1 sc in 2nd ch from hook and in each ch to end. Turn.

Scallop Row: Sl st in first sc, * 1 sc in next sc, 1 hdc in next sc, 1 dc in next sc, 1 tr in next sc, 5 dtr in next sc, 1 tr in next sc, 1 dc in next sc, 1 hdc in next sc, 1 sc in next sc, sl st in next sc; rep from * to end. Fasten off.

No. 6

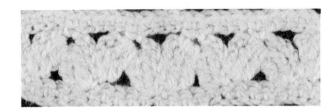

Chain a multiple of 5 plus 2.

Row 1: 1 sc in 2nd ch from hook and in each ch to end. Ch 4, turn.

Row 2: Holding back on hook the last loop of each tr, work 2 tr in first sc, yo and thru 3 loops (cluster), * ch 4, cluster in tip of last cluster, skip 4 sc, 1 sc in next sc, ch 4, cluster in same sc; rep from * to end. Fasten off.

Row 3: Join yarn to tip of last cluster. 1 sc in point, * ch 4, 1 sc in next point; rep from * to end. Ch 1, turn.

Row 4: 1 sc in each sc and in each ch to end. Fasten off.

No. 7

Chain 9 (or desired width for narrow end).

Row 1: 1 sc in 2nd ch from hook and in each ch to end. Ch 1, turn.

Row 2: 1 sc in first sc and in each sc to end. Ch 4, turn.

Row 3: 1 tr in back loop of 2nd sc and in back loop of each sc to end. Ch 1, turn.

Row 4: * 1 sc worked in back loop of next st and in back loop of corresponding st on row below; rep from * to end. Ch 1, turn.

Row 5: 1 sc in first and in each sc to end. Ch 1, turn.

Repeat from Row 2 for desired length.

Fasten off.

No. 8

Chain 2.

Rnd 1: 6 sc in 2nd ch from hook. Join with sl st to first sc.

Rnd 2: * Ch 2, 1 sc in next sc; rep from * around. 6 sps.

Rnd 3: * Under next ch-2 work (1 sc, 4 dc, 1 sc); rep from * around. Join with sl st to first sc and fasten off.

No. 9

Chain desired length.

Row 1: 1 sc in 2nd ch from hook and in each ch to end. Ch 1, turn.

Row 2: 1 sc in first sc, * ch 10, skip 1 sc, 1 sc in each of next 4 sc; rep from *, having an even number of loops. Fasten off.

Fringe: Cut ten 7-inch strands for each loop. Fold 10 strands in half. Hold 2 ch-10 loops tog, insert hook thru both, draw folds thru loop, draw cut ends thru fold and tighten for knot.

Knot 7 strands in every 2 loops, always crossing loops in the same direction. Trim fringe evenly.

No. 10

Chain desired length.

   Row 1: 1 sc in 2nd ch from hook and in each ch to end. Ch 1, turn.

   Row 2: 1 sc in first sc and in each sc to end. Ch 1, turn.

   Row 3: 1 sc in first sc, * wind yarn 3 times over a 1-inch piece of cardboard held at back, insert hook in next sc and thru loops on cardboard and complete sc; rep from * to end. Fasten off.